THE IRISH GARDEN

THE IRISH GARDEN

Jane Powers   WITH PHOTOGRAPHS BY Jonathan Hession

FRANCES LINCOLN LIMITED
PUBLISHERS

For Mary Davies

Frances Lincoln Limited
74–77 White Lion Street
London N1 9PF
www.franceslincoln.com

The Irish Garden
Copyright © Frances Lincoln Limited 2015
Text copyright © Jane Powers 2015
Photographs copyright © Jonathan Hession 2015

First Frances Lincoln edition 2015

All rights reserved.
No part of this publication may be reproduced, stored
in a retrieval system, or transmitted, in any form, or
by any means, electronic, mechanical, photocopying,
recording or otherwise without the prior written
permission of the publisher or a licence permitting
restricted copying. In the United Kingdom such licences
are issued by the Copyright Licensing Agency, Saffron
House, 6–10 Kirby Street, London EC1N 8TS.

A catalogue record for this book is available from the
British Library.

Designed by Anne Wilson

978-0-7112-3222-8

Printed and bound in China

3 4 5 6 7 8 9

FRONT ENDPAPERS MacGillycuddy's Reeks,
County Kerry.
BACK ENDPAPERS Nighttime at Kells Bay
Garden, County Kerry.
HALF-TITLE PAGE Wildflower meadow at
Salthill House, on the shore of Donegal Bay.
TITLE PAGE At the Bay Garden in County
Wexford, early autumn sees the grasses
(including *Miscanthus* and *Calamagrostis*) at
their best, while asters, *Verbena bonariensis* and
Rhus typhina 'Dissecta' add purple and red
notes to the scene.

Contents

Preface 6
Introduction 8

GRAND BIG GARDENS 12
Behind the gates of the Anglo-Irish gentry 14
Bantry House, County Cork 24
Mount Stewart, County Down 34
Birr Castle, County Offaly 46
Powerscourt, County Wicklow 58
Killruddery, County Wicklow 70

ROMANTIC INTERLUDES 82
Where nature and gardening mingle harmoniously together 84
Altamont, County Carlow 90
Mount Usher, County Wicklow 96

TAMING THE WILDERNESS 110
Gardens coaxed from savage landscapes 112
Caher Bridge Garden, County Clare 114
Kylemore Abbey, County Galway 122
Ilnacullin (Garinish Island), County Cork 128
Rowallane, County Down 134
Glenveagh, County Donegal 142

PAINTING WITH PLANTS 170
The gardens of passionate plantspeople 172
Mount Congreve, County Waterford 176
Talbot Botanic Gardens, Malahide Castle Demesne, County Dublin 182
The Dillon Garden, Dublin 190
Hunting Brook, County Wicklow 200

A LOVELY DAY FOR A WALK 192
Rambles through the rare and spectacular 194
Woodstock, County Kilkenny 202
Tullynally Castle, County Westmeath 208
National Botanic Gardens, Kilmacurragh, County Wicklow 214

A FEW FOLLIES AND FANCIES 226
The magical and the mysterious; the unexpected and the fantastic 228
Belvedere, County Westmeath 238
Kilfane Glen and Waterfall, County Kilkenny 244
Corke Lodge, County Wicklow 250
The Japanese Gardens, County Kildare 256
The National Botanic Gardens, Glasnevin, Dublin 262
Tropical Ravine and Palm House, Botanic Gardens, Belfast, County Antrim 274

FIELDS OF DREAMS 278
Where gardens grow from fertile imaginings 280
June Blake's Garden, County Wicklow 286
Salthill House, County Donegal 300
The Bay Garden, County Wexford 308
Lakemount, County Cork 316
Ardcarraig, County Galway 320

PARADISES REINVENTED 326
Old gardens carefully reawoken from the slumbers of gentle dereliction 328
Oakfield Park, County Donegal 330
The Master's Garden, Royal Hospital, Kilmainham, Dublin 338
Kells Bay Gardens, County Kerry 342
Heywood, County Laois 350
Glenarm Castle Walled Garden, County Antrim 354

GOOD ENOUGH TO EAT 364
Productive patches 366
Ballymaloe Cookery School, County Cork 370
Glebe Gardens, County Cork 376
Dunmore County School, County Laois 384

The gardens; contact details 392
Further reading 394
Index 395
Acknowledgments 400

Preface

IN THIS BOOK we have set out to give an account in words and photographs of the Irish garden today. We have included nearly sixty gardens – big and small, grand and cosy, old and new – on the island of Ireland. All those we have chosen are open and welcoming to visitors, and are gardens, in our opinion, that are worth spending some time seeking out. There are numerous others that are lovely or interesting in many ways, and we wish that we could have included them all. If we hadn't limited ourselves, however, you would have needed a wheelbarrow to transport this book.

Gardens can change dramatically from year to year. Inevitably, in the interval between *The Irish Garden* going to print and being published, there will have been metamorphoses in some of the places covered. Certain Irish gardeners are possessed of an almost supernatural dynamism and energy, and are continually pushing their plots into greater creative zones. We are in awe of their artistry and vitality, and have had to accept that our efforts sometimes could not keep up with theirs. Nonetheless, our happiest hours while making this book have been in those very gardens. We hope that you, the reader, will be able to share in our joy.

Jane Powers and Jonathan Hession
August 2014

Moss, ferns and bluebells clothe the rocky ground in Ardcarraig, the garden of Lorna MacMahon on the edge of Connemara.

Introduction

VISITORS TO IRELAND are often surprised at the 'palm trees' that make so many gardens appear to belong on a holiday postcard. How can such exotics survive in a place as far north as the plains of Alberta and the pine forests of Siberia? The answer lies in the tail of the Gulf Stream – the North Atlantic Drift – which wraps around this green island on the western edge of Europe.

The water's warm embrace creates the renowned 'soft' climate that allows those palm-tree approximations (in fact, New Zealand cabbage trees, *Cordyline australis*) to make their homes here, along with tree ferns from Australasia, bananas from Japan and true palms from four different continents. Plants from colder regions are also happy: rhododendrons and primulas from the Himalayas, lady's slipper orchids from the wetlands of Minnesota, edelweiss from the European Alps. So it is no surprise that Ireland, with its favourable climate, a range of plants that runs from the subtropical to the subarctic, and a landscape that varies from gently pastoral to savagely rugged, possesses some of the most interesting gardens in the world.

The island's mild conditions were observed as far back as the eighth century by the Venerable Bede, the English monk and scholar, in his *Historia ecclesiastica gentis Anglorum* (*Ecclesiastical History of the English People*). A translated edition from 1849 reads: 'Ireland, in breadth, and for wholesomeness and serenity of climate, far surpasses Britain; for the snow scarcely ever lies there above three days: no man makes hay in the summer for winter provision, or builds stables for his beasts of burden.'

Both hay-making and stable-building were later widely practised, but Ireland's climate has remained far balmier than that of its nearest neighbour. Irish gardeners have long revelled, somewhat boastfully, in the supposedly tender plants that thrive out of doors here. When the *Gardeners' Chronicle* (a journal covering both Britain and Ireland) reported in 1872 that it was not possible to grow any of the *Dracaena* or *Cordyline* genus outdoors, a flurry of 'Not so, sir!' letters arrived on the editor's desk. Correspondents declared that healthy and robust specimens of *Dracaena australis* (as *Cordyline australis* was sometimes then known) were growing in County Leitrim, in various parts of County Down, and all over County Dublin. (Of course, we now know that *Cordyline* is hardy in most of Ireland, where it grows like a weed, as it also does in the warmer parts of Britain – but at the time it was still a novelty, introduced half a century earlier for use as a stove house and semi-tropical bedding plant.)

From the middle of the nineteenth until the beginning of the twentieth century, Ireland's possibilities as a sort of hothouse for Britain caused some excitement among elite plantspeople. William Watson, curator of the Royal Botanic Gardens at Kew, made a special trip to visit Irish gardens in 1906. He was accompanied by Frederick Moore, curator of the Botanic Gardens at Glasnevin in Dublin. Their mission was to 'ascertain what had been done in the direction of establishing reputedly tender trees, shrubs, and perennial plants in the more favoured parts of the island'. Watson's notes in the *Kew Bulletin* are quoted extensively in the *Gardeners' Chronicle*. He reported that 'The things we saw . . . far surpassed our most sanguine expectations. Ireland is favoured with a climate, and in many parts, a soil most suitable to gardening; and fortunately a number of people who are in a position to do so are making good use of their gardens and estates by devoting them to what may be termed experimental horticulture.'

The visit was in the latter half of June, with daily rain in the morning and hot, sunny afternoons. Watson was thrilled with his findings: 'The vigour and healthy look of plants of all kinds under these conditions were delightful to behold. It might reasonably be said with regard to Irish gardening that the tools most needed are the saw, pruning hook, and knife.'

The summer in question, however, was not exactly typical Irish weather, which is damper, greyer and cooler. Far more characteristic were the meteorological conditions that Mr R. Fish, an occasional writer for the *Journal of Horticulture, Cottage Gardener and Country Gentleman*, encountered during his visit to Woodstock in County Kilkenny in 1863. He recounts that, although 'the thunder rolled and the rains poured', the head gardener, Mr McDonald, 'walked as unconcerned as if clothed with ducks' wings', while the ladies were 'not even holding their bonnets, and leaving

ribbons and crinolines to look after themselves'. Poor Mr Fish, alas, had been afflicted with 'twinges of rheums', and wanted nothing more than a warm, dry place to shelter.

For those of us who live in Ireland, imperviousness to rain is a matter of necessity. In the drier parts of the island – along the east and south-east coasts – rain falls on about 150 days of the year, totalling between 600 and 1,200 millimetres (23.5–47 inches) per annum, but in the wetter west it falls on 225 days, and the yearly total can be as much as 3,600 millimetres (142 inches). Admittedly, these torrential quantities fall only in mountainous areas, but gardens in Donegal and Kerry can easily average 2,000 millimetres (79 inches) per year.

Clearly, rain, combined with mild year-round temperatures (some areas rarely dip below freezing in the colder months), has been a powerful shaper of Irish gardens. Growth barely pauses for breath in winter in some regions, so that often trees increase quickly in height and volume, while foliage plants are lush and plump. When conifers from North America and rhododendrons and magnolias from the Himalayas were introduced in the nineteenth century, they took to the Irish soil and conditions with enthusiasm, and grew with gusto. The mild, moist climate – it must be said – has also hastened the demise of many gardens. The march of untamed vegetation across a space heretofore meticulously maintained can wreak havoc in a short period.

ABOVE, CLOCKWISE FROM TOP LEFT A gathering of *Cordyline australis* puts on a faux tropical show next to the sea in Dublin; the Broad Walk at Kilmacurragh in County Wicklow is carpeted with petals from *Rhododendron* 'Altaclarense'; *Deutzia purpurascens* 'Alpine Magician', raised at the National Botanic Gardens from seed collected in Burma by Reginald Farrer (in flower in Carmel Duignan's Shankill garden); *Primula pulverulenta* in Ardcarraig.

Apart from the climate, the other great influence on Irish gardens has been the British. Ireland was first colonized by the Anglo-Normans in 1170, and the part that is now the Republic did not achieve independence until 1922, when the Irish Free State seceded from the United Kingdom. For the most part, the non-Anglo-Irish were poor, and gardening, except for food cultivation, was a luxury. Even then, the produce was basic: J.C. Loudon, in his *Encyclopaedia of Gardening*, published in 1824, noted that 'the cottage-gardens in many districts contain nothing besides potatoes; and potatoes are the chief ingredients in the gardens of private gentlemen.'

One hundred and fifty years later, David Thomson published *Woodbrook*, his keenly observed memoir of his time as a tutor in the Roscommon house of the same name. In the 1930s Ireland of which he wrote, diversity had not increased greatly, at least in Munster. '[I]n the part of Ireland that I knew the potato reigned supreme, with cabbage plants as its subjects in an inferior plot nearby. Even on the sandy soil of Inishlacken and the Connemara mainland, we had found it impossible to buy carrots or parsnips. In Connemara many gardens were hedged by fuchsia bushes, beautifully red in flower, but no small flowers were to be seen, and between Carrick and Sligo I cannot remember even one house with roses, nasturtiums, marigolds, wallflowers or michaelmas daisies about it. . . . Most of the simpler seeds and seedlings could be bought in Carrick or Boyle, but were bought only by the Anglo-Irish and their gardeners.'

So, to generalize broadly, in times past, ornamental gardening was largely the preserve of the Anglo-Irish. Accordingly, all the older gardens in this book were originally made by those whose families came over, at one time or another, from England or Scotland. Some of the estates were auxiliary homes, and not the principal residences of the owners. Derreen in County Kerry and Lismore Castle in County Waterford continue in this mode.

The memory of dispossession among the 'true' native Irish rankled for centuries. In his *A Tour in Ireland*, published in 1780, the English writer Arthur Young noted: 'All the poor people are Roman Catholics, and among them are the descendants of the old families who once possessed the country, of which they still preserve the full memory, insomuch, that a gentleman's labourer will regularly leave to his son, by will, his master's estate.'

Relations between landlord and tenant ranged from the appalling – with rack-renting and evictions – to the benevolent. Many Irish demesnes have immense works that were commissioned as famine relief projects: roads, walls, buildings, follies and man-made lakes. Well-known constructions that were conceived to offer employment to the poor in hard times were Conolly's Folly at Castletown in County Kildare (now the symbol of the Irish Georgian Society) and the obelisk on Killiney Hill in south County Dublin. Both were built during the famine of 1740–41, which was as severe as the better-known Great Famine a century later. Among the gardens featured in this book, Altamont in County Carlow, Bantry House in County Cork and Powerscourt in County Wicklow all contain famine-relief works.

Several factors have rendered historic Irish gardens more fragile and ephemeral than those across the sea in Britain.

Our soft climate, as I mentioned earlier, can cause rampant growth to quickly erase man's work. And, while absentee owners may have created magnificent schemes at their Irish properties during times of abundance, when funds became tight these overseas extravagances were the first to suffer from retrenchment. Labour shortages in the First World War and the turbulent times around Ireland's War of Independence saw many gardens sink into dereliction.

Even after Ireland settled into a relatively comfortable state of nationhood, gardens – north and south – were bedevilled by adverse circumstances. In the Republic, these included the relative poverty of the country, economic recessions, and the association (among portions of the population) of grand gardens with years of British rule.

Low visitor numbers – the inevitable consequence of a small population – have also meant that it can be difficult for owners to fund the maintenance of their plots. A positive side effect of the last, however, is that most Irish gardens are rarely crowded. It's not unusual to find oneself entirely alone in the most beautiful of landscapes and planting schemes – even if the edges may be a little shaggy.

Recent years have seen great changes in the Irish gardening scene. Sadly, many gardens have closed (including the Robinsonian and romantic Fernhill in south County Dublin – erstwhile home of the Walker family). But other gardens, previously closed, have opened their gates anew. Airfield, in Dundrum, also in south County Dublin, has reopened after an extensive redesign by Italian-born British designer Arabella Lennox-Boyd. Lissadell, in County Sligo, which had been closed by a rights-of-way dispute, has cautiously reopened. In County Wicklow, the Royal Horticultural Society of Ireland is restoring the walled garden at Russborough House.

Irish gardens are unlike any others in the world. The older ones, made while Ireland was under British rule, contain elements of Englishness, but they are specific to this island on the edge of Europe. The plant palette, the atmosphere and the light could only be Irish.

A newer generation of plantspeople and garden-makers have added their plots to the inventory of Irish gardens. They make full use of the unprecedented plant choice available today, and rejoice in the possibilities offered by our unique climate. Ireland may be a relatively small island – almost exactly the same size as South Carolina, the tenth smallest state in the United States – but it offers a great diversity of landscapes. The silvery rockiness of the Burren, the stony wetness of Galway, the rugged majesty of the mountains north and south, the lake-rich pastures of the midlands, the misty blueness of our coasts: all these, and more, are celebrated in our gardens.

OPPOSITE The obelisk on Killiney Hill, commissioned by John Mapas during the famine of 1740–41 to provide relief to the poor.
ABOVE LEFT The Great Sugar Loaf mountain, seen from Powerscourt in County Wicklow.
ABOVE RIGHT Pictorial meadow and bee garden in the newly restored gardens at Airfield in Dublin.

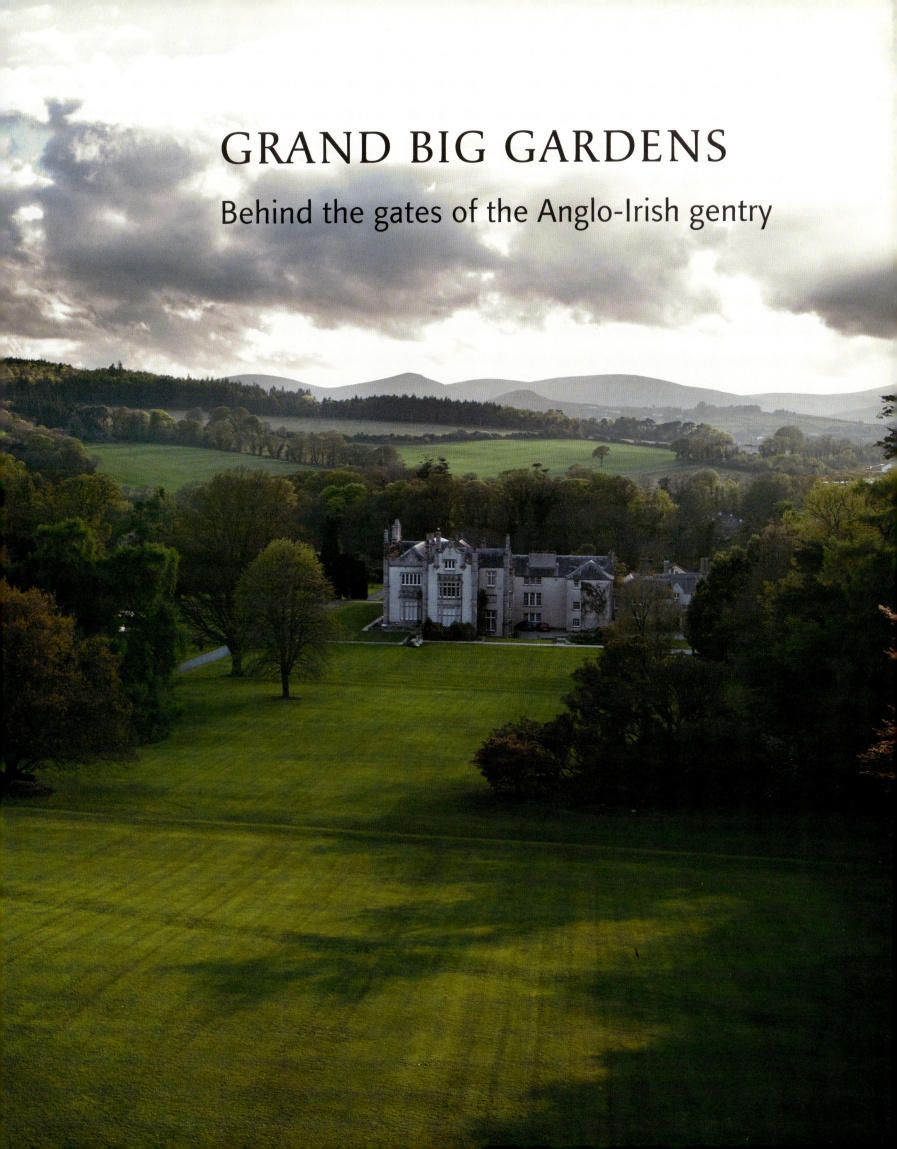

GRAND BIG GARDENS
Behind the gates of the Anglo-Irish gentry

IN THIS CHAPTER we encounter some of Ireland's most historic and grandest gardens – gardens that are showy, proud and formidable. If they were music, they would be a fanfare of trumpets: loud, triumphant and self-important. They announce: 'Look at us! We are here, we are great! Come celebrate our magnificence!'

Their swagger is underpinned by wealth, sophistication and a sense of privilege. The people who created these gardens were the Anglo-Irish elite of the day, confident, educated and worldly. Their houses were splendid and impressive, and the gardens that enfolded them were equally awe-inspiring.

Ireland is richly strewn with such gardens, in various states of repair, and I have included several in later chapters. Here, though, I have gathered the cream of the crop, the grandest of the grand. We range across the whole island, from the southern end where Bantry House commands the finest and loftiest of sea views, to Mount Stewart in Northern Ireland. The latter, filled with ostentatious surprises and exquisite, near-tender plants, was largely created by Edith, Lady Londonderry, at the beginning of the twentieth century. It still resonates with her energetic, egotistical and eccentric personality.

We pause in Birr Castle, in the centre of the island, a demesne with a weighty dignity and integrity. Here, over the centuries, the exceptional Parsons

PREVIOUS PAGES Acres of lush green lawn roll dramatically up to Killruddery House in County Wicklow.
BELOW Evening sun in springtime over the walled garden at Killruddery.
OPPOSITE The stable block at Bantry House emerges from the west Cork sea mist.

ABOVE Steps and terraces descend ceremoniously from Powerscourt House in County Wicklow.
OPPOSITE ABOVE Mount Stewart House in County Down, seen from the Spanish Garden.
OPPOSITE BELOW Birr Castle overlooks a spread of County Offaly parkland.

family, the Earls of Rosse, have made important contributions in the fields of horticulture and science. Three recent generations of tree men – the present Earl (Brendan Parsons), his father and his grandfather – have populated the garden and parkland with a collection of woody specimens that is outstanding in Ireland and Britain.

County Wicklow is larded with beautiful gardens, and has two remarkable Anglo-Irish gardens that we visit in this chapter: Powerscourt and Killruddery. They are entirely different from each other, despite the fact that parts of both shared a common designer, the utterly drunk, gout-afflicted, debt-ridden Daniel Robertson. Tiresome as these impediments were, the Scots architect was accomplished and in demand. The extravagantly theatrical Powerscourt was his best-known creation – although the untimely death of his employer in 1844 forced him to move on long before it was finished. At Killruddery, his work included beautifully wrought granite balustrades and stairs, as well as some fairly discreet Italianate gardens next to the house. Yet most of this County Wicklow garden is much, much older; its excellently enduring bones date from the 1680s, when the fashion for formal French gardens was at its peak, following the restoration of Charles II to the throne in England.

GRAND BIG GARDENS

The gardens that surrounded the erstwhile Antrim Castle on the banks of the Sixmilewater River in Northern Ireland were started a decade or two earlier than those at Killruddery. They were initiated by John Skeffington, the 2nd Viscount Massereene, and probably continued by his son, Clotworthy Skeffington, the 3rd Viscount. As at Killruddery, they are in the French mode, with long north–south axes formed by a canal and walks. More intimate Anglo-Dutch elements are also present. Antrim Castle, which was built between 1610 and 1662 and enlarged at the beginning of the nineteenth century, was gutted by fire in 1922 – possibly after an arson attack by the IRA. The ruins were demolished in 1970, and all that remains now is a sad and lonely Italianate tower in a corner next to the river. Because the gardens lack a building to anchor them, they seem a little unfocused, and the busy main road and the town of Antrim crowding in from the perimeter can be distracting.

Nonetheless, they are a valuable piece of garden heritage, especially since the owner, Antrim Borough Council, has recently completed a careful restoration. The ancient yews and the long canal are especially impressive, and it is not hard to imagine the aristocracy of Ulster promenading along the lime avenues. An Anglo-Norman motte, dating from the late twelfth century, is at the south end of the gardens. During the Victorian era it was embellished with a yew hedge that spirals to the top, and planted with Scots pines. Today it offers views across the gardens and the town of Antrim.

Another, much later garden that I'd like to mention here is Farmleigh, in Dublin's Phoenix Park. Now owned by the Irish nation, the Georgian estate had been in the Guinness brewing family since 1873 when it was bought by Edward Cecil Guinness, later the 1st Earl of Iveagh. The Office of Public Works acquired the 31.5-hectare (78-acre) property in 1999 for €29.2 million and spent a further €23

OPPOSITE The long canal at Antrim Castle is hedged in with lime and hornbeam and divided into two by a low cascade. A spectral coach and horses is said to appear on the last day of May each year, the night that its inebriated driver mistook the canal for a road and brought his passengers to a watery end.
ABOVE The conveniently placed Anglo-Norman motte was reincarnated as an ornamental mound in the early formal garden. The Scots pines and yew hedging were added in Victorian times.
LEFT The oval pond forms an impressive focal point near the end of one of the lime avenues.

ABOVE Irish draught horses graze the pasture at Farmleigh, a stone's throw from the busy streets of Dublin.

OPPOSITE ABOVE Architectural plants, such as cardoons and hostas, punctuate the length of the double border in the walled garden.

OPPOSITE BELOW The cutting border features cosmos, white and purple *Campanula latifolia*, and the Round Table delphiniums, including Black Knight Group, King Arthur Group, Guinevere Group, and 'Galahad'.

million refurbishing it. The late eighteenth-century house was extended during the Victorian era, and is surrounded by about 8 hectares (20 acres) of gardens and pleasure grounds, including a walled garden, walks and lawns. A generously proportioned fountain with a 21-metre (69-foot) basin is bordered by lime-green lady's mantle and catmint, their crisp colours evoking the coolness of the water. A sunken garden, dating from the early twentieth century, is in the formal style favoured then, and contains topiarized yew elements – a relative rarity in Ireland.

A 1.2-hectare (3-acre) ornamental lake has margins picturesquely dotted with naturalized daylilies. The rest of the estate is farmland – and it is a strange delight to see ebony-coated Kerry cattle and brawny Irish draught horses contentedly grazing in fields girdled by the sprawl of Dublin city.

Although the gardens are state-owned and much visited, they still retain a personal, private aura, and are lovingly tended by knowledgeable staff under head gardener Noel Forde. The American-born designer Lanning Roper (1912–83) was commissioned in 1969 by Miranda, the third countess of Iveagh, to help reshape the gardens and parkland. Roper visited twice yearly for most of a decade. His alterations included removing heavy conifers from around the house, and the planting of choice new trees to create vistas and congenial focal points.

The irregularly shaped Walled Garden dates from the early nineteenth century. It is an intimate space, much divided up, and, rather confusingly, with walks and yew hedges that have been placed with some formality but without resolute geometry. Gwendolen, the second countess, was responsible for this arrangement at the beginning of the twentieth century. The result is an intimate, idiosyncratic space with whimsically ordered compartments.

The main double border – a watercolour-like composition of peonies, cardoons, large-leaved hostas and other perennials – shoots diagonally from a decorative corner gate. It runs into a much longer walk, lined with ten pillars (the work of Lanning Roper), which are garnished with wisteria, the pale-pink, clove-scented *Rosa* 'Noisette Carnée' and the flouncy, violet *Clematis* 'Vyvyan Pennell'. Cut-flower and exotic borders, an orchard, vegetable patch, rose garden, herb patch and glasshouses are also concealed within the walls.

Although Farmleigh is respectful of its original nineteenth- and twentieth-century creators, it also contains work from the present era. Irish sculptor Brian King has contributed a monumental bronze sphere, while garden designer Mary Reynolds has made Bunchloch (Foundation Stone), a grassy landform with a granite bowl at its nucleus and concentric ripples representing the pathways of nine granite 'planets'.

OPPOSITE Topiarized yew, both inside and outside the gates of the sunken garden.
ABOVE Irish garden designer Mary Reynolds's landform, Bunchloch.
LEFT Irish sculptor Brian King's perforated bronze sphere is almost twice as tall as a human.

Bantry House

COUNTY CORK

Between the 1820s and 1850s, Richard White, Viscount Berehaven of Bantry House, travelled widely in Europe. The son of the 1st Earl of Bantry was eager to reinforce his family's recently minted noble status, and being an ardent admirer of the arts, he shipped crates of sculptures, paintings, tapestries and fine furniture to the west Cork house. He was keen, too, to improve the garden in a way that would exalt the family seat, embrace the surrounding landscape and – through its obvious magnificence – varnish the reputation of the Earls of Bantry with a deep layer of gravitas, sophistication and wealth.

He filled his European sketchbooks with picturesque vistas and classical details – summer houses, stonework, ornamental terraces, urns. He brought these inspiring images home to Cork and, over a couple of decades, constructed around the newly enlarged family home one of the most ostentatious gardens on the island. The site, on the south side of Bantry Bay, with the ground rising steeply up from the coast into a rocky hillside, was spectacular but challenging.

Berehaven turned the challenge into a triumph. He employed hundreds of men to reshape the land into seven terraces, ornamented with statuary and balustrades, and with Bantry House on the third level. His earthworks helped to disguise the new coach road that ran along the bottom of the property, separating it from the sea. His father had agreed to the construction of the road while Berehaven was travelling in Europe. This was a source of great distress to him, as the public way interrupted the dramatic flow of the gardens down to the shore.

On the other side of the grey stone and red brick house, he conquered the sharp gradient of the hill with a run of stairs ascending dizzyingly to the heavens, and interrupted by narrow terraces. Known as the Stairway to the Sky or the 100 Steps, the narrow and precipitous ascent siphons visitors irresistibly up its stone risers, as they seek the reward of the thrilling view from above.

The prize is well worth the heart-taxing, calf-searing climb. Below, Bantry House sits in stately aplomb, with its fourteen-bay exterior facing an Italianate box-delineated parterre, designed by Berehaven and flanked by two cupola-crowned, quadrangular stable blocks. In the centre of the parterre are a round fishpond and a dolphin fountain, encrusted with river stones and shells. Wisteria runs around a circular iron frame and makes blue and mauve thunderclouds of blossom in late spring and early summer. The climbers are famously of two different species, the

Early morning mist enshrouds the wisteria circle and parterre at Bantry House.

The French Invasion That Wasn't
Bantry House is famous for being magnificently prepared for an invasion that never happened. At the end of 1796, a fleet of forty-three warships set sail from Brest in France and headed towards Ireland. Led by General Lazare Hoche, and with around 15,000 men on board, including Irish patriot Theobald Wolfe Tone, the armada was intended to help the United Irishmen liberate Ireland from British rule. Richard White (father of Bantry House's chief grandifier) was the owner of Seafield House, as the estate was then called. Staunchly loyal to the British crown, he raised a militia of local men as soon as he heard rumours of a possible invasion. So when the ships appeared in Bantry Bay, the men, armed with muskets and cannon, were ready to repel the invasion. However, their services were not called upon. It was the worst winter in decades, and easterly storms scuppered the French admiral's plans. Twelve ships were lost, and the rest sailed raggedly back to France. Richard White, who had sunk huge funds into his troops, was made Baron Bantry in 1797 in recognition of his services to the king. In 1801, the title was upgraded to Viscount Berehaven, and in 1816, to Earl of Bantry. The earldom, according to the present owners of Bantry House, was the start of the family's financial troubles.

Japanese *W. floribunda* and the Chinese *W. sinensis*. The first twines clockwise, and the second anti-clockwise.

Beyond the house and its expansive lawns, Bantry Bay and its islands – Whiddy Island, Chapel Island, Horse Island – are spread out, while on the next peninsula the Caha Mountains trace a scalloped edge along the horizon. The mercurial west Cork weather ensures an ever-changing spectacle, as sea, sky and mountains shift their tones from muted greys and taupes to sunny Mediterranean blues and greens to the fiery palette of an Atlantic sunset.

Viscount Berehaven became the 2nd Earl of Bantry upon the death of his father in 1851, and he continued to improve the estate until his own death in 1868. Although married (to the wealthy Lady Mary O'Brien, daughter of the Marquis of Thomond of Dromoland Castle in County Clare), he had no children. His embellishments were designed for instant pomp and circumstance, and were executed as quickly as possible, often by an unskilled labour force. Some of the work was carried out during and after the Famine period, and was intended to provide relief and employment for the local population. But with little money coming in from rents, the grand designs suffered. Walls were built without foundations, and some structures were flimsily fashioned in timber, which did not last long in the aqueous west Cork climate. Part of the 2nd Earl's legacy, unfortunately, has been less-than-satisfactory work needing continual shoring up and fixing.

And Bantry House's finances – like those of many Irish big houses – have been precarious rather than comfortable for most of its history. Inheritance taxes, the Irish Civil War of 1922–3 (during which time the house operated as a hospital for both sides), and two world wars all took their toll on its resources and management.

The title of the Earl of Bantry became extinct in 1891, after the death of the 4th Earl, but the present owners, the Shelswell-Whites, are related through the female line. They continue to care for the house and gardens, and to attempt to reverse the dereliction that set in during the decades of difficult times. But with just two gardeners – including head gardener Lorna Finnegan – and a series of temporary student helpers, it is a battle to keep the garden from disappearing under a green tide of west Cork vegetation. Weedkillers, the refuge of many modern gardeners, are used only on the paths. During the 2nd Earl's incumbency, it is worth noting, between forty and fifty full-time gardeners and groundsmen were regularly employed

on the estate, and numbers were dramatically increased during the implementation of his various projects.

Today, despite its tiny staff, the demesne at Bantry House is magical. The 2nd Earl's creation still impresses, although not in the clean-lined and triumphant way that he had planned. The imposing geometry is there, but it is furred over with a coating of moss, ferns and other herbage. The house and its surrounding garden are like a classical clearing that blurs into a jungle of exuberant vegetation. There is a feeling of barely restrained decadence and decay that is mournfully attractive.

The view from the top of the 100 Steps, over a century and a half after it was conceived, remains one of the most majestic vistas in Ireland. The viewer experiences an interesting clash of centuries: the panorama of the bay is all Victorian watercolour, but drawn across with the lines of modern mussel farms, while the noise of traffic (from that pesky road) rises above the bird-song.

ABOVE The watchful figure of a bird, described in different sources as a heron or a stork (from the family crest of the Earls of Bantry), sits atop the parapet of the stables, with the cupola behind.

OVERLEAF The sun sets over Bantry Bay on an evening in late May.

ABOVE Steps at the edge of the formal garden lead off towards the woodland.
RIGHT Clipped box in terracotta pots attempts to maintain order in the garden, while ivy creeps up the balustrades below.
OPPOSITE The Stairway to the Sky is a daunting climb, but the brave-legged are rewarded with one of the best views in Ireland – across the house and gardens to Bantry Bay.

Parts of the gardens have been restored in recent years, and the family has wisely eschewed a slavish replication of a Victorian planting style. In front of the house, fourteen huge round beds have been planted with an exhilarating mix of red hot pokers, daylilies, Russian sage (*Perovskia atriplicifolia*) and palm trees. Nearby, in Diana's Bed, the goddess of the hunt rises from a many-textured green mound of strong foliage plants such *Miscanthus*, *Astelia* and *Melianthus major*.

On the west side of the house, the Sunken Garden was once a formal, box-edged rose garden. Now, after the tired old box hedges succumbed to blight, it is filled with airy plants such as giant oat grass (*Stipa gigantea*), gaura, *Verbena bonariensis* and evening primrose, and with cottagey species such as sweet pea and columbine. Bees, hoverflies and butterflies love the sheltered space full of nectar-rich flowers. Overhead, a century-old cordyline bad-temperedly drops its strappy, leathery leaves on to the joyful melée below.

Away from the house, a network of fern-lined paths spreads through the mixed woodland. The Stream Walk leads to an early twentieth-century, Japanese-style water garden made by Edward Leigh-White, who inherited after the death of his uncle, the 4th and last Earl. Another path ends at the sloping, 2-hectare (5-acre) Walled Garden. In the 2nd Earl's time it was formally laid out with box hedges and parades of yew trees among the espaliered fruit trees and other food-producing plants. Now it is given over to allotments and Mother Nature.

OPPOSITE Date palms, *Perovskia* and red hot pokers inhabit the fourteen round beds at the front of the house.
ABOVE Alliums, aquilegias and camassias in the Sunken Garden.
LEFT Japanese maple and red bridge in an oriental-style corner of the garden.

Mount Stewart

COUNTY DOWN

There is an earlier romantic landscape at the National Trust's Mount Stewart at Newtownards in County Down, but it is the twentieth-century garden that steals the show. Like its maker, Edith, Lady Londonderry, it is irresistibly flamboyant, self-centred and assertive. She and her husband, Charles Vane-Tempest-Stewart, the 7th Marquess of Londonderry, made Mount Stewart their principal home in 1921, when he was appointed Leader of the Senate and Minister for Education in the newly formed government of Northern Ireland. So, if it had not been for the partition of the island, this world-famous garden might not have been created by its owner with such attention to detail and with such devotion.

And if it had not been for the First World War, it would not have been made so swiftly, for much of the labour was carried out by a team of more than twenty ex-servicemen, newly demobbed and full of military discipline. Edith's garden, a series of compartmentalized gardens to the south and west sides of the house, was completed in less than ten years.

The mild climate helped the plantings to bulk up quickly. Mount Stewart nestles on the inner shore of the Ards peninsula, a bony downward-pointing digit on the east coast of Northern Ireland. The gardens are separated from the salt waters of the inlet of Strangford Lough by only a road and the Sea Plantation, an eighteenth-century land reclamation project. The sea proper – in the form of the North Channel to the east and Belfast Lough to the north – is just a few miles across the peninsula. With all this temperature-mitigating water, Mount Stewart is largely frost-free. Rainfall is relatively low for Ireland (about 800 millimetres/31 inches per annum), but the moist sea air brings in heavy mists and dews in warm weather.

Edith was energized by the balmy climate, and was happier here than in her other houses. Relations with her famously philandering husband improved for a time, and their fifth and last child, Mairi, was born here.

She was excited by the planting possibilities that Mount Stewart offered. She sought advice from Sir John Ross of Bladensburg, former Chief Commissioner of the Dublin Metropolitan Police, who lived about 96 kilometres (60 miles) away at Rostrevor House, overlooking Carlingford Lough. His garden – alas, no longer extant – was sheltered and mild, and boasted the largest collection of plants in Ireland in private hands. She turned also to Sir Herbert Maxwell of Monreith in

Mount Stewart House peers out from a screen of vegetation, including two huge domed bay trees acquired in 1923.

Mount Stewart's Powerful People

In 1744, Alexander Stewart, a landowner and linen merchant of Presbyterian Scots planter stock, used part of his wife's sizeable fortune to acquire a large tract of land in County Down. He built a modest house, which was later enlarged and named Mount Stewart. Alexander's son, Robert, became the 1st Marquess of Londonderry. Over the generations, the family achieved considerable status and power in both Ireland and England.

The 2nd Marquess, also Robert, was known by his courtesy title Viscount Castlereagh for most of his life (he outlived his father by only a year). He enjoyed many political appointments, among them Chief Secretary for Ireland. He was involved in the ruthless quelling of the 1798 Rebellion, during which 30,000 people lost their lives. He added to his unpopularity in Ireland by helping to set up the Act of Union in 1800, which abolished the Irish Parliament and handed its affairs over to London. In 1814 and 1815 Castlereagh represented Britain at the Congress of Vienna, along with his half-brother and fellow politician Charles Stewart, who went on to become the 3rd Marquess.

Immense wealth was brought to the family by Lady Frances Anne Vane-Tempest, the second wife of the 3rd Marquess. Her money allowed the Londonderrys to develop coalmines and railways, and a harbour at Seaham in County Durham. They also spent a large fortune on their residences, rebuilding houses at Seaham and Wynyard (also in County Durham), buying and extending Holdernesse House (which they renamed Londonderry House) in London's Park Lane, and refurbishing and enlarging Mount Stewart.

By the time the 7th Marquess, Charles Vane-Tempest-Stewart, succeeded to the title in 1915, the family owned 20,234 hectares (50,000 acres) of land in Ireland and England. They received an annual rental income of around £100,000 (the equivalent of several millions today), as well as enormous earnings from the Durham collieries. Charles was well connected (he was a cousin of Winston Churchill) and held many political posts during his lifetime. His wife, Edith, was a famed and lavish society hostess, who courted all who would advance her husband's career. At Mount Stewart the Londonderrys entertained royalty, fellow aristocrats, politicians, artists and literary figures at their many house parties. In the years before the Second World War, Hitler's foreign policy advisor Joachim von Ribbentrop visited twice, accompanied by a band of boorish SS men. Charles and his family paid a reciprocal visit to the Führer in Germany. These naive and unsanctioned efforts at diplomacy earned the Marquess the nickname of the 'Londonderry Herr'.

Between 1955 and 1986, the house and gardens at Mount Stewart were transferred in stages to the National Trust.

The Londonderrys' family burial ground, Tir Nan Og, is on a quiet hillside on the far side of the great lake.

Wigtownshire on the west coast of Scotland. The author and MP's garden, a quick hop across the North Channel, was famous for its rare and near-tender species.

When Edith began her transformation of the gardens, the long and low grey sandstone house was oppressively crowded by evergreen oaks (*Quercus ilex*). She had them chopped down – which must have been cathartic, as Mount Stewart had previously been the home of her late mother-in-law, Theresa, with whom she had had a sometimes difficult relationship. She spared the Scots pines, the big old yews, and the large planting of *Eucalyptus globulus* that embraced the garden. These last, grown from seed collected in South Africa in 1894, were usually used as temporary dot plants in bedding schemes, but in Mount Stewart's remarkable climate they grew into magnificent specimens. Now, over a hundred years later, they are a lofty and powerful presence, suffusing the air on hot days with their sharp, head-clearing resin, and bouncing their knobbly seed capsules on to the ground below.

Edith's first effort was the Italian Garden, which she began in the spring of 1919, before she and Charles took

MOUNT STEWART | 37

up residence full time. Her mother-in-law had died on 16 March of that year, and must have been barely cold in the grave when her successor set about the place. Although Edith had never actually been to Italy, this was no obstacle to her creative flow in designing her own salute to that country. The rigorously formal parterre beds and ponds she based on her mother's garden at Dunrobin Castle in Scotland; and for the stonework that surrounded it, she was inspired by pictures of Villa Gamberaia near Florence and the Villa Farnese, about 50 kilometres (31 miles) north-west of Rome. Her planting was idiosyncratic: instead of box – which she hated – for the parterres, she tried various woody plants that could be kept in shape with shears. Over the years, dwarf red berberis, hebe, heather, potentilla and santolina have all done the job as box substitutes.

Edith filled the beds with roses initially, but they did not like the sea mists, so she experimented with different kinds of plantings. She kept illustrated diaries on the garden's progress, and they detail her constantly changing ideas. She thought nothing of ripping out one year's planting and starting entirely anew the following season. By the middle of the 1930s, when she had become an accomplished plantsperson, she had designed her own unique system for the parterres: herbaceous plants with a strong vertical filling of standards and

climbers. She trained unconventional plants as standards, including geraniums, artemisia and ceanothus.

Mount Stewart's most photographed feature is its collection of Portland cement creatures. Many of these are on the Dodo Terrace, and are a humorous tribute to the Ark Club, which Edith had founded during the First World War. Its diverse members (eventually numbering around two hundred) were drawn from the worlds of politics, society and the arts, and they included Winston Churchill, Neville Chamberlain, Arthur Balfour, Sean O'Casey, and Lord and Lady Lavery. Among those immortalized in the garden are Edith's own father, Sir Henry Chaplin (who had been satirized in the *Westminster Gazette* as a dodo), and her fickle husband, Charley the Cheetah. Her favourite lurcher, Fan, occupies a position of prominence equal to that of her wayward spouse. The Mermaid of Mahee, a legendary figure from Strangford Lough, is here, along with Aesop's fox and crow, and other figures from various mythologies. Mount Stewart's chatelaine, never the shrinking violet, erected several effigies of herself as Circe the Sorceress – her Ark Club persona.

All the grey cement figures were designed by Edith herself, and fabricated by craftsman Thomas Beattie, from nearby Newtownards. Now, nearly a century old, they are beginning to show their brittle age, as the metal in their armatures

OPPOSITE The Portland cement creatures on the Dodo Terrace are representations of Edith's Ark Club, which she founded in 1915. Each of its members was given a badge with a dove bearing an olive branch.
ABOVE The figures surrounding the Italian Garden tell the story of Homer's *Odyssey*.

(which included old trowels, forks and cutlery as well as the expected chicken wire) has corroded over the years. The sheer number of whimsical creatures is overwhelming. They pop up everywhere – and include bunnies, squirrels and kittens – making parts of the garden look like a big house version of a cottage plot of gnomes, toadstools and wishing wells.

In this magically subtropical corner of Ireland, Edith obviously felt free to express herself. But the garden is strangely inward-looking, without much connection to the wider landscape. It is tempting to surmise that this was because Ireland was so turbulent at the time, and the Londonderrys' presence was not universally welcomed (they travelled in convoy with an armoured car in certain parts of Ulster). But, for whatever reason, Edith's Mount Stewart is an intense, fairytale world, full of frivolous myth-making (she had a kilted piper play at dawn each morning, as a hat-tip to her and Charley's Scots ancestors). And in the Shamrock Garden she casts herself in the role of an Amazon, in a rambling allegory depicted in topiary along the top of the yew hedge. This clover-shaped enclosure to the west of the house largely commemorates the legends of Ireland. The Red Hand of Ulster is picked out in bedding plants, while an Irish harp has been fashioned out of topiarized yew. There are more yew shapes: among them, crowns and Fomorians (mythological Irish beings). In some cases, the topiary pedestal is of English yew (*Taxus baccata*), while the upper part is grafted Irish yew (*T. baccata* 'Fastigiata').

The Shamrock Garden is one of the more sheltered parts of the 32-hectare (80-acre) garden and is planted with many winter and early spring-flowering specimens. These include camellias, mahonias, 'Nobleanum' rhododendrons and the rare Tasmanian *Atherospermum moschatum*, which has tiny, fragrant, magnolia-like flowers and scented foliage. It was also once home to a colony of tree frogs. Edith imported these so that she could listen to their strange piping song; but alas, this was a fleeting pleasure, as the tropical amphibians could not cope with the Irish winters, and soon died off. She loved exotic creatures, and after meeting Fuad I of Egypt at

The Sunk Garden was Edith's first foray into garden design. In spring it is filled with lavish plantings of tulips and forget-me-nots.

ABOVE Expertly pruned tree heathers mark the entrances of the Sunk Garden. The topiary harp is in the adjacent Shamrock Garden.

OPPOSITE In the Spanish Garden, the uprights of the tall Leyland's cypress arches can be seen mid-haircut.

a party in the 1930s, she received from him a gift of twenty-four flamingos. They lived for a time around the nineteenth-century lake on the far side of the house, but they too eventually went the way of the frogs.

The Sunk Garden, between the Shamrock Garden and the house, is surrounded on three sides by an elevated pergola, which, in turn, is protected by a tall Leyland's cypress hedge. Heat is retained by the stone piers of the pergola, and is reflected from the paving below, making it a Mediterranean basking ground for rare and almost tender climbers. Among these are Edith's original plant of *Lardizabala biternata*, a Chilean liana with near-black flowers. Other unusual species clambering over the grey stone and thick crossbeams include *Mutisia ilicifolia*, with improbable pink daisies and holly-like foliage, and *Jovellana violacea*, whose fuzzy lilac bells are splashed inside with egg yolk and measles. In recent times, as part of a garden conservation and restoration plan overseen by head gardener Neil Porteous, other interesting climbers, such as *Actinidia*, *Thunbergia* and *Aristolochia* have been added.

White-flowered tree heathers (*Erica arborea* and *E. lusitanica*) – expertly pruned to avoid legginess – make frosty white clouds of flower at each entrance to the Sunk Garden. Orange azaleas and bulbs brighten the first part of the year here,

ABOVE The octagonal Temple of the Winds looks out over Strangford Lough. It was designed by James 'Athenian' Stuart in the early 1780s for the 1st Marquess of Londonderry, and is based on the Tower of Andronicus Cyrrestes in Athens.
OPPOSITE The Mairi Garden was named after Edith's youngest child, and is planted in a blue-and-white colour scheme that runs through the year.

while later a constant parade of herbaceous plants is served up in the huge concave dish. A planting plan by Gertrude Jekyll exists for this section (and for various other parts of the garden as well). But Edith disregarded it, probably thinking that she could do better. And she probably did, having a more intimate understanding of the conditions than Miss Jekyll, and having an excellent head gardener, Thomas Bolas, to interpret her ideas.

Edith was not afraid to get her hands dirty. She took a special interest in composting, seeking the advice of compost expert Maye E. Bruce, who came to visit more than once. Miss Bruce had invented the 'Quick Return' method, which advocates using homeopathic amounts of various herbal preparations to accelerate the process. Such an idea was right up Edith's alley: she was a woman who embraced all things wacky and esoteric. She was fond of the Ouija board, spiritualism and astrology. Proof of this last interest is in her Spanish Garden (next to the Italian Garden),

where there is a carved stone zodiac table in the summer house. This garden was named because of the pale-green Spanish tiles on the loggia. The main event here, though, is the succession of vastly tall arches sculpted from Leyland's cypress – showing that in firm hands, this beast of a hedge can be tamed.

The Lily Wood, to the west of the Spanish Garden, is a more relaxed and less mannered area. Rhododendrons bloom here in spring, while eucryphias (*E. lucida* and *E.* x *nymansensis* 'Nymansay') flower in summer. Recent restorations have seen the addition of new land drains, and new plantings of woodlanders, including blue poppies (*Meconopsis* spp.), fragrant lilies, and great stands of the giant Himalayan lily (*Cardiocrinum giganteum*).

On the far side of the Spanish Garden, a path wends through the sombre and dark Peace Garden, where the family's pets are buried, and on into the Mairi Garden, also recently rejuvenated. The tropical palms *Bismarkii nobilis* (which are wheeled here when all threat of frost has passed), make a steely-blue-leaved centrepiece, while around them are blue-and-white-flowered plants: peonies, *Meconopsis*, the pure white rose 'Susan Williams-Ellis', *Hydrangea serrata* 'Crûg Cobalt' from Japan, and *Decaisnea fargesii*, which bears surreal metallic blue pods.

On the north side of the house the garden opens out into parkland and Mount Stewart's beautiful 3-hectare (7½-acre) lake. On the hillside across the water, the Italianate roofs of Tir Nan Og (Scots Gaelic for Land of the Ever Young) rise up among the pines and red-leaved Japanese maples. This is the family's burial ground, and the final resting place of Edith, Lady Londonderry, whose spirit still infuses this remarkable garden.

Birr Castle

COUNTY OFFALY

THE DEMESNE at Birr Castle in County Offaly is big, significant and historic. It is overlooked by a grey and formidable building, much castellated and betowered. If you are in an edgy mood, it might appear to be frowning down upon you, a stranger.

That unease, however, is misplaced. The Parsons family (now the Earls of Rosse), who have been here for nearly four centuries, welcome visitors to the demesne every day of the year. It is one of the great gardens of the world: a gracious and spacious landscape park, criss-crossed by two rivers and numerous other waterways, calmed by a nineteenth-century man-made lake and bordered by woodland. The pleasingly architectural formal gardens to the north of the castle contain – among other treasures – the tallest box hedges in the world. Eleven metres (36 feet) tall, they are said to have been planted sometime around the middle of the seventeenth century. Their terrifically lanky and exaggerated forms make a lofty, green-walled corridor that shimmies and sways when the breeze is robust.

There are many other venerable trees in the demesne, planted singly and in congenial groups. Together, these striking woody beings – beautiful of bark, and graceful in form and leaf – make up a famous and important collection.

Brendan Parsons, the 7th Earl of Rosse, is the present custodian of the castle and its 55-hectare (136-acre) demesne. He inherited following the death of his father in 1979, returning to Birr after two decades of work with the United Nations Development Programme in west Africa and Asia.

His ancestors, whom he describes as 'Elizabethan adventurers – or pirates, if you like', had settled in Youghal in County Cork before coming to Offaly to claim the castle (previously the stronghold of the O'Carrolls) and 516 hectares (1,277 acres) of land granted to them by James I. Sir Laurence Parsons, who was the brother of the Surveyor General of Ireland, made the journey from Youghal by sea in 1620. He and his entourage changed boats at the Shannon estuary, and then sailed up the river to Portumna, 20 kilometres (12 miles) from their new home. He styled it Parsonstown, a name that stuck for the next two and half centuries, until it reverted to Birr again.

Sir Laurence added substantially to the late Anglo-Norman castle, building flanking towers and other structures. He also developed a town, with strict ordinances as to how the houses were built and how the residents should comport themselves. Single women must not serve as barmaids, while those casting rubbish or filth in the streets would be fined. In the 1830s, his descendant, the 2nd Earl of Rosse, carried out further expansions to the castle, facing the building with limestone and adding crenellations and other decorations to give it the gothic flavour so popular at the time. He also

OPPOSITE The one-time king of the River Garden at Birr was this proudly vertical champion grey poplar. It was felled by a fierce storm in spring 2014.
ABOVE Birr Castle has been home to the Parsons family for nearly four hundred years.

> **The Leviathan of Parsonstown**
>
> Birr Castle is also renowned for science: for botany, of course, but also for photography, engineering and astronomy – disciplines that were pursued by members of the family over the centuries. The Leviathan is a 182-centimetre (72-inch) reflecting telescope built by the 3rd Earl in 1845. For over seventy years it was the largest telescope in the world, and the light-gathering potential of the huge mirror allowed the spiral nature of nebulae to be ascertained. The restoration of the instrument was initiated and overseen by the present Earl. The timber telescope tube is an 18-metre (59-foot) long beast, supported by immense battlemented and gothicized limestone walls. Its masculine and robust presence is in contrast to the ancient meadow – dating from 1620, or earlier – on which it sits. The vast grassy blanket is prettily embroidered with dandelions, buttercups, vetch and lady's smock. A path from the telescope leads to the Whirlpool Spiral, a planting of lime trees in the shape of the M51 galaxy. The 3rd Earl was responsible for discovering its spiral character.

made significant improvements to the town, and its wide streets and elegant buildings are now a well-preserved piece of Irish Georgian-style heritage.

Birr is in the very middle of Ireland, in the central plains, west of the Slieve Bloom Mountains. This is the coldest part of the country, where the benefits of the island's heating system, the Gulf Stream, are diminished. Recent harsh winters have whittled down the demesne's plant collection, sending many of the southern hemisphere plants to the compost heaps. Prolonged frosts and a temperature that fell to −18°C (0°F) dispatched three hundred species and cultivars, including members of the *Griselinia*, *Hoheria* and *Pittosporum* genera. But there are still thousands of different varieties of trees and shrubs. The majority are from Asia, and they are as happy here – or even happier – as in their native lands.

There are many champion trees at Birr. These are specimens of superior girth and height (or both), which have been measured and recorded by the Tree Register of Great Britain and Ireland (treeregister.org), an organization that celebrates notable trees on these islands. Champions are awarded blue labels, which are affixed to the trunks. Among the superlative trees are various magnolias: their health and vigour is surprising, as the soil here is predominantly alkaline. 'One of my father's most significant contributions to botany was showing how you can grow magnolias on lime,' says Brendan Parsons. A 'tiny bit of peat from the bog' and a mulch of bark chips create the right conditions.

At the time of writing there are over forty champions here, considerably more than in any other Irish demesne. This fact makes Birr's current incumbent glow with pride, for the 7th Earl is an ardent tree hugger and planter: 'My target is two hundred new plantings a year.' His father and his grandfather were also tree men, so the demesne has seen over a hundred years of constant and knowledgeable arboriculture, which is unusual for an Irish garden.

His grandfather, the 5th Earl (known as Ocky after his earlier courtesy title of Lord Oxmantown), was at Birr for only six years before leaving to fight in the First World War. He died in 1918 from injuries received in action. But his influence on the landscape was considerable. During his short tenure he reshaped the grounds to the south-west of the castle to form a series of terraces and slopes overlooking the River Camcor. He counted the great Irish tree man Augustine Henry among his friends, and was himself an ardent tree collector and subscriber to plant-hunting expeditions. His son, Michael, the 6th Earl, was a sponsor of Frank Kingdon-Ward and other seed collectors, as well as a plant hunter and botanist in his own right.

Michael married Anne Messel, a celebrated society beauty and good gardener with an artistic eye. She was the daughter of Lieutenant-Colonel Leonard Messel of Nymans in West Sussex, a great garden now owned by the National Trust. To commemorate her marriage to Michael in 1935, she augmented the formal gardens with an elaborate box parterre based on the R in Rosse, and a cloister of hornbeam hedges, inspired by those at Château de Beloeil in Belgium. She designed showy white seats on which her and her new husband's initials were elaborately entwined. The formal garden was completely restored in 1999 and 2000, and renamed the Millennium Gardens. The box parterre was reconstructed with 4,000 new plants, new herbaceous borders were installed, and

ABOVE The 3rd Earl's telescope: the 'Leviathan of Parsonstown' was for over seven decades the largest telescope in the world.
LEFT Yet another engineering feat at Birr: the oldest suspension bridge in Ireland, dating from the nineteenth century.
OVERLEAF Spring bulbs and bare branches in the sunset in Birr's parkland.

other remedial work was carried out. The old glasshouse was refurbished and once again filled to the brim with hundreds of tender geraniums, pinks, osteospermums, lilies and other flamboyant delights.

Links between Nymans and Birr Castle are still strong, and the two properties are officially twinned – despite some initial resistance. According to Brendan: 'My first rebuttal was that the National Trust couldn't twin with anywhere because it was a British institution and that twinning was a funny French habit.' The gardening teams regularly visit each other, and plant material flows back and forth.

Replanting continues in the Millennium Gardens: a lonely file of seven sombre Irish yews on the lowest of the three terraces has been given a matching line of twelve-year-old yews on the opposite side of the path. It will be many years before the adolescents achieve the self-important corpulence of the adults, but this is planting for the future – a constant theme at Birr. Outside the west-facing wall a recently planted cluster of Chilean plants enjoys a sheltered position. The group started over a dozen years ago with a single monkey puzzle (*Araucaria araucana*). It has been joined by the slow-growing mayten (*Maytenus boaria*), the Chilean plum yew (*Prumnopitys andina*), myrtle family member *Blepharocalyx cruckshanksii* and many others. *Berberidopsis corallina* clambers up the wall, brightening the grey stone with its distinctive coral-pink flowers.

A pretty bridge opposite the Chilean planting was designed by the present countess, Alison, an artist who trained as an archaeological draughtsman. The pale tresses of a golden weeping beech (*Fagus sylvatica* 'Aurea Pendula') make a satisfying contrast to the dark lines of the timberwork. The many other wooden bridges crossing the demesne's frequent waterways are the work of her mother-in-law, Anne.

Not far from Alison's bridge is a shell well, decorated from the collection of the late Mariga Guinness (the former Princess Marie Gabrielle of Urach, who married into the famous brewing family and who lived at Birr at the end of her life). The nearby Victorian fernery was the work of Brendan's great-great-grandmother, Mary, the third countess, who carried out numerous improvements, and who was an accomplished photographer.

Hornbeam arches in the Millennium Gardens.

Birr plants

The garden at Birr Castle has possibly more cultivars named for it and its inhabitants than any other Irish garden. Most famous is *Paeonia* 'Anne Rosse' (below), a hybrid between *P. lutea* var. *ludlowii* and *P. delavayi*. *Davidia involucrata* 'Golden Birr' is a pale-green-leaved handkerchief tree, believed to have arisen here. *Tilia* 'Alison Rosse' is a hybrid lime, the offspring of *T. mongolica*, named for the present Lady Rosse. *Magnolia* 'Michael Rosse', a cross between *M. campbellii* 'Alba' and *M. sargentiana* var. *robusta*, is an upright tree with pink goblets of flowers. *Fagus sylvatica* 'Birr Zebra' has yellow-green striped leaves, which become more pronounced as the season progresses.

Rosse-monikered plants that arose at Nymans, the family home of the sixth countess of Rosse, include *Lonicera etrusca* 'Michael Rosse' (a greyish-leaved honeysuckle, less rampant than the species, and with fragrant yellow flowers) and *Magnolia* 'Anne Rosse', a cross between *M. denudata* and *M. sargentiana* var. *robusta*.

ABOVE, CLOCKWISE FROM TOP LEFT
Among Birr's many champions are the tallest box hedges in the world; a golden weeping beech (*Fagus sylvatica* 'Aurea Pendula') bows mournfully over the bridge designed by Alison Rosse; *Juniperus recurva*; a miniature cascade of water in the Victorian fernery.

A short distance beyond the fernery, and over the Little Brosna River (water is everywhere here), the demesne enters the county of Tipperary. Brendan has been hard at work planting. There is a collection of Taiwanese plants, a grouping of Australian Wollemi pines (*Wollemia nobilis*) and a gathering of different species of limes which is planned to become a National Plant Collection of *Tilia* accredited by Plant Heritage, the National Council for the Conservation of Plants and Gardens.

An area known as Tír na nÓg is being preserved as a sanctuary for native plants including oak, ash, holly, hazel, spindle, yew and birch.

The Camcor and Little Brosna rivers feed into the lake, which was created by the 2nd Earl in the early eighteenth century. The weeping beech trees hanging mournfully over its edge were planted in the last century by Michael and Anne.

Near the castle, the River Garden (on the Camcor) is home to many fine woody specimens: the soil in the little valley is rich and alluvial. The rarest tree here dates from the 5th Earl's time. The tall and lean goat horn tree (*Carrierea calycina* from western Sichuan) is the British and Irish champion. It bears large ghost-white blossoms in summer, and is one of only two in Ireland (the other is at Rowallane in County Down).

ABOVE Daffodils and magnolias bloom in the River Garden in spring.

Also in the River Garden is a champion *Magnolia dawsoniana*. At 20 metres (66 feet) in height, and with a waistline of 2.6 metres (8½ feet), it is the tallest and fattest in Ireland. It was planted in January 1937 to celebrate the baptism of Brendan Parsons, born the previous year. It is beautifully shaped, its branches held up like candelabra. 'We have pruned and pruned and pruned it,' he says. 'We do massively more pruning on magnolias than most other gardens. We do it in July. The book says don't do it in midsummer. We found the book wrong. That's why we're controversial. We don't follow the books, and what a lot of people tell us. We found that the healing of the wounds, the callusing, is much better.'

Many of the trees at Birr are remarkably vertical and true. Is Lord Rosse a very orderly person? He laughs: 'Everyone says, "Brendan has a military background, he likes all his trees straight up, like soldiers on parade." It isn't true, because my favourite tree is flopping all over the place.' The tree in question, a *Juniperus recurva* (another champion), has a cluster of great brown limbs that splay outwards, just asking to be clambered over. The most perfect of Birr's trees, which had been the world's largest grey poplar (*Populus* x *canescens*) at 42 metres (138 feet) tall and with a girth of 6.28 metres (20½ feet), came a cropper in February 2014. A storm ripped through the demesne, toppling thirty trees, including the lofty

BIRR CASTLE | 55

A perfect specimen of Scots pine (on the right), with spreading limbs and pinkish-brown bark, grows by the mouth of the lake.

poplar. It was stricken in its prime, when it had stretched far into the sky, with a precisely shaped, oval crown – like a tree you might draw to fill a very tall piece of paper. It fell with admirable, soldierly exactitude, to lie scrupulously parallel to the river, offering a resting place for weary visitors.

Birr is full of superlatives: the oldest suspension bridge in Ireland – of intricate wirework dating from the early nineteenth century – is strung across the River Camcor. The first dawn redwood (*Metasequoia glyptostroboides*) recorded in Europe is also here. The tree, known previously only as a fossil, was discovered in China in 1944, causing jubilation among botanists. Not long afterwards Lord Rosse's father planted his own seedling, acquired through contacts in China. The Chinese connection is stronger than ever at Birr today, as Brendan and Alison's son Patrick, Lord Oxmantown, has married Anna Lin Xiaojing from Tianjin in northern China.

Powerscourt

COUNTY WICKLOW

IRELAND'S GRANDEST GARDEN is at Powerscourt, near Enniskerry in County Wicklow. In the high Victorian tradition, it is grandiose and magnificently, pompously grandiloquent. Its principal creators, the 6th and 7th Viscounts Powerscourt, subscribed to the idea of 'Why have only one of anything when it's possible have many, many, many?'

Visitors today – about 200,000 of them a year – step out from the house on to the dazzling gravel and enter an Italianate creation that resonates with confidence and privilege. Crowds of statues and clusters of urns are proudly raised on granite plinths. The terrain is arranged as if it is a vast amphitheatre, with a series of mown grass terraces cascading dramatically downhill. Flights of steps descend regally, their broad way book-ended by pairs of weighty granite spheres resting on pedestals. At the base is a 1-hectare (2.5-acre) oval pond ringed with towering, North American conifers. A pair of Pegasi – winged horses such as those that support the Powerscourt arms – rear up, muscles taut on shining thighs, nostrils flared and hooves pawing the clean Wicklow air. Above them and in the distance, the Great Sugar Loaf mountain rises. Its volcano-like form dominates the view, completing and giving reason to this garden. The sky and earth come together at its glorious, perfect peak. Although it is only 501 metres (1,644 feet) above sea level, its splendid isolation and well-defined lines give it a dignity beyond its modest stature.

Powerscourt House, the south-east face of which commands this prospect, was largely the work of the architect Richard Castle, designer of many notable buildings in Dublin, as well as Russborough House, Belvedere House (see page 238) and others. The Palladian house in Enniskerry was completed around 1740, and was built for Sir Richard Wingfield, who in 1743 became the 1st Viscount Powerscourt (the third iteration of the title, first created in 1618). It incorporates a thirteenth-century castle, originally owned by the Anglo-Norman le Poer family, from which the name Powerscourt derives.

The 9th Viscount, Mervyn Patrick Wingfield, sold the estate to the Slazenger family in 1961, who still own it. The house was gutted by fire in 1974 and remained

LEFT The Great Sugar Loaf makes a painterly backdrop to Powerscourt's pond, with its Triton fountain and winged Pegasi.
OVERLEAF Terraces ascend from the pond to the eighteenth-century house (with its hi-tech fibreglass domes).

a burnt-out and lifeless shell for twenty years. Eventually, it was refurbished and reroofed, with the copper domes being replaced by fibreglass ones (much to the dismay of purists). After an initial too-shiny period, they have now weathered to look almost indistinguishable from the real thing. The house interior – except for two rooms that have been faithfully restored – is now an upmarket shopping centre, but there is little clue of this new use from the exterior. And, as a bonus, for the first time the spectacular vista from the upstairs rooms, formerly enjoyed only by the Powerscourts and their guests, can now be seen by all. It is a pity that the north-west front of the house, which previously looked out on parkland, now faces a golf course. It might help matters to imagine the golfers as picturesque livestock, and to focus on the remaining majestic trees and the lime *allée* shooting off into the distance. The beech avenue, by which all visitors arrive, is likewise worth celebrating. Planted during the latter half of the eighteenth century, it retains some of the original trees, distinguished individuals with fat grey trunks and limbs.

The 25-hectare (62-acre) garden belongs mostly to two distinct periods. When the 1st Viscount was building his fine new mansion between 1731 and 1740, he set about making a garden that would provide a suitably sophisticated setting for his vastly expanded, conspicuous home. A map dating from 1760, by the French Huguenot cartographer and surveyor John Rocque, shows 'Powers Court' with some of its familiar formal elements. Among these are the amphitheatre-like design centred on the pond (later refined by the 6th and 7th Viscounts) and, to the south-west of the house, the Walled Garden. Also dating from this period, and still extant, are various tree plantings, a grotto built from tufa and a fishpond.

It was the well-travelled 6th Viscount, however, who around 1840 embarked on the Italianate extravaganza that greets visitors today. The making of the garden and the acquiring of the statuary, gates and other artefacts over two generations are recounted in near obsessive detail by his son, Mervyn Wingfield, the 7th Viscount, in *A Description and History of Powerscourt*, published in 1903. His father employed the clever but disaster-prone, doubly bankrupt and continually in debt architect Daniel Robertson to draw up plans for the Italian Garden and to supervise building the stone terraces by the house, which were based on the mid-eighteenth-century Villa Butera (now Villa Trabia) in Sicily. Robertson had another failing, which is famously described in the 7th Viscount's account:

> He was given to drink, and always drew best when his brain was excited with sherry. He suffered from gout and used to be driven about in a wheel-barrow with a bottle of sherry; while that lasted he was always ready to direct the workmen, but when it was finished he was incapable of working any more.

The brilliant architect's debts, moreover, followed him relentlessly, and he was dispatched to hide away in the dome on top of the house whenever the sheriff's officers arrived to arrest him.

The grand garden scheme stopped abruptly in 1844, when the 6th Viscount died from consumption on his way home from Italy, where he had been staying for his health. He was only twenty-nine, and his son, Mervyn, was seven at the time. Daniel Robertson moved on to other jobs in Wicklow, Carlow and Wexford before dying in 1849.

There was a fourteen-year hiatus before work recommenced. In the meantime, the 7th Viscount's guardians oversaw the making of roads and drives in the estate's deer park, giving much-needed employment during the Great Famine years of 1846, 1847 and 1848.

In 1858, after Mervyn had reached his majority, he threw himself into Powerscourt's garden project. He travelled to various grand gardens in Europe in search of inspiration, including Versailles, the Habsburg palace at Schönbrunn near Vienna and Schwetzingen Palace near Mannheim. He sought advice from landscape gardener James Howe and from the 'celebrated' William Brodrick (also known as Broderick) Thomas. The latter was an English landscape gardener whose work included improvements at the royal estate at Sandringham in Norfolk and at Westonbirt in Gloucestershire. Thomas 'came out on the terrace with an opera-glass, and looked about, and I pointed out to him the hillock in the centre. "Yes," he said, "you must take away that stomach;" and he also drew a plan of what he proposed.'

In the event, Lord Powerscourt and his Scots head gardener Alexander Robertson (no relation to Daniel, and 'a very clever man' with 'more taste than any man of his class that I ever saw') decided that both Howe's and Thomas's plans were 'not quite what was wanted'. They did, however,

decide to remove the 'stomach', as its bulge impeded the view to the pond.

Times were still hard for the Viscount's tenants, and they made willing workers: 'There were a quantity of poor people on the estate up at Glencree who were wanting employment, and we put them on the work at this terrace, at about six shillings a week. I had upwards of one hundred men on it at any one time, with carts and horses, and they were very glad of the employment.'

The soil-moving and landscape-shaping operations went on for years: 'We did part of it, and then stopped on account of the expense and waited until the following summer, and then began again.' The mess and the commotion as the men toiled like ants must have made a Breugelesque and busy foreground against the mighty and immovable bulk of the Great Sugar Loaf.

Eventually, the garden acquired its present form of slopes, terraces and walks. The excess soil and gravel had

The mosaic paving, made from stones collected from the beach at nearby Bray, shows the date of the Italianate garden's completion: 1875.

ABOVE While travelling in Europe, the 6th Viscount collected quantities of statuary, urns and other sculptural pieces. The figure of Diana in the background was bought in Rome. The winged figure in the middle is Victory, one of a pair – the other is Fame – commissioned by the 7th Viscount. They were made in Berlin in 1866 by Hugo Hagen after designs by the German classical sculptor Christian Daniel Rauch.

been deposited in the pond, which had been drained for that purpose. When it was refilled, the volume of water had been decreased by over half, taking pressure off the banks, which had been leaky. Lord Powerscourt had been busy too, travelling all over Europe buying artworks (and great quantities of antlers) for the house, and statuary, urns and gates for the garden. A 'sporting trip' to India where he bagged numerous animals – including bison, elephants, deer, wild boar and bear – yielded further treasures. He was the classic wealthy Victorian, buying and borrowing from others' more established cultures to demonstrate his own.

By 1875, the Italian Garden was complete. The upper terrace or 'perron', which had been started by the 6th Viscount, was finished off with a paved black-and-white mosaic of pebbles from the beach at Bray, nearby. The design for this, as well as that for the sundial and basin beneath it, was by Francis Cranmer Penrose, the British architect and astronomer.

The 6th Viscount had acquired marble replicas of the classical Apollo of the Belvedere, Diana and Laocoön while in Rome, and his son was, finally, able to place these on the upper terrace. The plinth for the last of these was a single, massive block of granite, quarried in the townland of Tonygarra in

64 | THE IRISH GARDEN

Glencree. It took over a week for a gang of workers to haul it from there on rollers and planks. Lord Powerscourt was much impressed by the image of his head gardener, Malcolm Dunn (Alexander Robertson's successor), superintending operations. He sat on the stone, 'enthroned, and gesticulating to the men from his elevated position, reminding me very much of the pictures of the ancient Egyptians commanding their slaves, probably the Israelites, moving obelisks and Nineveh bulls, etc., to their temples'.

Now every flat space in this part of the garden is liberally garnished with statues, vases or urns, while the granite steps bisect the space and descend triumphally to the pond. At the centre of the little lake a figure of Triton kneels, his thighs clad in a thick fabric of moss and a conch raised to his lips, while water shoots into the air and rains down all about him. It is a rough copy of Bernini's fountain in the Piazza Barberini in Rome, minus the supporting dolphins and scallop shells. In the 7th Viscount's time the water was thrown 30 metres (100 feet) high, but today's jet is considerably less powerful for fear that the pressure might crack the ageing merman's frame.

A boathouse built into the side of the bank is decorated with a margin of tufa rocks dug from a roadside in Enniskerry. They hang down from the archway like

ABOVE, CLOCKWISE FROM TOP LEFT
The Italianate gardens and the house; the basin and sundial on the retaining wall of the perron, designed by Francis Cranmer Penrose; the interior of the gothic boat house; the Triton fountain.

ABOVE Powerscourt's Japanese Garden was made in 1908, when the fever for all things Japanese (liberally flavoured with European elements) was sweeping across the houses and gardens of Europe's aristocracy.

RIGHT The Pepperpot Tower, completed in 1911, was based on the design of a pepper canister belonging to the Wingfield family.

teeth, so when you stand inside, it is easy to imagine that you have been devoured by a mythical beast.

The Italian Garden and its small lake form the core of Powerscourt, and are much photographed and much used as film locations. But there are many other parts to this remarkable designed landscape. If the visitor strolls to the east of the house and makes a wide loop of the garden and lake, a series of curiosities are revealed. The Pepperpot Tower is a fairytale, castellated edifice, surrounded by Italian cypresses and guarded by a circle of cannon, one of which is said to be from the Battle of the Boyne, and another from the Spanish Armada. The tower was built by Mervyn Richard Wingfield, the 8th Viscount, to celebrate the visit of George V in 1911. The design was based on a pepper canister in the Powerscourt dining room.

Nearby is a Torrey pine (*Pinus torreyana*), an endangered species native to a tiny portion of California. The tree here is a healthy individual about 25 metres (82 feet) tall, and the tallest and girthiest in all of Ireland and Britain. It is one of nearly twenty Irish and British champions in the garden. Powerscourt estate is also home to Ireland's tallest tree, a Douglas fir (*Pseudotsuga menziesii*) which lords it over the woodlands a couple of kilometres south of the gardens, and is nearly 62 metres (203 feet) in height.

The 7th Viscount was a prodigious planter, especially of the North American conifers that were being introduced to Europe in the latter half of the nineteenth century. These have grown swiftly in the relatively mild climate, where many years the temperature rarely drops below freezing. The garden and demesne are populated with their giant and unmistakable tapered physiques. In his estate as a whole, Lord Powerscourt added millions of trees: 'some 1,300 or 1,400 acres of plantation'. He was fond also of South American species, especially monkey puzzles *(Araucaria araucana)*, planting with his own hands a grove of one hundred trees near Dudley's Wood.

In the Tower Valley, not far from the outsize pepperpot, there is a fine Sitka spruce (*Picea sitchensis*), the tree that forms dense and unlovely cover in so much marginal Irish landscape. This is accompanied by two other handsome North Americans, a western red cedar (*Thuja plicata*) and a giant redwood (*Sequoiadendron giganteum*).

Not long afterwards, the visitor comes upon the Japanese Garden, nestling in a hollow. It was installed by the 8th Viscount in 1908, just as 'Japanese fever' was taking hold in Western Europe. As with other instances of japonaiserie of the period, it is a western fantasy, bearing little resemblance to a garden in Japan. It is, however, a delightful Edwardian set piece – with cherry trees, bridges and a pagoda – and should be enjoyed as such.

The Japanese Garden leads into the 1st Viscount's Grotto, which dates from the middle of the eighteenth century. Set into the hillside, it is a wonderfully creepy interlude, with steep tufa walls and rugged arches encrusted with ferns, moss and dense lime-green pads of *Soleirolia soleirolii* (which enjoys the common names of baby's tears and mind-your-own-business). The Grotto's rustic craftsmanship and simplicity are a welcome contrast to the opulence of the rest of the garden.

The walk behind the lake offers an opportunity to admire the full-on flamboyance of the house and of the angular, geometrical Italian Garden which strides imperiously down to the water. Further on, on the edge of a rhododendron walk, is the Pet Cemetery, the burial place of Wingfield and Slazenger dogs, ponies, cows and other faithful friends. It is much loved by children and adults alike. Only a cynic would fail to be moved by the little gravestones bearing words such as 'TOMMY, SHETLAND PONY, DIED MARCH 2 1936, AGED 32. ALSO HIS WIFE, MAGIC, DIED 1926'.

The eighteenth-century fishpond outside the Walled Garden was once known as the Green Pond, and is now the Dolphin Pond, after the fountain brought from Paris and installed the following century by the 7th Viscount. He also planted a line of eight Japanese cedars (*Cryptomeria japonica*), whose stately, arrow-straight march would now please him greatly. A multi-stemmed hiba or deer-horn cedar (*Thujopsis dolabrata*), also from Japan, makes a collection of at least thirty rust-and-grey striated trunks topped with glossy, fleshy leaves.

The Walled Garden can be entered here by one of the 7th Viscount's many ornate gates. The English Gate is embellished with wrought-iron roses, thistles and shamrocks – the emblems of England, Scotland and Ireland. The most decorative gate is one that was made for a church in Bamberg in Germany, and which Lord Powerscourt bought from a 'Mr Pratt, the curiosity dealer in Bond Street, London'.

The walled enclosure is home to one of the longest double herbaceous borders in Ireland, a bouncing, bold,

multi-coloured affair which, according to head gardener Michael Byrne, has over a thousand different varieties. Fruit walls, hothouses, rosebeds and a memorial to Julia, the 7th Viscount's wife, are also within the walls.

Powerscourt Waterfall, although it is not in the gardens, must be mentioned here. About 5 kilometres (3 miles) from the house, in the Deer Park, it is the tallest waterfall in Britain and Ireland, at 121 metres (398 feet) tall. The rattling, clattering cataract tumbles down a steep and wooded rock face, and was one of the country's earliest tourist attractions, an essential destination in County Wicklow. I'll leave you with the words of Mr and Mrs S. C. Hall, taken from their Dublin and Wicklow edition of *Hand-books for Ireland*, published in 1853: 'When fully charged ... the rapidity and fury of the descent is almost incredible; accompanied by an absolute roar, amid which the sound of the trumpet would be scarcely audible at the distance of a yard.'

OPPOSITE ABOVE The herbaceous border in the Walled Garden.
OPPOSITE BELOW The Bamberg Gate leads from the Walled Garden to an avenue of monkey puzzles planted by the 7th Viscount.
ABOVE Powerscourt Waterfall, one of the earliest tourist destinations in Ireland, and still much visited today.

Killruddery

COUNTY WICKLOW

SINCE THE GARDENS at Killruddery, Bray, were first laid out in the 1680s, Ireland has been buffeted by a series of wars and upheavals – both political and social. During times of change, countless gardens were swept away or substantially reshaped. And as landscape fashions inevitably altered, gardens were continually modified to fit the mood of the latest style. So, it is somewhat incredible – and thrilling – to come upon this instance of proud French geometry in County Wicklow over three centuries after it was conceived.

When it was constructed, its stern but beautiful Gallic precision must have seemed a surreal discipline imposed on to the raggle-taggle and rugged landscape of north Wicklow. Now, in the twenty-first century, with housing developments and industrial complexes lapping at the edge of the estate, the garden's orderly lines, symmetrical elements and heroic vistas are a historic treasure. No other garden in Ireland from the late seventeenth and early eighteenth centuries is as complete as this.

Killruddery has been connected to the Brabazon family since the middle of the sixteenth century, when William Brabazon came to Ireland from Leicester as Henry VIII's vice-treasurer and general receiver. His grandson, also William, was created the 1st Earl of Meath in 1627. The present Earl (the 15th) is John Anthony Brabazon. Known as Jack Meath, he is a forester, and is intimately acquainted with every tree in the 35-hectare (86-acre) garden.

The origins of the early garden are unclear. The design has been attributed to a French Huguenot named Bonnet, Bonet or Bonel. He was said to have been a pupil of the landscape architect André le Nôtre, who was Louis XIV's gardener and the designer of the park at the Palace of Versailles. The mysterious Bonnet-Bonet-Bonel was also said to have been previously in the employ of Sir

OPPOSITE AND BELOW The south face of Killruddery House is fronted by the twin canals known as the Long Ponds.

William Petty, originator of Ireland's Down Survey. Yet, no records have been found to prove that he actually designed the gardens at Killruddery. As garden and landscape historian Vandra Costello asserts in her book *Irish Demesne Landscapes: 1660–1740*, it is entirely possible that the gardens were designed by the man who is recorded as making improvements at the estate in the 1680s, Captain Edward Brabazon, later the 4th Earl. Edward Brabazon was a man of considerable talents in diverse fields. He was an accomplished soldier and horseman (commanding the 18th Regiment of Foot at the Battle of the Boyne in 1690 and at the Siege of Limerick, where he was wounded). He was also ranger of Dublin's Phoenix Park, and was responsible for managing the park's deer, enclosures and plantations. Later he was master of the Royal Hospital in Kilmainham, where he oversaw the garden. So it is quite possible that he was the principal architect of Killruddery's *jardin à la française*.

The green and formal creation nestles between the rocky protuberances of Bray Head and the Little Sugar Loaf to east and west, and the expanding towns of Bray and Greystones to north and south. The garden's axis is an unerring, direct line, now 1.5 kilometres (nearly a mile) long. Straight as an arrow, it shoots down the front avenue, passes invisibly through the house, continues between a pair of ornamental canals, and then zings triumphantly through an avenue of lime trees before burying itself in a distant woodland. If its long-dead creators could see Killruddery from the air (or from some computer in the hereafter running Google Earth), they would be well pleased at the persistence and perfection of its bold composition.

The early garden is laid out on the south side of the house. The twin canals, known as the Long Ponds, are like 168-metre- (552-foot-) long mirrors lying at the foot of the highly ornate mansion. Their watery surfaces hold a shimmering double of the mullioned windows, high chimneys and Dutch-style gables – occasionally erased into ripples by the skimming of a mallard coming in to land. At the far end of the *miroirs d'eaux* a round pond with a gravity-fed fountain throws up a lone jet of water. Beyond a water-filled ha-ha, the lime avenue marches off into forestry and farmland.

On the east side of the Long Ponds are the Angles, a *patte d'oie* (literally, goose-foot) arrangement of high hedges in yew, hornbeam, beech and lime. The tall, leafy walls enclose systematically radiating corridors, intersecting with pleasing – if slightly perplexing – regularity, and making a place for contemplative, romantic or playful walks. The 1.5 hectare (3¾-acre) space encloses twelve triangular lawns in its network, some of which are planted with specimen trees, including California redwood (*Sequoia sempervirens*), Wollemi pine (*Wollemia nobilis*) and *Eucryphia* x *nymansensis* 'Nymansay'. The rigorous, clipped lines of the Angles would not originally have been befuzzed by trees, but generations of Brabazons from the nineteenth century to the present day have been unable to resist an interesting woody plant. The toffee-coloured statues of plump putti that blend so harmoniously with the rusty autumn livery of the hornbeam hedges are made of cast iron and date from the mid-nineteenth century. They were manufactured by Barbezat & Cie, the French foundry that supplied the well-known bronze torchbearers outside Dublin's Shelbourne Hotel.

The Bowling Green, next to the Angles, was once a billiard-table-smooth lawn, but its tendency to flood has seen it go through several metamorphoses including a birch wood and a meadow. Now it serves as a smallish football pitch, watched over by a row of evergreen oaks (*Quercus ilex*) planted in 1693. Some distinguished-looking yews are onlookers too. Just over a hundred years ago they were neatly melded together as a boundary hedge, but labour shortages from the First World War onwards led to many of the hedges growing into trees and the lawns becoming hay meadows. Now most of the hedges have been whipped back into shape, and the lawns reclaimed. The garden staff, supervised by head gardener Daragh Farren, regularly clip 6 kilometres (3½ miles) of hedges and constantly mow 8 hectares (20 acres) of grass.

The lawns are one of the joys of Killruddery, generously cloaking the ground with a soft green fabric, sometimes folded into sloping terraces, sometimes rolled out into expansive flatlands. The feeling of openness and the inviting, springy surface prompt children to gallop and whirl, and the rest of us to wish that we could.

The best place to admire the spaciousness of the demesne is from the top of a rugged outcrop of ancient Cambrian quartzite and shale. Known simply as the Rock, the miniature mountain rears up abruptly on the east side of the garden.

OPPOSITE The view across the Angles of the Little Sugar Loaf mountain.
LEFT Colonies of snowdrops cluster at the feet of the ancient corrugated yews.

At its foot, many metres below, the intensely verdant lawn lies like a vast green counterpane. Great trees rise up from the edges: a stand of Australian blackwood (*Acacia melanoxylon*), misted with lemon-yellow blossom in spring; and beeches, including one that is swathed in a dark cloud of copper leaves. A European larch (*Larix decidua*), planted in 1750, rests its weighty old limbs on the ground; a Persian ironwood (*Parrotia persica*) makes a low mound that flushes maroon, red and orange in autumn; while a fine, upstanding Turkey oak (*Quercus cerris*) celebrates the birth of Jack Meath in 1941. A massive strawberry tree (*Arbutus unedo*) was pulled apart by a storm long ago, but undaunted, it continues to grow, forming a sprawling jungle of stems and branches. Its age is unknown, but its impressiveness (and that of all Killruddery's trees) was noted in 1822 by G.N. Wright in *A Guide to the County of Wicklow*: 'the arbutus is seen of an enormous size, and indeed every tree in the demesne appears to wanton in the luxuriance of its situation, for all have outstripped the usual limits of their specific growth'.

The pale, elegant house, with its gardens laid all around it, sits in the centre of the prospect like a precious gem. Beyond, the farm fields and forestry form a nicely balanced patchwork that spreads east and north of the Little Sugar Loaf. In the distance, the foothills of the Wicklow Mountains cut a gently undulating line on the horizon. It is hard to believe that this painterly vista is just kilometres from the busy town of Bray and less than an hour from Dublin.

After the heady heights of the Rock, the visitor might like to wander into the adjacent mixed woodland. The transition from light to dark and from open space to enclosure is frequent in the garden here. The continually changing moods make the journey infinitely interesting.

The wood, which is veined with numerous, broad and looping paths, has been rejuvenated over the last few years by the removal of holly, laurel and miscellaneous scraggly saplings. Now the splendid beech, Scots pine and chestnut trees can be better admired. At their bases, pretty, shade-loving perennials are mass-planted in drifts and pools. There are ferns, hostas, hellebores, dicentras, wood violets and *Geranium macrorrhizum* – all doing well in the heavy soil, lightened with leaf-mould. But also here are unexpected

Killruddery House in an early autumn dawn, when the trees are just beginning to flush and the dew is still lying on the lawn.

ABOVE The Wilderness, where, three centuries ago, the lime trees were originally planted in neat rows, now looking a little more casual.
RIGHT Pathways bordered by herbaceous plantings wander through the woodland.
OPPOSITE The Brabazon family amassed an important collection of garden statuary, mainly of zinc alloy and cast iron. Makers include Kahl of Potsdam, Barbezat & Cie of Seine-et-Oise and Geiss of Berne.

plants causing gardeners' eyes to light up with envy. Chatham Island forget-me-not (*Myosotidium hortensia*) – more usually grown as a precious, tiny clump – is planted en masse, while the North American shooting star (*Dodecatheon meadia*) is sprinkled about liberally. Rustic seats made from bits of logs invite the visitor to rest awhile, and listen to the full-throttle chorus of bird-song.

On the far side of the canals is another kind of woodland, the so-called Wilderness, part of the early garden. It was a place of extraordinary order, with lime trees densely planted in a rigid grid system – a mannered version of the wild wood, much favoured in gardens of the period. Now, three hundred years after it was first created, the carefully calibrated wood has lost its regularity, although at its north end a few evenly planted rows are still discernible. They are an appealing reminder of that time when the designed wilderness was a place of predictability and safety, in contrast to the real wilderness outside in the greater landscape.

Two other important elements that date from the early eighteenth century are the Beech Circle and the Sylvan Theatre. The first is a tall and wide cylinder of beech hedging – a leafy Colosseum – which conceals at its centre a round pond, 20 metres (66 feet) across. A quartet of statues representing the four seasons (the work of Barbezat & Cie) watch over the lily-padded water.

The Sylvan Theatre, still in use, is an intimate outdoor auditorium with grassy tiers of seating, snugly walled in by lofty bay hedges. It is said to have inspired Sir Walter Scott (who had stayed at Killruddery) to include in his novel *St. Ronan's Well* a little outdoor theatre where the characters dressed up and enacted a series of tableaux based on Shakespeare's *A Midsummer Night's Dream*. After the play, audience and players disperse about the gardens, where 'the old clipt hedges, the formal distribution of the ground and the antiquated appearance of one or two fountains and artificial cascades … gave an appearance of unusual simplicity

and seclusion, and which seemed rather to belong to the last than to the present generation'. It is possible that Scott was describing Killruddery here, for in 1824 when the book was published, the gardens would have been a century out of date.

That period, however, was one of the most prosperous at the County Wicklow estate. The 10th Earl, John Chambré Brabazon, who had inherited after his brother had been killed in a duel in 1797, made many changes to the house, and later to the gardens. From 1820 onwards, he remodelled and extended the house in an Elizabethan Revival style to designs by Richard Morrison and his son, William Vitruvius Morrison.

In the mid-1840s, he employed the famously intemperate but brilliant architect Daniel Robertson, whose tenure at nearby Powerscourt had been cut short following the unexpected death of the 6th Viscount. At Killruddery Robertson was responsible for the elaborate granite balustrading and steps at the front of the house. He also

OPPOSITE The squat Spanish chestnut between the Beech Circle and the Victorian parterre is one of the oldest trees in the garden; it was probably planted at the beginning of the eighteenth century.

ABOVE A round pond filled with water lilies is hidden within the Beech Circle.

ABOVE Performances are still held in the bay-enclosed Sylvan Theatre.

designed the small Italianate gardens to the west of the building, now prettily planted with catmint and roses. The scale is modest compared to that of the earlier garden, which is not a bad thing. To my mind it is the simple and brave geometry of Killruddery that makes it magical and unique, and the less this is diluted, the better.

The dainty ornamental dairy (now a tea room) that overlooks the small parterre is the work of Sir George Hodson, an amateur architect and artist who lived at nearby Hollybrook House, south of Bray. The adjacent Orangery was added in 1852 by the 11th Earl, and was designed by the Scots architect William Burn. It houses a collection of statuary collected by the Earl and his wife Harriot, gathered while on their Grand Tour.

During periods of the twentieth century Killruddery became a little woolly around the edges, and it dipped into that gracious decrepitude so common on Irish estates. But over the last couple of decades the demesne has become

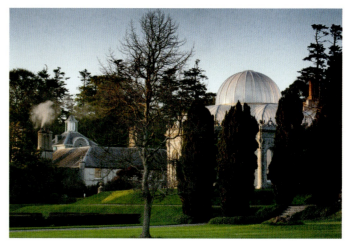

smarter, crisper and more assured, as energy and funds have been lavished on it. Jack Meath has put his forester's knowledge to abundant use, opening up the woodland and supervising remedial surgery on ancient trees and the Beech Circle, which suffered serious storm damage. In recent years, Anthony Ardee, next in line to the earldom, has been hard at work too, managing the farm with minimal chemical inputs and low stock levels so that the environment is rich in biodiversity. With his wife, Fionnuala, he has been bringing the nineteenth-century Walled Garden back to life. There is produce for the tea room and for sale, a small orchard and an increasing amount of soft fruit. A troupe of busy poultry and a few snuffly, rootling pigs are also quartered here. Visitors of all ages are catered for, and in such a way that the integrity of the demesne remains intact. It's a difficult task in a country with a population as small as Ireland, but the Brabazon family is negotiating it sensitively.

ABOVE, CLOCKWISE FROM TOP LEFT Killruddery's granite balustrades were designed by Daniel Robertson; the dome of the Orangery peeps over a procession of Irish yews; *Magnolia* x *soulangeana*, planted by the present Earl's mother, inside the Walled Garden; George Hodson's ornamental dairy.

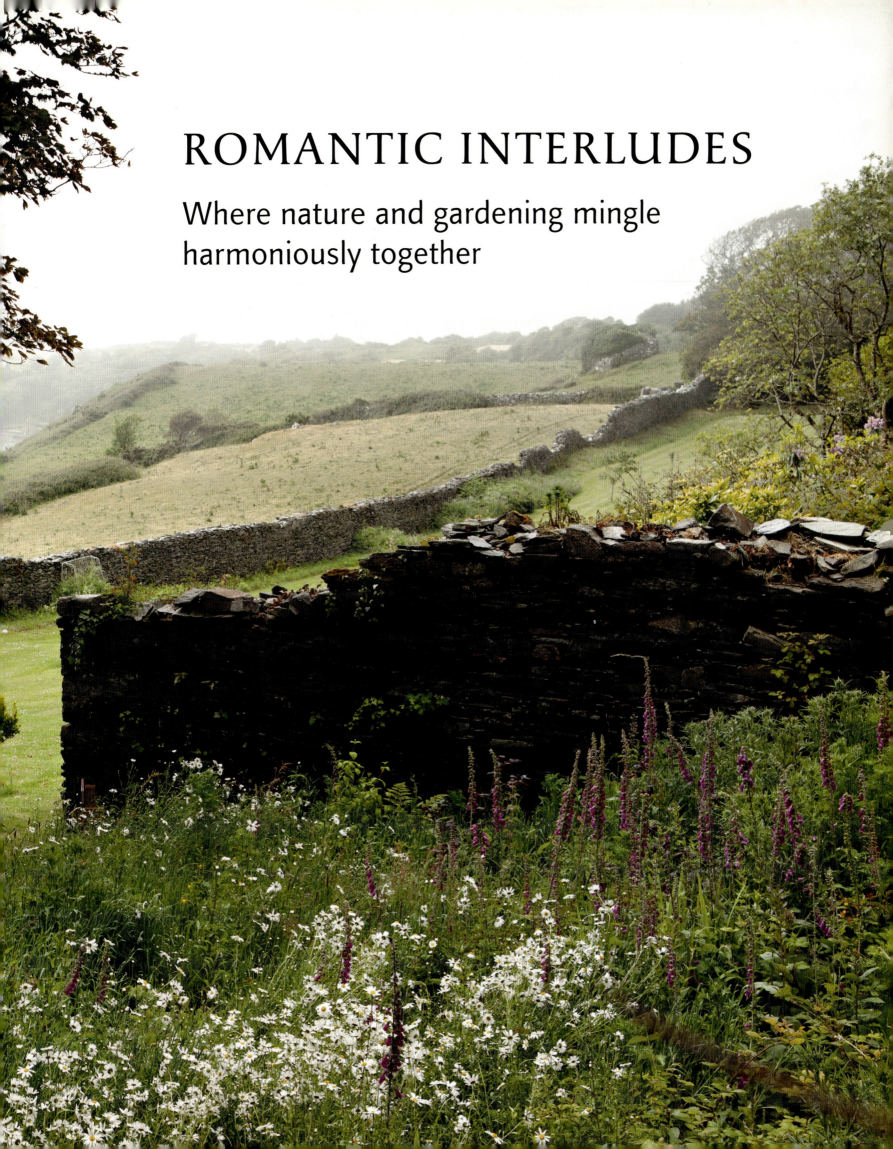

ROMANTIC INTERLUDES

Where nature and gardening mingle harmoniously together

NEARLY ALL THE GARDENS in this book are romantic in one way or another. The fact that they are in Ireland, with its abundance of water and green (two essential elements for a romantic garden), gives them an advantage. The gardens in this chapter, however, are more dreamlike than most. Enter their gates and you enter a parallel world, where daily concerns recede as the sights, smells and sounds take over your brain. These particular places offer a kind of intoxication by horticulture. Or rather, they are a potent cocktail where nature and gardening are blended together: it is not clear where one starts and the other ends, but the effect is narcotic.

Altamont, which you can read about in the following pages, is often referred to as Ireland's most romantic garden; Mount Usher – also here – frequently enjoys that title as well. But the garden that wins the award, from me anyway, is Annes Grove, a couple of kilometres outside Castletownroche in north-east Cork. It has been the home of Patrick and Jane Annesley since the mid-1970s, and has been in Patrick's family for generations. The eighteenth-century, seven-bay house, with its hipped, slate roof is stirringly beautiful in a faded and weary way. In the evening light, its Jersey-cream tones come alive, and the old glass in the many-paned windows shimmers and swells like dark liquid.

Its 12 hectares (30 acres) of gardens include, to the north of the house, a late eighteenth-century walled garden of brick-lined limestone. To the east and behind are a woodland garden and an ornamental glen through which the River Awbeg glides sinuously. Arthur Young in his *A Tour in Ireland, 1776–1779* approved of the 'beautiful glen' and 'agreeable scenery'. He also remarked that 'every thing about the place had a much nearer resemblance to an English than an Irish residence, where so many *fine* places want *neatness* . . .'

Over two centuries of Cork weather have banished any semblance of English primness, and Annes Grove today is quintessentially Irish, prevailing greenly under a mantle of moss and rampant vegetation. Much of what we see now is the creation of Patrick's grandfather, Richard Grove Annesley, who inherited the property in 1907, and gardened here – with the occasional hiatus – until his death in 1966.

Although the soil at Annes Grove is mostly limey, a strongly acidic seam meant that acid-lovers could be grown. Richard was a keen plantsman, and he acquired and planted extensively, making an exotic woodland garden above the river.

Crinodendron hookerianum, Embothrium coccineum, magnolias, rhododendrons and camellias thrive in the acid soil – which was boosted with peat hauled in from the mountains.

PREVIOUS PAGES At Drishane House in Castletownshend, foxgloves and daisies crowd the entrance to the newly planted orchard, while mist creeps in from Castlehaven.
OPPOSITE Annes Grove, near Castletownroche: in the river garden, a path through the bamboos opens into a clearing populated by sturdy perennials.
LEFT Bamboos arch gracefully as the River Awbeg slides darkly by.

ROMANTIC INTERLUDES | 85

Richard swapped plants with other collectors (including the Moores of Glasnevin and his distant cousin Earl Annesley of Castlewellan in County Down). He was also a sponsor of the plant hunter Frank Kingdon-Ward, and the *Rhododendron barbatum* and *R. wardii* in the woodland are probably original Kingdon-Ward collections.

Steep steps hurl themselves from the wooded ridge to the river garden below. They tumble and twist precariously until they arrive in the rampantly vegetated valley. When Richard inherited Annes Grove, the river glen, so admired by Arthur Young, had become silted up, and he employed English soldiers from nearby Fermoy barracks to clear it out.

The Awbeg, diverted around an island and split into channels, is crossed again and again by rustic wooden bridges. Richard's naturalistic plantings along the banks have grown to a jungle, so that every visit becomes an adventure and every visitor becomes an explorer – threading through groves of bamboo spears, ducking under prickly umbrellas of gunnera and creeping gingerly across swaying timber bridges. Overhead, a canopy of cypress, willow, cherry, and katsura (*Cercidiphyllum japonicum*) filters the light into chartreuse dapples. Occasionally, clearings open up, and gatherings of astilbe, daylily and *Primula florindae* mix casually with native meadowsweet, marsh valerian and purple loosestrife.

County Cork is the location for another of Ireland's atmospheric gardens, at Drishane House, the home of Tom and Jane Somerville in Castletownshend, on the north side of the Castlehaven inlet. The large family house was built at the end of the eighteenth century, and its walls are hung with slates in a style that was once prevalent in Cork. The thousands of individual shingles, in varying shades of blue, grey, mauve and purple, are like the scales on a gigantic fish. In the ever-changing marine light, the building morphs continually from dark and sombre to pale and iridescent. It is surrounded by 7 hectares (18

acres) of informal gardens that run down to the rocky shore. Lawns – their edges fringed with relaxed borders – flow outward from the house, while protective woodland skirts around the edges.

Drishane was for decades the home of Edith Somerville, who, with her cousin, Violet Martin ('Martin Ross'), wrote many books as Somerville and Ross. Best known of these are *Some Experiences of an Irish R.M.* and *The Real Charlotte*. A picturesque stone hut, supposedly Edith's writing place, sits on a hillside at the edge of the property. It enjoys spectacular views (mist permitting) across the waters of the inlet to Horse Island, and to the open sea beyond.

Derreen, a final romantic Irish spot, is in Lauragh, County Kerry, halfway along the upper flank of the rugged Beara peninsula. The garden covers about 24 hectares (60 acres) on the edge of Kilmakilloge Harbour, which is a bite out of the side of the Kenmare River estuary. In 1866, the rocky, scrubby, peaty property was inherited by Henry Petty-Fitzmaurice, fifth Marquess of Lansdowne. He was a descendant of William Petty, Oliver Cromwell's surgeon-general and the creator of the historic Down Survey of Ireland. For most of six decades – aside

OPPOSITE Drishane House, glimpsed under the spreading limbs of a massive Monterey cypress (*Cupressus macrocarpa*) on the lawn.

ABOVE The woodland paths are lined with montbretia (*Crocosmia* x *crocosmiiflora*), which has naturalized in the south west of Ireland.

from his stints as Governor General of Canada and Viceroy of India – the marquess was at Derreen for three months every year. From 1870 onward, he employed dozens of men to plant shelter belts of conifers and to construct a vast network of drainage channels to take the water away from the boggy soil. In the famous 'soft' Kerry climate, with two metres of rainfall per year and hardly any frost, his shrubs and trees grew magnificently. The *Gardeners' Chronicle* of 1 December 1906 reported in awestruck tones the heights of various woody specimens, previously considered too tender for cultivation in the open air. 'Griselinia littoralis planted in 1882 was 30 feet high, Veronica Traversii [*Hebe traversii*] 15 feet, Acacia dealbata 50 feet, Eucalyptus globulus 80 feet, Azara microphylla 25 feet...'

Today, while those same plants are impressive (the *Griselinia* is the tallest in both Britain and Ireland), it is the marquess's extensive tree fern grove that gives this garden its otherworldly character. The ferns, *Dicksonia antarctica*, natives of Australia and Tasmania, were planted around 1900, and the largest are now several metres high. Their green, ostrich-plume crowns tremble and swish under a canopy of oaks, conifers, rhododendrons and eucalyptus. Moss has clothed their rhizomatous trunks in moisture-retentive towelling, and opportunistic seedlings of ivy and other plants (including ferns) have germinated in the moist creases. The *Dicksonia* have also multiplied by spores dropped onto the welcoming woodland floor, and miniature forests of fernlings have arisen. The massed tree ferns have a magical presence: you'd think twice about passing under their eerie fronds at night. Even in the watery, emerald daylight in this corner of Kerry, their spirit is powerful.

A mass planting of *Dicksonia antarctica*, dating from the beginning of the twentieth century, at Derreen in County Kerry.

Altamont

COUNTY CARLOW

Faulty drains are rarely a good thing. But it is to the dodgy drains at Lumclone in County Carlow that we owe the garden that now exists eight miles away at Altamont, near Ballon. In 1923, when the Lecky Watsons had had enough of the blocked pipes and bad smells at their family home, they upped and moved to the vacant Altamont – an older house, but with better plumbing. They rented it for a year, to allow remedial work to be carried out on their errant drains.

At the family's new billet the gardens were unkempt and wild, with lanky grass surging up to the drawing room door. But, down a gentle slope from the house, an overgrown path led between heavy, unclipped Irish yews to a romantic and glassy lily-pad-covered expanse of water.

This lake, a hectare (2½ acres) in extent, had been dug out by hand – by over a hundred men, it is said – as part of an employment scheme created in the lean post-famine 1850s by the then owner, Dawson Borror. Borror, whose father had been a landscape architect, had made considerable changes to the demesne. He added beds, borders and terraces, the yew-lined broad walk, and various garden buildings. He laid out many paths, including the still-exciting one that threads through the 'Ice Age Glen' on the far side of the lake – a place of gigantic, mossy boulders, enlivened by a fern-edged stream and overhung by ancient sessile oaks. It then continues along the River Slaney and rises steeply from the banks via the bluebell-fringed granite stairway of One Hundred Steps.

Even before the Borrors' improvements, Altamont had good bones. The house had been built around 1720, on the site of a much older dwelling, possibly a convent. In the following decades it was enhanced, probably by the St George family, with roadside and avenue plantings of beech and a cool, cloister-like, tree tunnel – also of beech – now called the Nun's Walk. More beeches were planted as specimen trees throughout the demesne, as were cedars, chestnuts, limes and *Rhododendron arboreum*. A walled garden was added in the late eighteenth century.

When the Lecky Watsons arrived two hundred years after the house was built, Isobel fell in love with the dreamy atmosphere of the garden, and the green and reflective magic worked by the trees and water. As the time approached for the move back to Lumclone, she increasingly felt she couldn't leave, although her

Damp-loving perennials such as *Ligularia*, *Hosta* and the native *Lythrum salicaria* thrive on the lake margins, while Corona North's two 'bice green' *Chamaecyparis lawsoniana* 'Erecta Viridis' catch the evening light.

husband, Feilding, was keen to go home. In the end they stayed, buying Altamont. He had perhaps been swayed by the soil – good acid soil. He knew all about growing things, having previously been a tea planter in Ceylon. At his new home, he threw himself into propagating and growing rhododendrons. It was the golden age for plant-hunting in China, and there was seed to be had from expeditions, if you knew the right people. Feilding did, counting among his many gardening friends Sir Frederick Moore, the curator of the Dublin Botanic Gardens. Altamont became one of a few gardens in Ireland where acid-loving plants – which didn't like the soil in the Botanic Gardens – were sent by Moore. Feilding was skilled at germinating rhododendron seed, and he also received packets from Kew, Edinburgh and other botanic gardens, swapping the seedlings with fellow enthusiasts, and building up a formidable collection.

His younger daughter, Corona, also became a keen gardener, helping her father in the big old Victorian greenhouse, and planting and staking his seedlings. This was only fitting, for he named her after a prized rhododendron. As she told me a couple of years before her death in 1999, 'I was lucky that the favourite at the time was 'Corona' and not 'Bagshot Ruby'.'

Feilding died in 1943, and the gardens, without his guiding hand, became neglected. Corona was in England working as a driver in the FANY (First Aid Nursing Yeomanry) during the Second World War, while her mother and her sister, Diana, tried to make ends meet by taking paying guests. Gardening activities were confined to mowing the grass and clipping the big yews.

When, after the war, Corona was asked by the demobilization officer what she would like to do, she expressed an interest in learning to hybridize rhododendrons. So, in a manoeuvre straight out of an Evelyn Waugh story, she was sent to agricultural college at Cirencester in Gloucestershire. 'There I was taught to grow very good carrots and cabbages, and that sort of thing.' The staff were 'extraordinarily nice and kind', but the subject of rhododendrons never came up.

After learning to grow excellent vegetables, Corona got a job in England, which lasted for nine seasons, working with horses and hounds. Each year in late spring, after the Badminton Horse Trials, she returned to Ireland laden with plants. 'The little car that I'd bought over there would be full to the eyebrows' – much to the amusement of the Irish

customs officials at Rosslare. She would spend the summer moving her father's rhododendrons, and planting her own treasures all around the lake. The ground was choked with brambles and scrub, but she 'just made holes where I thought things would grow'. She was a young woman, still in her twenties, but she was planting for the future, 'thinking . . . would it look nice in twenty years' or fifty years' time?' She remembered how 'everybody laughed at me for planting trees', but she had an insatiable hunger for them. As her father had before her, she sent off flotillas of letters looking for difficult-to-find specimens. The now-defunct Watson's nursery in Killiney, County Dublin was the conduit for many such plants. She was especially proud of the dawn redwood (*Metasequoia glyptostroboides*) that they managed to get her from Kew – 'one of the first available seedlings' – shortly after the species' introduction to cultivation in 1947.

Now, in its seventh decade, it shoots up from a damp bed on the lake's edge, steadily gaining height, and taking on

rusty tones in autumn before dropping its scale-like leaves. Nearby, others of her favourites planted at that time are in good health: swamp cypress (*Taxodium distichum*), tulip tree (*Liriodendron tulipifera*) and a beautiful handkerchief tree (*Davidia involucrata*). Across the water is a many-textured treescape, with certain individuals standing out from the picture: a tall Douglas fir, an Atlantic cedar, and a pair of venom-green conifers on a promontory. These last two, *Chamaecyparis lawsoniana* 'Erecta Viridis' (still doing well) made Corona happy because they reminded her of the 'bice green' cake of pigment of her childhood paintbox.

Corona continued to plant for another half-century, enjoying love affairs with various woody genera along the way, including *Cornus, Acer, Sorbus, Nothofagus* and, of course, *Rhododendron*. She travelled the world in search of trees, and was a member of the International Dendrology Society.

She was keen on herbaceous plants too, and on bulbs, collecting daffodils and snowdrops from old and abandoned

OPPOSITE Lily pads crowd the nineteenth-century man-made lake at Altamont in County Carlow, one of the coldest parts of Ireland; beech trees line the Nun's Walk; early in the year, snowdrops grow at their feet.

ABOVE, CLOCKWISE FROM TOP LEFT The temple in the Sunset Field; *Galanthus* 'Wendy's Gold' keep their flowers tightly closed during a cold spell; Irish yews are clipped into an arch over the Broad Walk; *Cornus* was one of the many woody genera collected by Corona North.

ABOVE AND RIGHT
The Corona North Commemorative Border is filled with plants donated by her friends.

demesnes. She loved scented plants, and grew roses and lilies all along the Broad Walk. In 1966 she married Garry North, a 'varminty-looking young man in a deer-stalker hat and knickerbockers' whom she had met one winter when she hosted a skating party on the frozen lake. She and her new husband moved to the keeper's cottage on the far side of the lake, and she began to strike out from there, planting her trees in a ribbon arboretum and creating a bog garden.

A devastating New Year's Eve frost in the early 1970s killed almost all of her father's rhododendrons and the very old *R. arboreum* specimens planted by the Borrors. The trees, after a dry summer and a mild and moist extended autumn, were full of sap instead of being dormant. The deep chill, so cold that it was off the thermometer's gauge, caused the trees to split their bark explosively. The sound – heartbreaking to hear – was like gunshot ringing out across the lake.

After her mother's death in 1985, Corona moved back to the big house, and continued to reclaim the 16 hectares (40 acres) of gardens, woodland and lake – while farming the rest of the 40-hectare (100-acre) estate. She was adept at gardening on a shoestring. She extended the Broad Walk's hedging with bits of box plants that she had received from other gardeners, including Lady Levinge in Bunclody. And when she wanted a temple as a focal point in the Sunset Field – which connected the lake to the woodland – she bought a reconstituted stone item and trusted that the weather would put a dignified patina on it (it did, but the proportions still lack gravitas).

She died in 1999 at the age of seventy-six. But, determined that her and her father's work would not be wasted, she had left the house and garden to the nation. It is now managed by the Office of Public Works: the garden is maintained in her style, with her head gardener, Paul Cutler, keeping things going as she would have wished. Her collections of plants are being maintained and added to. At the time of her death, for instance, there were around thirty-five named snowdrops. Now there are close to two hundred. Not all are on show, but there are plenty to keep the public amused during Altamont's annual Snowdrop Week.

And then there is the Corona North Commemorative Border, full of plants with Irish connections. Corona died before her final project was completed. But, in the words of her friend Assumpta Broomfield: 'She believed we would do it. She had great faith in people. Had her last wish been to build a tower in the sky, there would be a tower in the sky!'

Corona North Commemorative Border

If you were in a hurry you might pass right by the simple gate leading into Altamont's eighteenth-century walled garden, and thus miss the main event of the summer: an all-singing, all-dancing double herbaceous border. It is a spectacular piece of floral pageantry — 70 metres (230 feet) long by 7 metres (23 feet) deep on either side — with each of its several parts having a distinct colour scheme. In midsummer, the upper reaches on one side vibrate with yellow and blue (including *Achillea*, *Lysimachia punctata* and the spires of many monkshoods), while facing them are the mauve, pink and lemon inflorescences of (among others) campanulas, geraniums and *Thalictrum flavum*. Further down, cool blues and purples — including *Aster* x *frikartii* 'Mönch' and a good deep form of *Campanula* 'Pritchard's Variety' — gaze frostily across the path at the hot petals of dahlias, daylilies, monardas and other fiery flowers.

Finally, the borders curve around to embrace a round pool, and complement its water with luxuriant foliage: ligularias, hostas and two rodgersias with Irish connections. The first of these, 'Irish Bronze', arose in the famous Ballawley nursery in Dundrum (which ceased trading in the 1950s), while 'Perthshire Bronze' was brought to Ireland by Dublin gardener Helen Dillon from her family's home in Scotland.

The border was designed and planted in the millennium year by Corona's friend Assumpta Broomfield, Robert Miller (who now manages it), and a team of volunteers.

Eighteen months after Corona's death, the border was formally opened, with hundreds of special plants from gardeners all over Ireland (and from farther afield). Over the years, inevitably, some have been lost and have had to be replaced with more robust varieties. But many remain. From the tiny snowdrops in early spring to the last brave asters, perennial sunflowers and deep-red sedums, the border continues to honour a great Irish plantswoman.

Mount Usher

COUNTY WICKLOW

Mount Usher in Ashford, County Wicklow, is one of the world's most gently enchanting gardens. The River Vartry is a constant and mesmeric presence as it traces its bowed course through the 9-hectare (22-acre) plot. A series of low weirs manipulates the flow into a succession of little falls and glassy reaches. The rushing glide of the water is always audible and always euphonious. Interspersed between the miniature cascades, the flat stretches of river reflect the sky and the many spectacular plants along the banks. In autumn the watery mirrors double the flaming leaves of black tupelo (*Nyssa sylvatica*), sweet gum (*Liquidambar styraciflua*), Persian ironwood (*Parrotia persica*), Chinese *Stewartia rostrata*, Japanese maples and other anthocyanin-flushed individuals.

The garden is home to over four thousand plant varieties, including numerous rarely seen specimens. There are trees of lofty height and heroic girth, among them over two dozen champions of all Britain and Ireland. Plants from the southern hemisphere grow energetically in the acid soil and humid air: the collections of eucalyptus and southern beeches (*Nothofagus*) contain some of the tallest and most corpulent in these islands. But this slice of County Wicklow wears its mantle of botanical eminence graciously. Its beginnings as a garden over a century-and-a-half ago were modest: then, it was planned as a place of beauty and of escape, and it has retained these essential qualities through several changes of guardianship. Today, its many-layered character continues to enthrall garden lovers, plantspeople and romantic souls alike.

In the middle of the nineteenth century, the property, then a mill, was leased by Sam Sutton. He was befriended by Edward Walpole, a Dublin businessman, who came regularly to Ashford to go walking in Wicklow. Walpole, who stayed at the nearby Hunter's Hotel (still extant today and little changed) soon began to take a room at Mount Usher Mill instead. When Sutton's lease expired in 1868, his guest was so enamoured of the area that he procured the lease for himself, acquiring the mill and just over an acre of land.

Walpole planted trees, and replaced the miller's sensible potatoes with flowers. And thus the garden was begun. But it was when three of his sons – George, Edward junior and Thomas – took over the lease in 1875 that the gardens as we now know them began to take shape. Over the years they added to the land,

The Vartry River, which bisects the garden at Mount Usher, is spanned by cobwebby suspension bridges.

and in 1927 Edward junior's son, Edward Horace (known as Horace), bought the freehold and built a new house (the mill had been gradually crumbling thanks to its disintegrating mortar). In 1946 he brought the plot up to its present size.

Both George and Edward junior were eager plantsmen, and Thomas was a gifted engineer. While his brothers were engrossed in plants and plant lists, he busied himself with the river. He designed the weirs to control its flow, and built the first of the cobweb-thin suspension bridges that still stretch between the two banks. His careful hand with the river was entirely complementary to his brothers' vision for the gardens. For they had espoused the ideas of William Robinson, the irascible and opinionated Irish-born gardener, writer and publisher whose doctrine of naturalistic gardening was then catching hold in Britain and Ireland.

Following Robinson's principles, and with advice from Sir Frederick Moore, the curator of Glasnevin's Botanic Garden, the brothers created a remarkable garden where plants, river and landscape make a harmonious whole. Moore, who first visited in 1885, was impressed by the favourable climate (the river and the nearby sea keep the worst of the frosts away) and by the excellent soil, alluvial with pockets of clay. He was convinced that 'practically any plant that would live outdoors in the British Isles would grow there' (writing in 1926 in *Mount Usher 1868–1928: a short history*, compiled by E.H. Walpole). At that time, southern hemisphere species were still a rarity, but Mount Usher was well furnished with *Crinodendron, Pittosporum, Escallonia, Olearia, Azara* and other genera from the far side of the world.

Moore especially admired the 'stately groups of *Cordyline australis*, which give a peculiarly tropical look to their surroundings'. The palm-like New Zealand cabbage tree did so well here that Edward junior freely distributed its seeds to other gardeners in the area. His generosity was an act with which some of today's gardeners would take issue, for the cordyline is now (unfairly, I think) reviled by some because of its near-indestructible, leathery leaves (which make convenient plant ties when torn into strips).

Lady Phylis Moore (Frederick's wife), was also keen on cordylines, especially *C. indivisa*: 'by far the finest species of the genus', as she wrote in *Irish Gardening* in 1921. Its broad, copper-marked, olive-green leaves are over a metre long, giving it a jungly demeanour. It is too tender for some gardens, but it still thrives at Mount Usher, adding its superbly architectural form to the plantscape.

The brothers Walpole, and after them, Horace, took great care when placing plants, making sure that each was given a position where it would thrive and get along with its neighbours. With so many choice spots – in woodland, in clearings, in grassy areas, and along the river and the little rivulets that coursed through the so-called 'Island' by the house – the result was dreamily naturalistic and free from formal artifice. It perfectly embodied William Robinson's recommendation in his book, *The English Flower Garden*, that 'the best kind of garden grows out of the situation, as the primrose grows out of a cool bank.'

The plants here were not just well-placed and thriving, they were – many of them – rare and distinguished. The Walpoles' initial strategy for the garden was brilliantly conceived and executed, so now there are communities of unusual species from disparate regions living congenially together. A multinational assembly of aristocratic trees planted near the banks of the Vartry is typical of the garden's diversity. Two champion (one for height, the other for girth) Chinese firs (*Cunninghamia lanceolata*) are flanked by an umbrella pine (*Sciadopitys verticillata*) from Japan, which is, in turn, shouldered by a New Zealand rimu (*Dacrydium cupressinum*), which stands near to Ireland's tallest tulip tree (*Liriodendron tulipifera*) – a native of North America. At their feet, smaller trees and shrubs congregate, while perennials gather casually on the edges of paths and waterways. Tens of thousands of bulbous plants – snowdrops, crocuses, daffodils, scillas, dog's-tooth violets, anemones, bluebells, fritillaries, lilies, colchicums – have naturalized in grassy areas and in the woodland. Mount Usher is beautiful in all seasons, but especially in spring when the bulbs embroider its contours with a light-emitting, spirit-lifting tapestry of colour.

In 1980, Horace's son, Robert Basil, sold Mount Usher to Madelaine Jay, the current owner. Although her previous life in County Kildare had involved horses rather than horticulture, her approach towards the garden was sensitive and intelligent. She told me some years ago: 'When I heard that it was for sale, I was worried that it would be sold and demolished. It was maybe a little run down, but I fell in love with it. My one ambition was to keep it the way it was, and not to "improve" it.'

Weirs made to the designs of Thomas Walpole manipulate the river into a series of tiny falls and glassy reaches.

ABOVE Daffodils clothe the ground under a centenarian Mexican blue pine (*Pinus hartwegii*).

RIGHT A paperbark maple (*Acer griseum*) rises out of a scilla and anemone carpet that is speckled with daffodils.

OPPOSITE Crocuses and dog's-tooth violets (*Erythronium dens-canis*) are among the bulbs that erupt in their thousands in springtime.

In fact, she went a step further in the ecological direction, and prohibited the use of pesticides, weedkillers and artificial fertilizers. Such organic methods were revolutionary in Ireland at the time, particularly in large gardens open to the public.

In 2007, Mrs Jay and her family leased the gardens to the Avoca company, run by the Pratt family. The ethos of Robinsonian planting continues, as does honouring the legacy of the Walpoles and their gardeners. As head gardener Sean Heffernan (who has been here for a dozen years) says, at times the garden feels 'quite ghostly. Trees and shrubs were planted with such care that you can almost feel the old head gardeners checking up on you.'

The gardens are still chemical-free, and wildlife is abundant. Trout and salmon swim in the Vartry, while shy dippers and kingfishers, nodding moorhens and coots, and primeval-looking herons also make their homes here. Wild animals did not always meet with such a cordial reception. F.W. Millard, who had an interest in alpine plants, wrote in *Mount Usher 1868–1928: a short history*:

> Intersecting the garden is the famous Vartry river, a pellucid and ever-flowing stream, and the banks were at the time of my visit being transformed into a rockery. The only disadvantage was that otters esteemed the alpines as beds, and ruined many a promising display, but I think that means have since been found for dealing with such unwelcome visitors.

Today, otters are cherished in this watery haven. They are not often visible, but the whistling calls between mother and cubs can be heard at night, and in the morning the mud is embossed with their webbed and clawed footprints.

The gardens are more mature than when Millard was writing, and the denser tree canopy precludes the mass growing of alpines. Yet, many of the other plants that are mentioned in his early account are still here. Among them are the 'somewhat difficult Himalayan Rhododendron'; *Mutisia*, 'generally so miffy and untrustworthy'; and *Lapageria* and 'giant lilies' (*Cardiocrinum giganteum*) in the woodland.

At Mount Usher, the different sections of the garden flow seamlessly into each other with no formal arrival or departure points. An exception is just inside the entrance, an ante-room hedged in by a thick and high wall of beech, planted in 1927 by Horace Walpole. Formerly the orchard, it now contains a lively herbaceous border, augmented by cosmos, sunflowers, sweet peas and other annuals in summer. The unsuspecting visitor might think: 'Ah, a garden of rooms follows', and prepare for a Sackville-Westian creation of interlinked enclosures neatly divided by hedges. But beyond the arched opening in the beech periphery, the layout is dictated entirely by the river and the gently sloping land on either side.

The visitor immediately encounters trees of great beauty and interest, and plantspeople do a double-take at the immense Bosnian pine (*Pinus heldreichii*) and the mournfully drooping Chinese coffin juniper (*Juniperus recurva* var. *coxii*) – both of which are Irish champions. A cluster of purple-leaved Japanese maples (*Acer palmatum* 'Atropurpureum') borders the grassy way as it tilts down towards the water. A fine specimen of the rusty and ragged paperbark maple (*Acer griseum*) is cleverly placed at a junction of paths

ABOVE Martagon lilies are emerging among the bluebells in the eucalyptus grove, where nearly three dozen trees shoot up to the heavens.

RIGHT A handkerchief tree (*Davidia involucrata* var. *involucrata*) hangs out its white bracts above an unruly mass of azaleas.

which amble variously off through the woods and along the Vartry's banks. The meanderings may seem aimless, but some cleverly lead to vistas, while others pause to consider strategically planted trees and shrubs.

There are few straight lines in the garden. One of these, on this side of the river, is the Azalea Walk: a broad grass path bordered by about a hundred azaleas that make a brassily raucous springtime display of oranges, yellows, reds and pinks. Above them, a large handkerchief tree (*Davidia involucrata* var. *involucrata*), planted in 1930, proffers scores of snowy white bracts, signalling its complete surrender to the unruly army of colour below. Also here are several other elite trees, including two champion centenarians: the very rare Tasmanian cedar (*Athrotaxis selaginoides*) and the Mexican blue pine (*Pinus hartwegii*, sometimes known as *P. montezumae*). The latter's branches hold clouds of exquisitely arranged needles, as if each has been meticulously engraved by a heavenly hand. Two of its seedlings – plump, rounded specimens – are planted at the far end of the garden.

Next to the Azalea Walk is Mount Usher's famous eucalyptus grove, at the south-east end of the garden. Its first specimens were planted at the beginning of the twentieth century, when the hardiness of the newly introduced trees was still uncertain. It was a time, wrote the awestruck F.W. Millard, 'when people were cossetting with them in pots as window plants', and he marvelled that 'specimens are to be seen as much as eighty feet high, not single ones, but row on row.' Now, the same trees have grown to twice their previous heights, and their trunks – some smoothly patchworked, some deeply corrugated – stretch impossibly high into the sky. In all, there are about thirty trees of twenty different species. Bluebells wash the ground with an azure haze in spring, while in summer *Lilium martagon* raises its many-belled stems in dignified shades of mauve, pink and purple.

ABOVE The Vartry River rushes over a weir, while twin seedlings of the famous *Pinus hartwegii* grow companionably on the bank.

RIGHT *Rhododendron barbatum* is covered in clusters of startling deep crimson flowers.

At the edge of this antipodean plantation is a solid but graceful metal bridge, erected in 1927, the year Horace Walpole bought the freehold. It offers a place to pause and contemplate what William Robinson described as 'the silvery River Vartry... gentle as it falls over its little rocky weirs in summer, but swollen and turbid after wintry storms'. The river margins are hung with a many-textured fringe of plants: strappy cordyline leaves, big green plates of *Darmera peltata*, carefully cut maples, frondy ferns, the fading powder puffs of hydrangea heads.

Across the bridge, and in a woodlandy area, various rhododendrons call out for admiration. A pair of 'Loderi King George' are delightful with their richly toned, red-brown, knobbly kneed trunks, pink buds and fragrant white flowers. A little farther, *R. barbatum* presents a surreal picture with its near-purple bark (the same colour as oxblood shoes) and scarlet trumpets. The garden's *Eucryphia* collection (including two related Mount Usher cultivars of *E.* x *nymansensis*) is nearby. It was started in the Walpole era, and added to by Mrs Jay's head gardeners.

The trees in the adjacent collection of *Nothofagus* are too lofty to be seen easily from below, but there is an opportunity to admire the impressive embonpoint of Britain and Ireland's fattest Dombey's beech (*N. dombeyi*). It was planted in 1928, and has since acquired a waistline of 5.2 metres (17 feet).

ABOVE On the area known as the Island, primulas including *P. japonica* 'Miller's Crimson' and the canary-yellow *P. prolifera* gather on the margins of the rivulets.

OVERLEAF A conical *Eucalyptus urnigera* with diagonally striped bark towers above its neighbours; to its right is a multi-stemmed *Stewartia pseudocamellia*, underplanted with viburnums and azaleas. The mixed planting of the Island area behind is visible to the right again and includes cordylines, a pink-flowered *Rhododendron* 'Gauntletii' and a *Ginkgo biloba* sending its tall leader into the sky.

The Palm Walk shoots up towards the house, and is a double parade of twenty or more *Trachycarpus fortunei*, with hairy, dark trunks like the legs of gigantic tarantulas. Birds harvest the tough fibres to use as building material for their nests.

On the far side of the house is the Island, a marshy piece of land veined with tiny streams fed by the Killiskey River (the tributary of the Vartry that originally powered the wheel in the old mill). Primulas in candy-coloured variety clothe the ground in May, while above them the roll call of Mount Usher's patrician trees continues. There is room to mention only a few: the Japanese *Betula maximowicziana*, which has uncharacteristically large leaves – beautifully buttery in autumn; *Malus hupehensis*, bearing dainty, berry-sized crab apples; *Magnolia x veitchii*, with its elegant tracery of branches and waxy pink flowers; and Brewer's weeping spruce (*Picea breweriana*), which is melancholically dressed in sadly drooping branchlets.

Beyond the Island the garden narrows to its smallest width, a narrow stretch on either bank of the Vartry: the Riviera and the Contra Riviera walks. On quiet days, a heron can be seen hunched in the shallows, waiting for its next meal to come swimming downstream.

ABOVE A heron waits for dinner to come swimming by.
RIGHT The upper and narrowest end of the garden, with its Riviera (left) and Contra Riviera walks.

TAMING THE WILDERNESS
Gardens coaxed from savage landscapes

WHAT POSSESSES A PERSON to go to an extreme place, where all is rugged and wild, and make a garden?

The reasons seem to be very different, depending on when the operation takes place. Earlier garden makers poured money and labour into contrived creations where the landscape was subjugated or excluded. Man's (oh-so-fleeting) mastery over nature was demonstrated in disciplined scenes of mown lawns, clipped hedges and orderly borders.

But for those who make gardens in wild places today, the intent is usually to be at one with nature, to celebrate that wildness, and to tread gently on it. Carl Wright, who has made his home in the Burren in County Clare, is one such gardener. In his small acreage, the rocky landscape has not so much been tamed, as whispered into a temporary compliance.

Another garden that now also harmonizes cordially with the rhythms of the land is the National Trust's Rowallane, in County Down. When the Reverend John Moore started to create it in 1858, he was quite happy to use dynamite to blast through the rock, but his nephew, Hugh Armytage Moore, wielded a more benign hand after he inherited in 1903. His interventions were few, although his plants were many. His garden of choice specimens sprawls over the lumpy, bumpy terrain of the drumlin-laced county. He was more interested in getting plants into the ground than pulling the ground asunder.

At Kylemore Abbey in County Galway, on the other hand, the wealthy Mitchell Henry moved roads and cottages in the creation of his extensive Connemara retreat in the 1870s. Unlike John George Adair, who ruthlessly evicted scores of people in County Donegal while making his estate at Glenveagh, Mitchell Henry rehomed his tenants into housing that he continually improved. Henry's walled garden was a triumph of Victorian innovation and engineering that left the bleak Irish wilderness and weather out in the cold. The former was kept at a safe remove behind

the tall walls of the enclosure, while the latter was tightly excluded by his range of twenty-one glasshouses.

At the beginning of the twentieth century, John Annan Bryce acquired the near-barren Ilnacullin, also known as Garinish Island, off the coast of West Cork. His dream, and that of his wife, Violet, was to make an island paradise where a subtropical jungle would surround a structured and classical core designed by their friend, the architect Harold Peto. Although the collapse of their finances forced them to severely curtail their plans, they continued with their extraordinary undertaking. The resulting garden, like the others in this chapter, is a monument to singlemindedness.

PREVIOUS PAGES The walled garden at Kylemore in Connemara, first created by Mitchell Henry in the 1870s.
OPPOSITE The kitchen garden at Glenveagh Castle, the Donegal retreat of Philadelphia man Henry McIlhenny.
ABOVE, CLOCKWISE FROM TOP LEFT The Italian garden at Ilnacullin, County Cork; rhododendrons on the drive at Rowallane in County Down; an ancient cordyline at Kylemore, resprouting after a harsh Connemara winter; Carl Wright's stonework at Caher Bridge Garden in the Burren.

Caher Bridge Garden

COUNTY CLARE

THE BURREN, in north County Clare, is just one vowel away from 'barren', and at first sight it seems like a godforsaken place. 250 square kilometres (about 100 square miles) of grey limestone, with little or no soil and few trees, it is one of the most extensive karst landscapes in Europe. It was famously descibed in 1651 by one of Cromwell's men, Edmund Ludlow, as 'a country where there is not enough water to drown a man, wood enough to hang one, nor earth enough to bury them'. Fittingly, 'boireann' in Irish means 'rocky place'.

Yet, in reality, this rocky place is one of the most diverse regions in Ireland. Over 600 different flowering plants live here, about 70 per cent of the country's native flora. Among them are nearly two dozen orchids, and strange arctic and alpine visitors such as mountain avens (*Dryas octopetala*), hoary rockrose (*Helianthemum canum*) and spring gentian (*Gentiana verna*) which spread here after the ice melted 11,000 years ago. There are many animals too: rare butterflies and birds, red squirrels, Irish hares, pine martens, otters, stoats and eight of Ireland's ten bat species.

The light is magical: reflected off the pale stone and diffused by the moisture in the atmosphere, it makes the air luminous and sparkling. Sunsets and sunrises wash the vast limestone undulations with a surreal pink radiance. Even in the wooded and grassy areas, the stone is an abiding theme. It elbows its way out of the thin soil and is gathered up into the walls that line the roads and flow across the fields. These are some of the most beautiful walls in Ireland, and they are treasured by the people of north Clare. Nearly every house has a carefully built stone boundary, often lined with hawthorn – which in late spring is covered with an effervescence of blossom that rivals the cherries of Japan for poetic buoyancy.

All this stone, though, makes gardening hard, hard work. No one knows this better than Carl Wright, whose 3.5-hectare (8½-acre) Caher Bridge Garden is near the village of Fanore. Fanore, incidentally, is the longest village in Ireland, thinly strung out along 8 kilometres (5 miles) of coast. And Carl's patch is probably the rockiest garden on the island. When he bought the property at the tail end of the 1990s, the house – virtually derelict – was surrounded by a layer of limestone rubble over Burren limestone pavement. A dense thicket of blackthorn, hazel and hawthorn had winkled its roots into the sparse soil underneath.

LEFT Carl Wright's plantings flow into the Caher River. The bridge is part of the Burren Way walking trail: passing hikers are surprised and charmed by the watery garden below.
OVERLEAF The limestone landscape of the eastern Burren, near Carron, County Clare.

ABOVE Carl transformed a 'damp mucky spot' at the edge of the river into a pond garden.

OPPOSITE, CLOCKWISE FROM TOP LEFT *Arisaema nepenthoides*; *Geum rivale* 'Bellbank'; bogbean (*Menyanthes trifoliata*); *Omphalodes cappadocica* 'Starry Eyes', which was discovered by Eithne Clark in her garden, Woodtown Park, in Rathfarnham, Dublin, around 1981; the fairy foxglove (*Erinus alpinus*), a native of central and southern Europe that has colonized walls all over the Burren; *Astrantia major* 'Berendien Stam', happy in the shade here; primulas, which are everywhere in the garden in late spring and early summer; *Hosta* 'Frances Williams', one of the dozens of varieties of hosta here.

Over a period of two years, Carl rebuilt the house and the boundary walls, using the rubble underfoot. He added more walls (no shortage of building materials here), incorporating nest chambers for the birds. The birds approved heartily, and began moving in even before the walls were completed.

Carl cleared the scrub from the front of the house, leaving some of the multi-stemmed, heavily coppiced hazels – and digging out and replanting others. Each new planting hole had to be wheedled out of the ground with a crowbar, but Carl had his heart set on these mature hazels that had been configured by nature. 'I do not like new gardens. I wanted this garden to look like it had been here for hundreds of years.' And indeed it does, merging seamlessly with the surrounding landscape. The house, which is swathed in *Rosa* 'New Dawn', faces north, so the front plot is shady and cool in summer, offering a nice spot for dozens of hosta varieties. Among his favourites are the gently puffy, gold-centred

'Stained Glass' and the peculiar 'White Feather', which has so little chlorophyll that its leaves have a waxy, ghostly pallor.

In spring, the front garden is brighter, and is awash with snowdrops, daffodils and hellebores, followed by erythroniums and aquilegia.

The Caher River, which drains parts of the Burren, runs along the edge of the property. It has as much influence on the garden as the rock. Soon after moving here, Carl hired a digger and carved out a section next to the river – 'it had been just a damp mucky spot' – to make a dreamily pretty pond garden. He has planted it carefully: near the house there are plants of garden origin including bergenia, euphorbia and the little Irish navelwort *Omphalodes cappadocica* 'Starry Eyes'. But as it draws closer to the river, he uses natives such as bogbean, branched bur reed, marsh marigold and yellow flag. A stand of pollarded willows (*Salix alba*) turns brilliant orange in winter. Carl's water garden can be seen from the road above, which bridges the river here. The quiet route is part of the Burren Way walking trail, so hikers who stop to take a breather on the bridge get a nice surprise when they turn their eyes to the water below.

The river is usually a well-behaved watercourse, but after prolonged downpours it turns into a fast-moving, foamy torrent, beloved of kayakers. It overflows dramatically as well, swiftly turning Carl's riverside creation into a miniature Atlantis. The water recedes as quickly as it floods, so there is usually little damage, just a tidemark of leaves and other debris on the lawn. This part of the river is famous among botanists, as it is one of only a handful of places in the British Isles where the hybrid sterile pondweed *Potamogeton x lanceolatus* has been recorded. A cross between *P. coloratus* and *P. berchtoldii*, it was discovered here by the local amateur botanist and nurseryman Patrick B. O'Kelly in 1891. The Burren man's name survives in the flora of Ireland in O'Kelly's spotted-orchid (*Dactylorhiza fuchsii* var. *okellyi*), which produces scented, milky-white inflorescences late in the season.

O'Kelly's namesake is one of several wild orchids that bloom in Caher Bridge Garden, in a meadowy strip along the river. Others here include the early purple orchid (*Orchis mascula*) and the daintily cartoonish bee orchid (*Ophrys apifera*). Carl is intensely knowledgeable about the flora and fauna of the Burren, and he maintains about two-thirds of his acreage as a nature reserve. At the back of his house, native ash, hazel and holly woodland marches mossily uphill until it peters out among the pale limestone contours. The woodland is home to dozens of fungi – and Carl knows the name of each one. Wild animals are plentiful: a sociable fox, 'Edward', visited for years, coming into the kitchen for his dinner; and a pair of pine martens moved into the loft to raise their noisy family. Feral goats live in the mountains, and during very cold weather 'they come down and help themselves to bits of the garden.' In spring, the call of the cuckoo is a constant *ostinato* amid the other sounds of the Burren.

While the outer edges of Caher Bridge Garden are barely cultivated, the area immediately behind the house is where its owner indulges his obsessions with building and planting. This is an intensive place, furnished with limestone-faced terraces and raised beds which are filled with tons of imported topsoil – all sieved by hand. For Carl is an inveterate plant collector, and the thin and stony ground offered few places for roots to nestle. His inventory of plants would have Patrick B. O'Kelly turning green in his grave with envy. He has around two hundred snowdrops (including the Irish 'Castlegar' and 'Drummond's Giant'), over a hundred daylilies, and many dozens of ferns and daffodils. He's also rather fond of arisaemas, geraniums, geums, hellebores and saxifrages. Primulas spring up everywhere in May and June. And, because he is originally from Devon and lived in Somerset, 'there are quite a few Margery Fish plants'. In honour of the great British cottage gardener, he grows, among others, the ferny-foliaged, lilac-flowered *Polemonium* 'Lambrook Mauve'.

There are thousands of plants here, in super-detailed arrangements. For the non-plantsman, this could be dizzy-making, but fortunately, there is much else to admire, particularly in the stonework. Carl has chosen to echo the arches of the bridge spanning the Caher River. So, circles and semicircles occur again and again, and give the garden coherency. The haze of native woodland too is a constant reminder that this rocky, meticulous garden is on loan from a savage landscape, patiently waiting to march back in to reclaim its territory.

LEFT Native hazel, ash and holly woodland crowds into the back garden. The ash trunk on the right is home to twenty-seven species of lichen.
BELOW Carl's stonework contains secret chambers for nesting birds; the circular theme is based on the arches of the bridge over the Caher River.

Kylemore Abbey

COUNTY GALWAY

The Victorian era was a time of great inventions and extravagant ambitions. For those with money, it was possible to realize near impossible dreams. Mitchell Henry, born in Manchester in 1826, was a man with such dreams. The son of Alexander Henry, a well-off textile merchant and Liberal MP for South Lancashire, he trained as a surgeon and became a senior consultant at Middlesex Hospital in London before he was thirty. Among his feats in the operating theatre was the removal of a gallstone so large that half was sent to the Museum of the Royal College of Surgeons in London and the other half to its sister institution in Dublin.

With the death of his father in 1862 he inherited the very prosperous family business, A & S Henry, and abandoned his medical career. Not long afterwards, he set about acquiring land in Connemara – a place that was dear to him and to his much-loved wife, Margaret. He put together an immense estate near Renvyle – 6,000 hectares (15,000 acres) of bog, mountain and lakes. Kylemore, as it was called, was outstandingly beautiful and remote, 78 kilometres (48 miles) from Galway city. Getting there from the Henrys' lavish home at Stratheden House in Knightsbridge, London, required a serious amount of travel by train, boat and carriage. The gothic castle that Henry commissioned at Kylemore must have offered near-surreal comfort after the journey across the desolation of post-famine Ireland. Designed by Samuel Ussher Roberts and James Franklin Fuller, it was completed in 1871, and had around seventy rooms, including thirty-three bedrooms.

The building was faced with 'Kingstown granite', brought by sea from the quarry at Dalkey in County Dublin, on the far side of Ireland. The pale-grey, castellated and turreted pile sits on the edge of Pollacappul Lough, where its massive grandeur is doubled by its wavy reflection. Mitchell Henry planted around 300,000 trees on the estate, mostly oak, ash, sycamore and conifers. Some of these swathe the hillside behind the castle, giving it a dramatic backcloth of greenery. The name Kylemore – Coill Mór – means 'big wood' in Irish, but by the time the Henrys arrived there were few trees left in this rocky and boggy part of Connemara.

The fairytale castle needed a fairytale garden – in the requisite prim and proper Victorian style. The badly drained, boggy soil was no barrier to Mitchell Henry's fantasy, nor was the 1,600 millimetres (63 inches) of rain per year – much of it falling in that special soul-mouldering drizzle that occurs on at least two out of three days

Kylemore Castle, the Victorian pile built by Manchester-born Mitchell Henry, is reflected in the waters of Pollacappul Lough.

RIGHT The steep gradient of the land in the walled garden is evident in the lawn and beds that slope abruptly downhill from the restored glasshouse.
BELOW The plants in the double herbaceous border are arranged in four graduated tiers: carefree mingling was not encouraged in Victorian gardens.

in this part of the west of Ireland. Nor was he put off by the cold winds wheeling off the Atlantic, less than 4 kilometres (2½ miles) away. And the road to the town of Clifden that ran through the middle of the newly formed demesne? That just needed to be moved to a more convenient location on the far side of the lake.

Accordingly, while scores of men were erecting the castle, another workforce, about a mile to the west, was building one of the largest walled gardens in Ireland, and possibly the only one built on a bog. Fortunately, Mitchell Henry's principal architect, Roberts, was also a drainage specialist. The 2.5-hectare (6-acre) stone and brick enclosure was constructed in a fold in the landscape, with Doughruagh Mountain on one side and Diamond Hill on the other. The remains of the old Clifden road ran in the main gate and out the far side, acting as an important artery through the enclosure. The French head gardener, James Garnier, worked with the inventive Birmingham glasshouse designer, James Cranston. The resulting complex on the south-facing slope of the garden consisted of twenty-one interconnected glasshouses. In the eternally damp weather, they offered a warm and sheltered place for the ladies to take their walks. Heating was supplied by three boilers, one of which – patented by Kerryman John Cowan – was fired by a lime kiln. Anthracite (shipped from Wales) and limestone (the local rock) were layered in the kiln and burnt: the resulting lime could be used to make mortar, or to bring down the acidity of the soil. In time, the kiln produced enough lime to sell – and the glasshouses were, in effect, heated for free.

Each of the glasshouses was specially designed for its purpose: there were four vineries, a palm house, a plant house, a stove house, and – it being the height of pteridomania – two ferneries with elaborate rockwork and arches clothed in rare ferns and mosses. There were fruit houses in plenty – for growing nectarines, peaches, melons and tomatoes. An entire house, 22 metres long and 8 metres wide (72 feet by 26 feet), was devoted to bananas. When the Henrys were not in residence at Kylemore Castle, the bananas, carefully wrapped in cabbage leaves, were sent to their London home.

Mitchell Henry was keen on new technology: dynamite was used here for the first time in Connemara, to blast the rocks for the rock garden. Later he had his own electricity, using a turbine powered by the water from a small lake on Doughruagh. He also installed an industrial standard fire hydrant system in the walled garden and on the estate farm.

Beyond the remarkable glasshouses, the rest of the walled garden was a model of Victorian horticulture. It was divided into two parts by a stream, margined with a strip of woodland – which acted as a shelter belt, as well as an artificial wilderness. Here, safely ensconced among the ferns and bluebells, family and visitors could play at being bucolic while the real wilderness was kept at bay by the high walls. On the east side of the miniature sylvan retreat was the flower garden, with rigorously formal beds and perfect lawns. To the west were the kitchen and herb garden, the rockery, ponds for irrigation, and a double herbaceous border – this last protected from the sight of the rude vegetables by high hedges.

Mitchell Henry was reputed to be a good employer and landlord, paying a more than fair wage, and continually improving his tenants' cottages and amenities. He was deeply involved in the area, becoming MP for Galway from 1871 until 1885, supporting Home Rule for Ireland. Sadness came in 1874 when he lost his beloved Margaret to dysentery while they were in Egypt. A few years later, a daughter was killed in a riding accident. His income, perhaps drained by the Connemara enterprise and his lavish London lifestyle, slowed to a trickle. Stratheden House was sold around 1900, and in 1902 Kylemore went too, at a great loss. Mitchell Henry died in 1910 at the Regent Hotel in Leamington Spa, leaving £425.

Kylemore's next owner was the Duke of Manchester, whose American father-in-law, Eugene Zimmerman, largely funded the purchase. Alas, the Duke was rather fond of gambling, and the Connemara estate changed hands again about a dozen years later when it was bought by property speculator Ernest Fawkes. Finally, in 1920, a neglected and somewhat shrunken estate of around 4,000 hectares (10,000 acres) was sold to the present owners, a community of Benedictine nuns who had fled from Ypres during the First World War.

I first saw the walled garden at Kylemore Abbey (as it is now called) in 1996. A corner of cultivation had been bravely defended by Sister Benedict, who since 1958 had been raising vegetables for her fellow nuns and for the girls' school that the community ran. But the rest could not have been more forlorn. The glasshouses, except for a few sad bones, had been levelled by winds and weather. A mat of rough grass, scrub, brambles and weeds covered the soil. A few hulking conifers and huge cordylines – grown to heroic proportions while no one was looking – pushed up through the undergrowth. The noble, arched gateway and its stepped walls had been invaded by ivy. Insistent suckers and stems had wrestled the crowning limestone shield to the ground – where it lay in an undignified bed of silverweed and dock.

The nuns had been hard at work though – raising funds for the garden's restoration. Through bank loans, government-sponsored employment schemes and the EU-funded Great Gardens of Ireland Restoration Scheme, they gathered together enough to fund a £1.5 million restoration. Now, the abbey and gardens welcome around 200,000 visitors per year. On a busy day, 1,400 people pass through the restored walled garden.

What do they see? Well, despite the valiant and tireless efforts of the restoration team and the seven gardeners, they don't get the full effect of Mitchell Henry's creation. Only two of the twenty-one glasshouses have been restored. The footprints of the other houses are still there, laid out like a life-sized blueprint. Interesting as it is to see this, it leaves a disconcertingly empty space along the north wall.

The walled garden has been restored along historic lines, and the design style and all the plants are pre-1900. The late Victorian principle of man-over-nature-at-all-costs looks wrong to our twenty-first-century eyes. To my mind, the gardens presented an opportunity for a contemporary landscape architect to celebrate and complement the natural surroundings while responding to the garden's extraordinary legacy.

Instead, visitors arriving through the painstakingly refurbished gateway are greeted by an immense counterpane of green lawn into which dozens of ornate flower beds are inscribed. Bedding plants have a hard job in the west of Ireland at the best of times – with the wind, the rain and the wet soil. But old cultivars, with their short flowering periods and their increasing susceptibility to pathogens, can be miserable. The head gardener is constantly challenged, and has, in some cases, resorted to newer varieties, such as *Myosotis* 'Blue Ball' instead of an older forget-me-not. The beds are faultlessly maintained, but the struggle is evident, especially in wet summers when plants are slow to flower.

The warm west-facing wall on either side of the entrance gate has been replanted with old varieties of pear – including 'Comice', 'Emile d'Heyst' and 'Louise Bonne of Jersey'. They are doing well, and their yellow, orange and red fruits glow like lanterns against the red bricks.

The central wilderness is charming, with its woodland of beech, chestnut, lime, swamp cypress, monkey puzzle and holly. There are precious elms here too, unaffected by the fatal Dutch disease. The stream is lined with ferns, including the very ornate European chain fern (*Woodwardia radicans*), the shuttlecock fern (*Matteuccia struthiopteris*), and the sensitive fern (*Onoclea sensibilis*). Montbretia (*Crocosmia x crocosmiiflora*), the corm that has naturalized all over the south-west of Ireland, is planted en masse here, blanketing the ground with its bright-green sword leaves and tiny flame-coloured trumpets.

The west section of the garden, beyond this delightful and mannerly wilderness, is largely given over to food production. There are four big plots (subdivided into smaller beds) that facilitate a four year rotation: potatoes, roots, brassicas and legumes. Only heirloom varieties are grown: the leguminous veg include the climbing French bean 'Cosse Violette', with purple pods; runner bean 'Painted Lady', with white-and-red bicolored flowers; and the mauve-flowered mangetout, 'Carouby de Maussane'. Among the venerable spuds are 'British Queen', 'Duke of York', Epicure', 'Salad Blue' and 'Shamrock'. The last, despite its name, is an old British variety.

The vegetable area is bisected by the double herbaceous border, backed by an escallonia hedge. At around 80 metres (262 feet) long, it is one of the longest in the country. Its subjects are planted in the Victorian mode, with perennials in four height-graduated tiers. Lofty characters such as Shasta daisy (*Leucanthemum x superbum*) and globe thistle (*Echinops sphaerocephalus*) are in the back row, and squat ground-huggers such as the elephant-eared *Bergenia cordifolia* and the pink-tipped *Persicaria affinis* take up their positions at the front of the border. Plant varieties – all in cultivation for over a century – are not mingled, as in modern herbaceous plantings, but keep themselves to themselves.

Despite the restoration's adherence to somewhat oppressive criteria, the walled garden at Kylemore is an exceptional and unforgettable place. The gardeners, led by Anja Gohlke, are a dedicated and careful crew, trimming, snipping, planting, pruning and manicuring every inch of the garden. The contrast between this enclosed rectangle of intense cultivation and the wild country outside its walls could not be greater.

ABOVE Montbretia (*Crocosmia x crocosmiiflora*), which has colonized much of the south-west of Ireland, brightens the artificial wilderness.
LEFT Red drumhead cabbages and pot marigolds are planted in the kitchen garden.

Ilnacullin (Garinish Island)

COUNTY CORK

THE BOAT RIDE to Garinish Island in West Cork is only minutes long, but its watery drama puts you in a fine mood to visit one of Ireland's most remarkable gardens. As the vessel chugs slowly through Glengarriff Bay, it pauses by a seaweed-draped rock where harbour seals sway and loll blobbily, their dark eyes turned obligingly to the tourists' cameras. An instant later, you disembark at the little quay and enter a fantastical world.

The 15-hectare (37-acre) rocky island, also known as Ilnacullin (Irish for 'island of holly'), has an interesting history. In 1805, the British built a Martello tower – believed to be the first in Ireland – at its highest point. These small round forts were erected as a chain of defence around the coasts of Ireland and Britain, to ward off possible invasions from France. After a decade or so, the troops departed, and the island was inhabited by only a handful of people who grew potatoes and raised a few cattle on the poor, peaty soil.

A century later, this rugged and windswept shred of land was acquired by John Annan Bryce and his wife, Violet (née L'Estrange). They bought it from the British War Office, but an annual ground rent of £80 was to be paid to Bantry House estates. The Belfast-born Bryce was a Scottish Liberal MP and businessman who regularly took holidays at nearby Glengarriff Castle, and he and Violet were keen to create an island paradise on the unpromising-looking terrain. It's true that it was windblown, treeless and nearly barren, but the mild maritime climate offered great potential. Frost was a rarity, and the mean annual rainfall of 1,850 millimetres (73 inches) meant that near-tender plants would grow swiftly and safely. As a young man, Bryce had lived and worked in Asia, where he took a keen interest in the flora of India and Burma, and wrote papers which he submitted to the Royal Geographical Society in London. The possibilities of Ilnacullin's topography and conditions must have excited him.

They also excited the Bryces' friend, Arts and Crafts architect Harold Peto, whom they employed to make their island dream come true. Peto was an experienced garden designer. His Italianate garden at his home at Iford Manor in Wiltshire and his work at West Dean House in West Sussex (including a famous pergola) bore witness to this. Garinish Island, with its glorious views of mountains and sea, and its hilly profile, spoke to Peto. According to Violet, 'He went up to the Martello tower from whence it is possible to see most of

The 'Casita', an Italian tea-house, is dwarfed by the bulky mass of the Caha Mountains.

the island, and, waving his magic wand, produced what is undoubtedly one of the most beautiful gardens in the world.'

Violet, it is said, was keen to provide local employment, and the plans were ambitious enough to keep a hundred men in work from 1911 until the outbreak of the First World War. Peto also produced designs for a house: a massive, sprawling structure on many levels. It was to incorporate the Martello tower, which would contain a garden room, a music room, and – built on to the top – Violet's sitting room. However, the collapse of the Russian market after the war seriously affected the Bryces' finances, and the huge, overblown palazzo was never started – which may not be a bad thing. When they were on the island, the Bryces lived in the much smaller Gardener's Cottage, which was built around 1912.

Peto planned the garden so that its heart would be rigorously and beautifully formal. Outside this highly civilized classical nucleus, the wild island flora would blend with exotics from all over the world to create a jungle. Beyond this, the sea and the mountains would hold the island in their strong embrace.

It was an ambitious scheme, requiring dynamiting of rock to provide planting pockets, and – probably – some importation of soil on to the island (although Violet, in later years, vehemently denied that soil had been brought in). Shelter belts of Scots and Monterey pine, and of cypress, fir and spruce, were planted to break the strength of the winds sweeping in from the north Atlantic.

The jewel of Ilnacullin is the Italian Garden. At the south-west end, a small pavilion in honey-coloured Bath stone has neat Palladian lines, with tripartite openings separated by marble columns. It offers a place to stand and gaze at the rock-strewn waters of the bay and at Sugarloaf Mountain, whose conical 574-metre (1,883-foot) peak stands like a rugged sandstone pyramid among the angular Caha Mountains. Turn your back on this spectacular natural

prospect, and the opposite view is one of man-made artistry: a still, aquamarine-tiled, rectangular pool over which a bronze Mercury is eternally poised in wing-footed flight. The statue is a copy of a sculpture made by the Flanders-born Renaissance artist Giambologna. On the far side of the pool the view is completed by a low Casita, or Italian teahouse, also featuring Bath stone and marble, and hung with curtains of wisteria.

Peto's and the Bryces' cosmopolitan tastes were evinced in salutes to Japan as well as to the classical world. At the beginning of the twentieth century Britain and Ireland were fixated upon Japan, especially after the 1910 Japan-British Exhibition in London. So, the lines of the Casita are reminiscent of oriental architecture, and the paving around the pool is home to several bonsai. *Nandina domestica*, the so-called sacred bamboo (although it is not a bamboo), an important plant in Japanese culture, grows on the perimeter. A backdrop of pines, rhododendrons,

OPPOSITE Holes were dynamited in the rocky terrain a century ago to provide planting pockets for the trees that we see today.
ABOVE The highly formal Italian Garden is in stark contrast to the wildness outside.

ABOVE The rough landscape of the Caha Mountains is continually celebrated. Here it is seen from the Grecian Temple.
RIGHT The Martello tower, perched on the highest point of the island, is believed to have been the first built in Ireland.

camellias, bottlebrushes (*Callistemon*), fuchsias, tea trees (*Leptospermum scoparium* cv.) and other exotics gives this area an otherworldly atmosphere. The mood is somewhat jarred by the incongruous mix of clashy-dashy modern bedding plants that fill the sloping beds around the paving's edge in high summer.

On the far side of the Casita, in a boggy area where turf for fuel was once cut, Peto had the land drained before laying out a perfectly smooth lawn for tennis and croquet. The preternaturally green sward and its broad gravel apron (which at one time was a sand tennis court) is surrounded by a screen of woody plants: magnolias, rhododendrons, Chinese lantern trees (*Crinodendron*), ceanothus, olearias and many others. Beyond the lawn, he constructed a walled garden.

The Jungle is a wild interlude of New Zealand tree ferns, big-leaved rhododendrons, and rarities such as the white, cup-flowered *Schima wallichii* from China and the chocolate-leaved *Brachyglottis repanda* 'Purpurea' from New Zealand.

This dense subtropical woodland borders the Happy Valley, a long, grassy clearing with a marshy pool at its lowest point. At the south-west end, the skeletal Grecian Temple frames the rough majesty of the Caha Mountains. At the other end, wide steps rise to the Martello tower, and to various viewing points. There are important plants lining the Happy Valley, pushing up between the hard grey humps of the rocky island. Among them is a specimen of the slow-growing weeping Huon pine (*Lagarostrobos franklinii*) from Tasmania. This is one of many antipodean near-tender species at Illnacullin. Others include the black-barked and olive-green-leaved kauri (*Agathis australis*), which is of the same family as the monkey puzzle; the celery pine (*Phyllocladus glaucus*), whose sign proudly declares it as one of the largest specimens outdoors in Britain and Ireland; and the pendulous rimu (*Dacrydium cupressinum*), which started life in a glasshouse at the Botanic Gardens in Glasnevin. The aromatic, multi-coloured *Pseudowintera colorata* is over 6 metres (20 feet) tall here, whereas in its native New Zealand it grows as a shrub. Some plants, however – *Gaultheria*, *Griselinia* and *Leptospermum*, for example – do rather too well, and have self-seeded all over to become weedy nuisances.

Annan Bryce died in 1923, but Violet remained on the island. In 1928, she hired Scotsman Murdo Mackenzie as head gardener. Illnacullin, which had become neglected in the last years of Bryce's life, was hugely overgrown. Mackenzie and three under-gardeners spent the first three years of his tenure clearing away the weeds and rampant plants. After that he began ordering plants with gusto; often choosing bright cultivars over the more understated species plants that had been favoured by Bryce and Peto. Under his care, the gardens were opened regularly to the public, and his annual wage of £100 was supplemented by 10 per cent of the income from the entrance fees. A dedicated worker, he spent the last fifty-five years of his life in the garden – even after he retired.

Roland L'Estrange Bryce took over the running of the garden from his mother in 1932 and worked closely with Mackenzie. Violet died in 1939. Roland followed her in 1953, but not before bequeathing the island to the Irish state – which now runs it.

At the time of writing, and for at least the last fifteen years, Ilnacullin has been a garden fraught with problems. Parts are over-maintained (and with a municipal flavour that is entirely at odds with what should be an island paradise), while others are barely cared for at all. Paths and important vistas are flooded by a tide of *Griselinia* seedlings, yet the ground under some trees and shrubs is inexplicably bare, leaving the soil looking naked and uncomfortable. Portions of the gardens have been regularly cordoned off, misspelled signs remain uncorrected, and the unique combination of climate and setting is patently under-celebrated.

This state of affairs may stem from the number of visitors (around 60,000 per season) that set foot on the island's fragile – but over-advertised – fabric. Many of them have no interest in gardens or horticulture and stumble about the rough terrain like dazed sheep.

Perhaps more energy is being directed into managing people than the gardens? My sincere hope is that by the time you are reading this Ilnacullin will have somehow regained its magic and integrity, and will once again be a place that does credit to its wildly romantic creators.

Rowallane

COUNTY DOWN

County Down, especially around Saintfield, is drumlin country. The landscape is gathered into gently contoured knolls, smooth and curvaceous in all their parts. Hedgerows and roads swoop rhythmically over the mellow hillocks. In places the countryside looks as if it has been drawn by a child, each hill a green half-oval neatly defined by the dark lines of hedge and wall.

On the avenue to the garden at Rowallane, therefore, it is delightfully and curiously right when you come across two prehistoric-looking cairns of river-rounded rock rising from the moss and heather. Each stone in the pair of conical mounds is a hefty granite egg – a petrified drumlin in miniature.

These primitive piles were the work of the Reverend John Robert Moore, who started to create the estate in 1858, first buying up farmland in the townland of Creevyloughgare, and a while later, more fields in the adjoining Leggygowan. Just before the Reverend began building the estate, an unexpected interlude in his life had come to an end. He had married when he was fifty, but his experience of wedded bliss was fleeting: his wife died after just a few years. Two years later, aged fifty-seven, he embarked on the work of creating what was to become one of the most important gardens in Ireland, and which he was to call Rowallane, after the home place of his Scots antecedents, the Muirs.

His family had traditionally served as agents to the Earl of Annesley's estate at Castlewellan, 32 kilometres (20 miles) to the south of his new County Down acquisition. His sister, Priscilla Cecilia, had married the third earl, but had been left a widow after ten years. Her son, William, the fourth Earl, was only eight years old when he succeeded, so the Reverend – one of the trustees – stepped in and managed the estate for many years.

When it came to creating his own territory, Reverend John Robert Moore chose a modest style – a world away from the ostentatious Scots Baronial castle that his nephew built at Castlewellan in 1856. The house was two storeys, and

OPPOSITE Doubly lovely: hydrangeas are mirrored in the pond in the Pleasure Grounds at Rowallane.
ABOVE The Reverend John Robert Moore amused himself by building cairns of river-worn rock on the avenue to the garden; one of the Reverend's pair of crouching lions on the avenue.

relatively plain. He allowed himself a more ornate stableyard though, with a lofty bell tower and a few crenellations and diminutive turrets. Could these architectural fripperies – applied only to the out-offices – have been a little poke at the young Earl's extravagances?

Ironically, the Reverend's sister, the widowed Lady Annesley, was critical of her brother's expenditure of £76 on one of the avenues at Rowallane. He employed an engineer to blast a way through the rock so that the drive would proceed levelly, and so that it was dramatically bordered here and there by craggy walls of dynamited whinstone (the local basalt).

He also built a handsome garden enclosed with elaborate walls of brick and whinstone. Raised ribs of dark tiles were inserted in regular courses. Pierced with holes, they offered a way of attaching plant-support wires without causing damage to the structure. Throughout the rest of the demesne he indulged himself in a highly personal and mostly vernacular style: no two sets of gate posts were alike. Some were topped with totemic stones, others with roundels, still others with snaggle-toothed crowns of rock. A pair of crouching lions guarded the drive – nothing unusual in that. But they faced the 'wrong' way, so that arriving visitors were greeted by a brace of amply scrotumed rear ends, while those departing from the house were faced with stony glares.

The Reverend Moore joined several fields together to make a large pleasure ground, and – in the manner of all those who want to leave a beautiful demesne for posterity – he planted trees. Thanks to his work, Rowallane is abundantly furnished with stately groupings of Deodar cedar, Scots pine, beech and other fine trees.

It was this well-made estate that a nephew, Hugh Armytage Moore, inherited in 1903. Formerly a lieutenant in the Royal Dublin Fusiliers, he went on to become the estate manager at Castlewellan, as well as chairman of the County Down branch of the Ulster Volunteer Force. He was also a plantsman – in an era that was one of the most exciting periods of plant-hunting ever, especially in China. Hugh was in correspondence with the important collectors of the time, and received material from George Forrest, Ernest Henry Wilson, Frank Kingdon-Ward and others. He had connections with various gardens, including the botanic gardens in Edinburgh and in Glasnevin. The curator of the latter, Sir Frederick Moore, and his wife, Phylis – a knowledgeable gardener in her own right – were regular visitors to the County Down property. He also had close ties with the famous Slieve Donard Nursery in Newcastle, and with the equally renowned Daisy Hill Nursery in Newry.

The structure that his uncle had established allowed Hugh to concentrate on horticulture and botany, rather

RIGHT Giant redwoods (*Sequoiadendron giganteum*) and rhododendrons on the avenue.
OPPOSITE The stableyard at Rowallane is oddly ornate, with grandiose crenellations and soaring bell tower. In autumn the leaves of *Acer palmatum* and *A. p.* 'Sango-Kaku' are alight with colour.

than building. When he started planting outward from the house and began to commandeer the farmland for his acquisitions, he kept the old field boundaries intact. He was far too focused on his plant collection to be pulling down walls and designing new spaces. The low enclosures, moreover, offered shelter to his infant woody specimens. Today, Rowallane – which is owned by the National Trust – has a pastoral atmosphere, with fieldstone walls running hither and thither, continually punctuated by rustic gates. The 21 hectares (52 acres) of gardens have been gently laid over the land. There is still a working farm of 69 hectares (170 acres), and the sound of lowing cattle and baaing sheep regularly interrupts matters horticultural.

There are echoes of farm life in the names of the garden's sections: in the Paddock, with its delightful wildflower meadow (home to both the lesser and greater butterfly orchids, *Platantera bifolia* and *P. chlorantha*), and in the Spring Ground, where the calves were first put out in that season.

Rowallane Plants

Hugh Armytage Moore was a selector of plants, as well as a collector. He kept a vigilant eye on batches of seedlings and on volunteers that appeared in his gardens – pouncing on those with superior attributes. It is to his skills of discernment that we owe the existence of excellent cultivars such as the candelabra primula 'Rowallane Rose' and the wall shrub, *Chaenomeles* x *superba* 'Rowallane Seedling' – the original of which is still here. The sterile *Viburnum plicatum* f. *tomentosum* 'Rowallane Variety' still grows in the walled garden. The large-flowered *Hypericum* 'Rowallane Hybrid' was discovered in the gardens by Hugh's friend, Leslie Slinger, of the nearby Slieve Donard Nursery.

ABOVE Herb and salad beds in the Inner Walled Garden are given the formal treatment with neat box edging and cylinders. The central axis of the four rectangles is marked by a *Magnolia stellata*.

RIGHT Rhododendrons and old Irish daffodils on the Spring Ground.

Here, watched over by the Reverend's lofty pines and beeches, is a collection of Hugh's rhododendrons and azaleas, including scores of cultivars in clashing tones of mauve, pink, ultraviolet, deep red, orange and yellow. The grass is salted with old Irish daffodils – their simple, ingenuous flowers looking slightly aghast at the brash statements being trumpeted by the rhododendrons. The Hospital, nearby, is a sheltered area where poorly livestock were grazed. Now it is the quarters of several of Rowallane's important plants: a champion *Paulownia tomentosa*, a collection of maples, and a huge and uncharacteristically spreading handkerchief tree (*Davidia involucrata*). This last was grown from Ernest Wilson's wild-collected seed by Veitch – the nursery that employed the plant hunter specifically to find this species. Hugh bought a pair in 1904 for fifteen shillings. The partner tree, which was planted in the walled garden, has since gone to meet its maker, but it has been replaced by a clone, propagated from its material.

Rowallane's head gardener, Averil Milligan, is much taken up with managing an ageing collection. As she points out: 'generally by the time something is a champion tree it means it's heading into the nursing home.' Therefore, the genetic material of the garden's historic and significant specimens is preserved through rejuvenatory pruning and through being propagated and grown on into new plants. Natural decrepitude has been hastened in some cases by the disease sudden oak death (*Phytophthora ramorum*), which has appeared in the gardens. Older ericaceous plants are especially susceptible.

Just outside the Hospital is a very old but only recently famous tree: *Carrierea calycina* from western Sichuan. The goat horn tree arrived in the garden in 1919, having been purchased for three shillings and six pence from Slieve Donard Nursery. Ninety-one years later, in 2010, it flowered for the first time. This tree and another in Birr Castle are believed to be the only two surviving specimens from the seed collected by Ernest Wilson in 1908.

Hugh Armytage Moore's inheritance of Rowallane coincided with the Edwardian rage for rock gardening. His Rock Garden was immense, and the envy of all. He uncovered giant outcrops of whinstone in land to the south of the house, and filled pockets of soil with naturalistic groups of choice alpines. He felt that no plant should outshine the next: instead the visitor was to be drawn ever along in a pleasurable journey of exploration. The adjacent tiny waterway gave him a habitat for moisture lovers such as primulas, hostas and ferns.

Today's small staff of five gardeners and helpers does not allow for the cultivation of tricky alpines – the prima donnas of the plant world – so the Rock Garden is home to species that don't mind the shallow and dry soil. The annual rainfall is around 1,000 millimetres (39 inches), but the rock heats up quickly and parches the ground. The pretty *Boenninghausenia albiflora*, a member of the rue family with dainty white flowers, does well, as do Mediterranean species such as *Cistus*.

Hugh was fond of hydrangeas also, and the outer part of the Walled Garden has a collection of about a dozen different forms – all recent plants propagated from Rowallane's original stock. One of his favourites was the mauve-flowered, white-bracted *H. aspera* subsp. *sargentiana*, which has large, strokeable velvet leaves and furry stems.

The Inner Walled Garden is a formal space, with a green lawn and orderly paths overhung with century-old magnolias (*M.* x *watsonii* and *M.* x *veitchii*) and other treasures, such as a fine and healthy *Hoheria lyallii*. In spring, the peonies – both herbaceous and tree varieties – are a speciality. There are great gatherings of *Meconopsis*, including 'Slieve Donard', a hybrid between *M. grandis* and *M. betonicifolia* raised in Scotland but introduced by the Newcastle nursery. By late summer, the soil is obscured by mounds of perennials and biennials luxuriating in the warmth and shelter of the old walls. Spires of *Verbascum* rise skywards, their creamy tones matched by the plantings of variegated hostas at their feet. Blue agapanthus, jelly-coloured crocosmias, powdery campanulas and highly scented lilies crowd the beds. On the walls above are the Reverend Moore's pierced tiles. Threaded through with wires and supporting the stems of climbers, they are still doing the job allotted to them in the middle of the nineteenth century. Rowallane, engineered by the Reverend and planted by his nephew, is a garden that was meant to last.

OPPOSITE Ferns and *Alchemilla mollis* cling to the sides of a little pond for dipping watering cans, clay pans and plant pots in the Outer Walled Garden.

ABOVE, CLOCKWISE FROM TOP LEFT A quiet corner of the Inner Walled Garden with *Verbascum chaixii*, *V. c.* 'Album', variegated hostas, and *H. sieboldiana* var. *elegans*; elegant *Meconopsis* x *cookei*, a cross between *M. punicea* and *M. quintuplinervea*; *Hydrangea aspera* subsp. *sargentiana* and the Reverend's specially built walls (the dark tiles were pierced with holes for plant wires); *Hoheria lyallii*, from New Zealand.

Glenveagh

COUNTY DONEGAL

There are few places in Ireland more wild than the former Glenveagh estate in County Donegal. Now making up the largest part of the 16,000-hectare (40,000-acre) Glenveagh National Park, it is dominated by the great rumple of the Derryveagh Mountains and their accompanying lakes and bogs. Powerful weather systems sweep in from the Atlantic, bringing bands of precipitation and blustery showers, which dump as much as 1,980 millimetres (78 inches) of rain per annum. Water washes down the rocky slopes, through the blanket bogs and is gathered into swiftly flowing streams dyed the colour of tea by the peaty soil. The vegetation is mostly hard-worn and sinewy: wind-sculpted holly and rowan, wiry heather, coarse rushes and resilient purple moor grass. The roads are narrow and looping, and require a careful hand at the wheel – not just because of the topography, but because of the occasional blackface sheep obstinately parked on their surface.

It is this supremely rough and remote terrain that is the surprising setting for one of Ireland's most lush and enthralling gardens. Now owned by the Irish state, the 11-hectare (27-acre) Glenveagh Gardens, under the imaginative and careful hand of head gardener Seán Ó Gaoithín, is a salutary model for how to manage an intensive and sprawling space while keeping it vibrant and true to the spirit of the creators.

In the 1880s and 1890s, Cornelia Adair planted belts of Scots pine to diffuse the harsh winds whipping off the mountains. She planted *Rhododendron ponticum* too, little knowing that this pretty thug of a plant would become the invading enemy in a continual territorial battle today.

Her pines, however, still give a gothic splendour to the estate. And, combined with the high sides of the valley and the deep waters of Lough Veagh, they help to ameliorate the climate.

The two most extensive sections of today's garden were also laid out by her. In a boggy patch to the north-east of the castle, she had the land drained and levelled to create the liberally lawned Pleasure Grounds (0.8 hectare/ 2 acres). Among her plantings that survive here are tree rhododendrons (*R. arboreum*), some fine specimens of purple-leaved Japanese maple (*Acer palmatum* f. *atropurpureum*), some lofty Chusan palms, and thick clumps of bamboo. On the south-east flank of the castle, she made a kitchen garden (0.4 hectare/1 acre) in the hollow where the granite for the building had been quarried. She also introduced red deer to the estate, importing animals from the ancient, post Ice Age herd in County Kerry, and from Scotland and Germany.

During the First World War, Cornelia offered accommodation to 30 convalescing Belgian soldiers. Those who were well enough constructed a path above the Pleasure Grounds, which became known as the Belgian Path.

After her death in 1921, Glenveagh passed to Cornelia's grandson by her first marriage, Montgomery Wadsworth Ritchie. He had little time for Glenveagh, which suffered over the next few years. During the Irish Civil War it was first occupied by the anti-Treaty forces, and then by members of the opposing Free State Army. Later, it was rented to a British war veteran, Captain Geoffrey Gathorne-Hardy, who used it as a hunting lodge.

Eventually, in 1929, things started looking up for the neglected and looted estate when it was bought by Arthur Kingsley Porter, a fabulously rich Harvard professor and internationally renowned mediaeval scholar. He and his wife, Lucy, went to work repairing the castle and its demesne. But their tenure was cut short: just four years later, Porter disappeared without a trace from Inishbofin Island in County Donegal.

Lucy, keen to distance herself from a place with such sad associations, rented the property to Philadelphia man Henry Plumer McIlhenny and his mother, Frances. Henry was an art collector and connoisseur, becoming curator and (later) chairman of the board of the Philadelphia Museum of Art. His grandfather, born in Carrigart, County Donegal,

Glenveagh Castle nestles in woodland at the side of Lough Veagh.

A Cruel Emergence

The origins of the estate at Glenveagh were mired in singular misery and injustice. John George Adair, originally from Bellegrove in Queen's County (now County Laois), was a land speculator and money broker who began to amass property in Donegal in 1857. His holdings included the Glenveagh, Derryveagh and Gartan estates – an area of over 28,000 acres – and he had shooting rights over another 14,000. Elsewhere in Ireland, he bought and sold considerable chunks of land in his home county, and in King's County (County Offaly), Kildare, Kilkenny and Tipperary. At the time of his death in 1885, he also co-owned a 1.3-million-acre ranch on the Texas Panhandle, the J.A. Ranch (still extant, although somewhat smaller).

Adair's relations with his Donegal tenants were poor, and his treatment of them was abysmal. In April of 1861, just a decade after the Great Famine, he evicted 244 people – 85 adults and 159 children – from the sixteen townlands of Derryveagh. Twenty-eight houses were levelled or de-roofed, rendering them uninhabitable. Over half of those turned out of their homes sailed to Australia, others moved in with friends or family, still others went to the workhouse in Letterkenny. Some died.

Six years later, Adair married American widow Cornelia Ritchie, and began to build a grand hunting lodge, designed with the help of his first cousin, John Townsend Trench. Glenveagh Castle, completed in 1873, is in the Scots Baronial style: much battlemented, and with a four-storey, turreted keep. The great, granite building – which was later enlarged – sits mid-way along the 5.5-kilometre (3½-mile) shore of Lough Veagh, commanding views up and down the glen.

Adair died suddenly in 1885 in St Louis, Missouri. Cornelia, who was more popular locally than her late husband, spent a good deal of time at Glenveagh. It was she who took the first steps to beautify the estate that John George Adair had so heartlessly created.

had emigrated to Columbus, Ohio, where he invented the McIlhenny gas meter, a device that provided the foundations for the family's very considerable fortune.

In 1937, Henry bought Glenveagh to use as a summer home, and became the third American in a row to own this remote patch of Donegal, with its grandiose granite pile. He immediately began to whip the garden into shape. 'Until 1939 my days were spent eliminating weeds, burning bamboo and cutting ivy out of the trees,' he wrote in the book *In an Irish Garden*.

Renovations were interrupted by the Second World War, when Henry served in the United States Navy (spending nearly a year and a half on board the USS *Bunker Hill*). In 1946, he renewed his efforts at his Donegal home, and applied himself to learning how to garden on the acid soil and with the copious amounts of rain. He sought guidance from many quarters including from the Earl and Countess of Leitrim, who lived at nearby Mulroy, and who ran a nursery which provided him with many of his plants.

The American landscape architect Lanning Roper, who had been his classmate at Harvard, visited frequently, advising on plantings and design. The great plantsman James Russell, from Sunningdale Nursery in Surrey, was already involved. 'He had apparently wild ideas which proved to be excellent, and introduced many rare and tender plants to the gardens.' The Swiss landscape designer Walter Bruger was likewise pressed into service. Henry McIlhenny had a finely tuned eye, and a strong sense of how his creation should take shape: 'I wanted to avoid having a garden beginning anywhere and ending nowhere.' He also hated bare soil, and planted densely to avoid being offended by this condition.

Lough Veagh makes up the garden's lengthy northwest boundary, and a series of cultivated clearings spreads upwards through the woods, joined together by a network of paths. The highly gardened spaces and the untamed Donegal terrain leak repeatedly into each other: there is no doubt that this is a garden, but it is a garden that is not afraid to live intimately with nature. One minute you are walking through the highly horticultured interlude of the Pleasure Grounds – and the next you are climbing through glacial boulders into a native wood of oak, holly, rowan, birch and hazel. A little later you are looking down over the moss-furred branches onto the sleekness of a well-mown lawn far below. Both the garden and the wilderness continually celebrate and acknowledge each other in carefully crafted vistas from one to the other.

Henry McIlhenny's tenure at Glenveagh lasted until 1983, when he donated the castle and gardens to the Irish state. He had already sold the rest of the estate to the Commissioners of Public Works so that it could be made into a national park. He was a famously sociable man, enjoying the sobriquet of the 'first gentleman of Philadelphia' in his hometown. His house parties at Glenveagh were glamorous, international affairs with guests including Greta Garbo, Grace Kelly, James Stewart and Yehudi Menuhin. Throughout his time in Ireland, he drew on his vast fortune to furnish the house with Victorian and Georgian pieces, and to bring structure and elegance to the gardens with good design, sympathetic planting and carefully chosen statuary.

Henry had at least eight full-time gardeners at Glenveagh. Now there are half that number, but the place is still looked

BELOW LEFT Henry McIlhenny's walks through the garden at Glenveagh often led him to this favourite view of the lough.
BELOW RIGHT Steps lead from the garden into the native woodland.

after in a way that he would recognize and – I hope – approve of. The practice of horticulture has not been sacrificed to the pursuit of maintenance, as is the case in some state-owned Irish gardens. Many plants are grown from seed which head gardener Seán Ó Gaoithín sources from specialist nurseries and botanic gardens. The entire plant collection is constantly monitored, with an inventory compiled every five years. Only species that will not impact on the native holly-oak woodland are acquired, while invasive species are vigorously removed. Among these are *Alchemilla mollis* (which Seán has replaced in some areas with the Irish heath, *Erica erigena*), *Gunnera tinctoria*, *Hoheria populnea*, *Gaultheria mucronata*, *Rhododendron ponticum*, and – surprisingly – *Dicksonia antarctica*. Yes, the impressively showy Tasmanian tree fern is a plant that, according to Seán, 'self-sows all over the bloody place'.

The Kitchen Garden is still in the *jardin potager* format laid out by Lanning Roper, and is defined by dainty box hedging and topiary. Its formality is emphasized by the untamed woodland crowding in on three sides. Long-term crops such as soft fruits, artichokes and herbaceous perennials are now grown alongside the more labour-intensive vegetables and cut flowers. Among the last are the dahlias, a favourite of Henry's: dozens of vases were displayed throughout the house when he was in residence. His chosen varieties are still here, and include the purple and white 'Edinburgh', the lemon-yellow water-lily 'Glorie van Heemstede', the red pompom 'Kochelsee', and the single 'Matt Armour', which was selected here in the 1930s by the man who was head gardener for the Kingsley Porters and Henry McIlhenny alike.

The soil in the Kitchen Garden is delicious and black, and about a metre deep. Local tradition says that during Cornelia Adair's time it was brought in by the people from the region, who were paid a penny per cartload. (The soil in the Pleasure Grounds was imported in the same manner.) Each year in late autumn and early winter annual crops are removed and the ground is systematically manured, dug over and piled into broad, high ridges. This allows the soil to shed water during the damp months, and to warm up in spring. At the beginning of the growing season, the ridges are knocked level and planted.

The Kitchen Garden was laid out by Lanning Roper; Cornelia Adair's Scots pines protect it from the worst of the winds.

THE IRISH GARDEN

ABOVE Box spirals and edging lend formality to the Kitchen Garden, while the woodland forms a dramatically wild backdrop.
RIGHT The head gardener's cottage, with herbs, perennials and a fine specimen of *Cordyline indivisa*.

This vibrant mélange of productive crops and ornamentals is watched over by the picturesque gardener's cottage and the battleship-grey gothic orangery, the latter designed by Philippe Jullian, a French art historian, writer, illustrator and jack-of-all-aesthetic-trades. The south-east-facing conservatory is home to a collection of expertly grown tender plants. Hectically coloured *Streptocarpus*, *Impatiens*, *Pelargonium*, *Hippeastrum* and *Clivia* nestle among the calming foliage of ferns and palms.

The Kitchen Garden shares a surreal beauty with the Pleasure Grounds: both are theatrical spaces whose contrivance is emphasized by the naturalistic surroundings. The latter, with its elongated sunken lawn, echoes the topography of Lough Veagh. While the framework and many of the important trees were Cornelia Adair's, the bulk of the planting is James Russell's and Lanning Roper's.

Russell came here first in 1953. He added to the existing rhododendron collection, planting varieties with outsize, jungly leaves or with gorgeous scent, among them *R. sinogrande*, *R. falconeri*, *R. ciliatum*, *R. lindleyi* and *R.* 'Polar Bear'. (More recent acquisitions have pushed the number of rhodo varieties to over two hundred.) Nurserymen can tend to see gardens as places to display as many different specimens as possible, but Russell was an accomplished designer with plants. Besides Glenveagh, he worked in at least two hundred gardens in the British Isles and Europe. In the Pleasure Grounds, he underplanted the trees – the rhododendrons, maples, *Magnolia tripetala* and *M. salicifolia*, *Nothofagus obliqua* and *N. cliffortioides*, and others – with highly textured swathes of perennials. He favoured massed groups of beefy species such as *Aruncus*, *Hosta*, *Astilbe* and *Rodgersia*. Lanning Roper, who first came to Glenveagh in 1959, favoured this kind of planting also. It looks right to our eyes, but during the 1950s and 1960s such naturalism was going against the grain. At that time, shrubs and trees were not usually combined with waves of perennials.

Roper had a painterly approach to gardens, and was fascinated by the misty light in Glenveagh. He used silver foliage to add an ectoplasmic shimmer to his plantings. One of his signature plants was the shrubby *Brachyglottis* (Dunedin Group) 'Sunshine', with felt-backed, pale-green leaves and acidic yellow daisies. The gardeners were ordered to remove the flowers, so that the foliage could glimmer freely, unimpeded by the gaudy inflorescences.

Irish Plants

Irish cultivars form an important part of the collection at Glenveagh, and include several Donegal cottage roses and other county specialities, such as the 'Gortahork' cabbage (*below*). This is an old drumhead variety, grown by generations of the Sweeney family on the north-west coast. It is thought to be descended from the early nineteenth-century Cow Cabbage or, in Irish, Cál Eallaigh, traditionally used both for human food and animal fodder. Unique to Glenveagh is the 'Matt Armour' dahlia (*bottom*), a vibrant single red, raised in the 1930s from a packet of seed, and propagated vegetatively ever since. Deep crimson *Rhododendron* 'Mulroy Vanguard' was first named at Glenveagh, but it originated in Mulroy House in north Donegal. Irish apples and potatoes feature in Glenveagh's walled garden, as do archaeophytes (useful plants introduced prior to AD 1500) such as Scots lovage (*Ligusticum scoticum*) and Alexanders (*Smyrnium olusatrum*).

OPPOSITE AND ABOVE A great diversity of trees is happy in the Pleasure Grounds: they include rhododendrons, Chusan palms (*Trachycarpus fortunei*), tree ferns (*Dicksonia antarctica*), blue Atlantic cedar (*Cedrus atlantica* Glauca Group). The lawn mimics the sinuous lines of Lough Veagh.
LEFT Lanning Roper used massed plantings of perennials as ground-cover, a practice that was innovative during the 1950s and 1960s (and that looks exactly right today).

ABOVE Head gardener Seán Ó Gaoithín's pavilion in the Pleasure Grounds uses classical one-in-seven proportions.

RIGHT The two gazebos in the Rose Garden are roofed with shingles made from pines harvested at Glenveagh.

OPPOSITE Genveagh is full of theatrical moments, as here in the Italian Terrace on the Belgian Walk.

In the Pleasure Grounds, the long north-west facing border is now a masterful tapestry of lustrous and dark foliage woven together. There is *Brachyglottis* in plenty, as well as *Astelia, Elaeagnus* 'Quicksilver', *Eucryphia* x *nymansensis* 'Nymansay', *E. glutinosa* and blue cedar (*Cedrus atlantica* Glauca Group). Sombre notes are added by – among others – the fiercely masculine lancewoods from New Zealand, *Pseudopanax ferox* and *P. crassifolius*. Lilies, of all varieties, were favoured by Henry McIlhenny, and they still raise their glorious trumpets all over the gardens. Those in the Pleasure Grounds include *L. auratum, L. martagon, L. speciosum* var. *album, L.s.* var. *rubrum*, and cultivars such as Imperial Silver Group and Golden Splendor Group. Earlier in the year, the ground is washed with spring bulbs: a sequence of snowdrops, crocuses, daffodils, bluebells and leucojums flow from one into the next.

Two Balinese temple guardians, ferocious but benign mythological characters, are a startling presence amid the lush growth here. The stone figures are part of the collection of statuary, urns and other pieces that Henry dispersed about the gardens. He was passionate about good craftsmanship, as well as art. Benches were made by local blacksmiths, and a pair of circular gazebos in the Rose Garden (adjacent to the Kitchen Garden) were roofed with shingles made from Glenveagh pines. The respect for craft continues today: Seán Ó Gaoithín designed a small pavilion for the Pleasure Grounds using classical one-in-seven proportions, based on a particular fireplace in the castle. Seán's shelter is made from unfinished locally grown larch, and its pinky-silvery tones echo the bark of one of Cornelia Adair's majestic Scots pines standing nearby.

Much of the garden at Glenveagh takes the shape of a journey along paths through the woodland. Each is lined with an interesting meld of introduced and native flora, and each has its own character. Walter Bruger's Swiss Walk – where azaleas and woodlanders such as hellebore and lily of the valley grow under pine trees – mimics the flora of Switzerland. The Belgian Walk, meanwhile, passes through many moods, the most surprising of which, perhaps, is where it is lined with the spiny *Fascicularia bicolor*. In autumn, this South American bromeliad produces incongruous baby-blue flowers nestling in rosettes of fire-engine red.

Glenveagh's paths may seem to wander idly, but often they are strategically kinked to hide what lies ahead and what has been left behind. The visitor here is always in the moment. And it is this series of carefully planned moments that makes a visit to this richly planted, historic and beautiful garden utterly unforgettable.

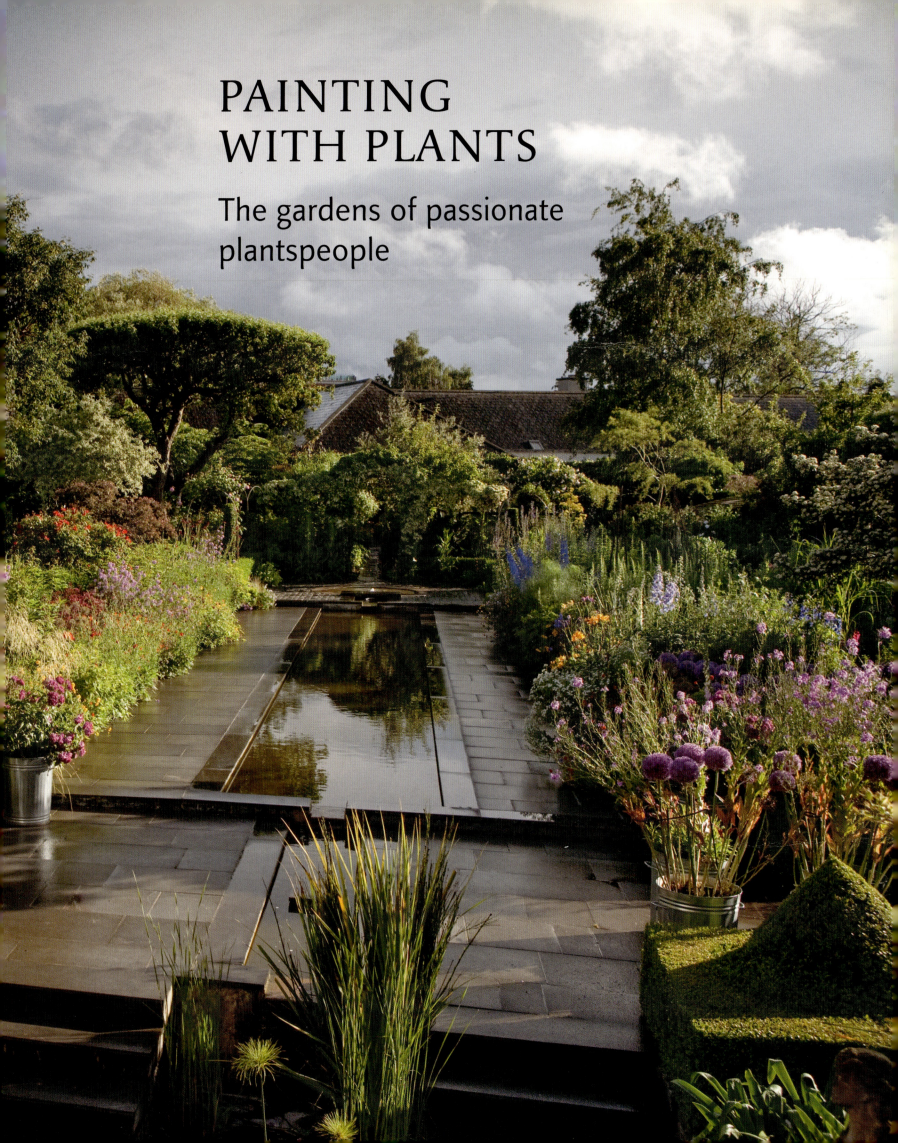

PAINTING WITH PLANTS

The gardens of passionate plantspeople

PREVIOUS PAGES After the rain at the Dillon Garden in Dublin.
ABOVE, CLOCKWISE FROM TOP LEFT Airy perennial planting at Hunting Brook, near Blessington in County Wicklow; the Dillon Garden; Talbot Botanic Gardens in Malahide; Mount Congreve in County Waterford.
OPPOSITE The perfect lawn in Carmel Duignan's back garden acts as a peaceful pause between the bustling borders.

IRELAND is a plantsman's paradise. Its maritime climate and varied topography offer conditions that gardeners in other countries can only envy. It is not unusual to see specimens from widely different biomes in the same garden. Alpine, Mediterranean, woodland, grassland and subtropical species may often find themselves gathered together in a single, pan-global community of plants.

Faced with so much choice, certain gardeners – especially during the last century – habitually lost the run of themselves, delightedly shoe-horning in hundreds of disparate plants. The endeavour sometimes resulted in a horticultural hotchpotch, a glorious, mismatched ragbag of plant life.

It is easy for us to poke fun at such gardens – we, with our twenty-first-century eyes, and our ability to have almost any plant we desire, thanks to the mechanisms of globalization and the internet. Until recently, it was no easy matter to obtain a rare plant. Letters were written, pleas were

delivered and deals were made. If you had collected seed yourself, or somehow acquired cuttings of a special treasure, your bargaining position was strengthened. For much of the last century, in some circles an Irish gardener's status was measured by just how many rarities he or she had. And if nobody else had them, so much the better.

Two of the gardens in this chapter – Mount Congreve in County Waterford and the Talbot Botanic Gardens in Malahide, County Dublin – were largely made during those fiercely acquisitive and competitive times. At Mount Congreve, the late Ambrose Congreve furnished his garden with hundreds and thousands of plants during a period of over eight decades. He was probably the most audacious have-it-all plantsman Ireland has ever known, and his Waterford garden – although a bit shaky in recent years – remains a monument to his massive appetite for plants.

At the Talbot Botanic Gardens at Malahide Castle, the late Milo Talbot, the 7th Baron of Malahide, carried on a twenty-three-year love affair with southern hemisphere species. He was scientific and single-minded, and deeply concerned about providing agreeable conditions for his plants. Aesthetics sometimes fell by the wayside. His garden, which has been undergoing a sensitive restoration, is unique in these islands, and a valuable repository of well-documented plant material.

The other gardens in this chapter have also been made by ardent plantspeople. Helen Dillon gardens in Dublin city, while Jimi Blake has created Hunting Brook on farmland in County Wicklow. Each – as they will happily admit – has gone through an intense and immoderate collecting phase. But both have come out the other end equipped with the artistry and knowledge that comes from minutely considering the possibilities of thousands of different plant varieties. They have perfected the art of painting their garden canvases with immense and varied palettes of plant matter.

ABOVE A *Tetrapanax papyrifer* 'Rex' of heroic proportions dominates a corner of Carmel Duignan's garden.
OPPOSITE *Schefflera taiwaniana* backs up the graceful grasses, *Molinia caerulea* subsp. *arundinacea* 'Transparent' and *Miscanthus sinensis* var. *condensatus* 'Cabaret'.

So, too, has Carmel Duignan, the owner of the smallest garden in this book — but also the plot with the most plant species per square metre. Her cottage, in the village of Shankill in County Dublin, is part of a 1930s county council development, with each house built on a 0.1-hectare (quarter-acre) lot, which at the time was considered the right size for working families to raise plenty of vegetables. But when Carmel moved here in 1987, the land was lumpy and fallow. It had seen no vegetables for many years.

Its blankness pleased her, and she set to digging out rubble, laying paths and making borders. Her brother, meanwhile, rolled up his sleeves and built her a retaining wall between the back patio and garden. While she mixed the cement for him, she had a close look at how wall-building worked, and decided she could probably do this sort of thing for herself in future. So she did. Now, although in her mid-seventies, she is completely labour-

sufficient, and is undaunted by bricks and mortar, lofty ladders or whining chainsaws.

The extraordinariness of Carmel's garden is announced by a herd of giraffe-necked giant Canary Island bugloss (*Echium pininana*) stretching over the boundary. They beckon you in, past the trumpets and bells of phygelius and fuchsia, and on into the back garden.

Although there must be over a thousand different plant species and cultivars, there is no feeling of clutter. The patio is punctuated with well-placed troughs of interesting specimens, while in one corner, an immense, twelve-year-old *Tetrapanax papyrifer* 'Rex' – with freakish, 1-metre- (39-inch-) wide leaves – claims a space for itself.

The back of the house, which faces south-west, offers a warm wall for heat-lovers such as the sweetly scented South American climber *Mandevilla laxa* and the Mexican bush mallow, *Phymosia umbellata*. Nearby, dieramas and grasses sway in the breeze, throwing an airy veil over the border behind them. The rectangular plot is bisected by a broad band of smooth, green lawn, which acts as a peaceful interlude between the crowded borders.

They may be crowded, but they are not chaotic or awkwardly exhibitionist – as the gardens of plant collectors so often are. Carmel has a rare talent for harmonious compositions, artfully combining colours and balancing leaf shapes and weights. For instance, one dynamic collaboration includes the wispy *Molinia caerulea* subsp. *arundinacea* 'Transparent', backed by fountainy *Miscanthus sinensis* var. *condensatus* 'Cabaret', which is in turn lorded over by the palmate-leaved *Schefflera taiwaniana*.

The last belongs to the *Araliaceae* family, of which the best-known member is the common ivy (*Hedera helix*). But it is the 'aristocratic ivies' that reign here: besides *Schefflera* (of which she has several species) and *Pseudopanax* (ditto), there are members of the *Tetrapanax, Metapanax* and *Aralia* genera. All have supremely architectural leaves that immediately confer a jungly flavour upon a garden.

Carmel has been fixated on various plant families over the years, eagerly riffling through the pages of the *RHS Plant Finder* to find the choicest and most serviceable of each. Her heavy soil is perfect for clematis, a clan with which she enjoyed a dalliance some years ago. She still has about thirty different varieties: favourites include the dusky and double *C. viticella* 'Flore Pleno', which dates from Elizabethan times, and *C. tibetana* subsp. *vernayi* 'Glasnevin Dusk' with chunky, near-brown tepals, which was collected in Tibet by Irish plantsman Seamus O'Brien. It is one of many plants with an Irish connection that Carmel grows.

There is not enough room here to give more than a tiny taster of this remarkable Shankill garden. Its modest size and charming artistry make it attractive and accessible to those who know nothing about plants. And for those who do, it soon becomes apparent that its owner is an uncommonly good plantswoman. She is, in fact, one of the grand dames of Irish gardening. Like her garden, she is eminently approachable and full of surprises.

Mount Congreve

COUNTY WATERFORD

Mount Congreve Gardens sit on a bend of the River Suir at Kilmeaden, about 8 kilometres (5 miles) west of Waterford city in the south-east of Ireland. The area is a gentle landscape of rolling green fields: rich pasture for a thriving dairy industry. The climate is benign – moderated by the waters in the broad arc of the river and in the Celtic Sea 10 kilometres (6 miles) to the south. Belts of beech, oak and conifers planted generations ago give shelter to the 30-hectare (70-acre) plot, which dips down to the river. The soil is acid, very acid: between 4.5 and 5 pH. As its erstwhile owner, the late Ambrose Congreve, told me contentedly a few years ago: 'It is the optimum pH for growing plants.'

To Big House gardeners of a certain era, 'plants' meant woody specimens, especially rhododendrons, magnolias and other Asian and North American species. Ambrose Congreve, who died in 2011 aged 104, was a man from another time. His remarkable demesne reflects a mode of gardening that he learned in the 1920s and 1930s and never deviated from.

He was born in 1907 in London, at 3 Savile Row (a house made famous in 1969 when its rooftop was the venue for the Beatles' last live concert, which featured in the film *Let It Be*). Congreve dressed nattily and lived extravagantly, eating the best food, smoking the best cigars (even in his final years) and surrounding himself with liveried house staff.

The massive Waterford house had been built around 1760 for John Congreve, his great-great-great-grandfather. The property had passed directly from father to son (all alternately named John and Ambrose) until the final Ambrose, whose marriage yielded no offspring. At the time of writing, the future of the garden is unresolved. It was supposed to be taken over by the Irish state some years ago, but legal and financial complications have hampered the process. I hope that by the time you are reading this, the handover has been effected and the gardens are secure.

Ambrose Congreve met his horticultural mentor when he was sixteen, and his admiration for him was still strong when I interviewed him eighty-seven years later. 'I fell under the influence of Mr Lionel de Rothschild' – who was then creating his own garden at Exbury, in Hampshire, a property he acquired in 1918. The banker and Conservative MP was 'the best gardener in the world in the

Massive plantings of *Magnolia campbellii* and *M. sargentiana* var. *robusta* frame the vista of the River Suir and the Waterford countryside. The lower *M.* x *soulangiana* have been drastically pruned to bring them back into shape.

mid-1930s'. He was certainly one of the most generous, plying his protégé with plants that he sent, carriage paid, across the sea to the Waterford garden during the 1920s and 1930s. Many are still thriving, including a plantation of big-leaved *Rhododendron sinogrande* in the woodland. The younger man was a good student, eagerly espousing Rothschild's ideas and putting them into action in his own garden.

Chief of these was that plants were to be in arranged in 'biggish groups', and never dotted around as singletons. So, instead of planting one magnolia, azalea or whatever, the idea was to group together five, ten, twenty or even a hundred, all of the same variety. Nowadays, advances in micropropagation and a globalized trade in plants have made previously rare specimens much easier to acquire, but in times past such mass plantings were possible only for the very rich and the very well connected. Ambrose Congreve was both of these, and his collection of abundantly repeating woody plants is world-renowned.

Most spectacular are his stands of magnolias, which he claimed to be the largest planting in the world: 'I suppose we must have planted two hundred tree magnolias – I should think so.' Among them are the voluptuously flowered *M. campbellii*, *M. sargentiana* var. *robusta* and *M. sprengeri*. These can be seen in throngs (no loners here!) around the gardens, with a stupendous plantation on both sides of a walk that rolls downhill towards the River Suir. Over a hundred magnolias are here: *M. campbellii* and *M. sargentiana* var. *robusta* raise their lavish blooms to the sky, while at their feet many different cultivars of *M. x soulangiana* compete for attention. The grass underneath is planted with thousands of snake's-head fritillaries. It is not an easily forgotten sight – which is exactly what its owner intended. He was unabashedly ostentatious, referring to his garden as a 'folie de grandeur'. It is, in parts, like a horticultural Vatican, overwhelmingly furnished with showy specimens.

Accordingly, there are numerous walks (many miles in all) that are bountifully lined with massed plantings of various genera. Some – such as the kilometre- (0.6-mile) long *Hydrangea macrophylla* walk – are very effective. Mophead hydrangeas always look good in a throng, and here the swollen trusses of pink, blue and indigo make the path a dreamy, fantastical interlude. The peony border in the Walled Garden, frothed up with catmint and backed by blue-spired delphiniums, is likewise a treat. But I am less moved by a forty-strong parade of dwarf Japanese maples (*Acer palmatum* var. *dissectum* Dissectum Atropurpureum Group) next to another woodland path. To my mind, these little gems, with their cascading branches and delicate leaves, deserve to be seen as single specimens, or as part of an artfully arranged group, instead of bobbing along brownly in an orderly procession.

Other paths are frilled with ruffles of pieris, camellia, mahonia, azalea, wisteria and feijoa (*Acca sellowiana*). They go

OPPOSITE White wisteria forms frothy cascades in the Walled Garden.
ABOVE Red hot pokers hoist up their fiery torches in the June border.

ABOVE, CLOCKWISE FROM TOP LEFT The chinoiserie railing alerts the visitor to the little pagoda in the quarry below; an easily portable bench, which Ambrose Congreve claimed as his own design; climbing hydrangea billows around a doorway in the Walled Garden.

OPPOSITE An artificial waterfall tumbles into three small pools edged with ferns, *Lysichiton americanus* and the native *Iris pseudacorus*.

on and on, jubilantly irrepressible in their abundance. There are rhododendrons by the tonne as well. Mount Congreve has over 2,000 varieties of rhodo, 600 of camellia and 300 different Japanese maples. The plant inventory here is 120 pages long. There is no doubt that this is one of the world's largest and most important collections of acid-loving plants.

A simple plant that is unexpectedly poignant is a Mass bush. This hawthorn tree, carefully cordoned off in the woodland, marks one of the places where people would congregate in secret during penal times.

Another idea that Ambrose Congreve adopted from Lionel de Rothschild was that different areas should shine during different seasons. This is most apparent in the Walled Garden, where there are borders devoted to May, June, July and August. Surprises around every corner were another requirement. In the Walled Garden, a door opens to reveal a pond shaped like the racecourse at Ascot – which delights horsey visitors who spot the resemblance. And at

different points in the woodland, the explorer comes upon a classical temple, a tumbling waterfall and – cradled inside a quarry – a Chinese pagoda, shining like a jewel.

In the years after the Second World War, the Mount Congreve gardening team competed at Chelsea Flower Show. The garden's owner explained: 'It amused me doing it. I put up thirteen gardens, and got thirteen golds before the trade did – so they got rather annoyed at me. Private people in those days didn't really do it.'

Mount Congreve's garden director from the early 1960s was Herman Dool, who had originally come from Holland to work in a nursery. He transferred his services to the Waterford estate and stayed for thirty-nine years. He was awarded the Order of Orange-Nassau, a Dutch royal honour, for his efforts. Ambrose Congreve also garnered many awards for his services to horticulture, including a CBE, a RHS Veitch medal, and an honorary doctorate from Trinity College, Dublin.

The garden, since his death, has been looked after by head gardener Michael Murphy, curator Michael White and a team of around ten gardeners.

Talbot Botanic Gardens

MALAHIDE CASTLE DEMESNE, COUNTY DUBLIN

THERE IS A CURIOUS FRAGRANCE on the breeze around Malahide Castle on warm summer days. It is sweet and coconutty, redolent of exotic places and of sunnier climates than that of Ireland. It ambushes the nose again and again with its dessert-like aroma. A particular New Zealand daisy bush, *Olearia* 'Waikariensis', is responsible. It is liberally dotted about the demesne, and is just one variety in a collection of around fifty olearias.

Southern hemisphere plants are a speciality here on the edge of the Malahide Estuary in north County Dublin, where 10 hectares (25 acres) of the 100-hectare (250-acre) Malahide Castle Demesne are given over to the Talbot Botanic Gardens. This is the legacy of Milo, Lord Talbot, the 7th Baron of Malahide, who inherited in 1948 after the death of his cousin James. A diplomat for the British Foreign Office, Milo travelled widely, and had strong links with Australasia, especially Tasmania, where his family had established a sheep station – also known as Malahide – in the 1820s.

The Talbots had been at the Irish Malahide since the end of the twelfth century, having arrived during the Anglo-Norman invasion. As a reward for his military efforts, Richard Talbot was granted the lands and harbour of Malahide by Henry II in 1185. Aside from a brief unseating under Cromwell's rule, the family – a succession of thirty Talbots – was resident here for eight centuries.

The oldest part of the existing castle dates from the fifteenth century. The building was added to regularly, until it arrived at its present much towered and turreted configuration. It enjoys a lordly position overlooking a Brownian landscape park accented with gentle man-made undulations and punctuated by fine trees. Two specimens that probably date from the park's creation in the late eighteenth century are a majestic cedar of Lebanon and a great, crouching sessile oak whose weighty limbs have descended to kneel arthritically on the ground.

The demesne is rich in historical remnants, including the ruins of a mediaeval abbey. Hefty iron rings set into the ground at various locations were once the mooring points for airships during the First World War. The Sea Scout Zero blimps and their three-man crews set off from here to patrol the Irish Sea for German submarines.

An ancient sessile oak rests its limbs on the ground in front of Malahide Castle.

Malahide Castle left the Talbot family in 1976, three years after sixty-year-old Milo's sudden death on a Mediterranean cruise. His sister, Rose, saddled with immense inheritance taxes, auctioned off most of the castle's contents and sold the property to Dublin County Council for £650,000. She emigrated to Tasmania, but returned regularly to Ireland, doing the rounds of her friends in the big country houses and castles.

Following the reorganization of Dublin's local authorities in 1994, the newly formed Fingal County Council assumed ownership of the demesne. Over the years, the garden – underfunded and with too few effective staff – became a little weary and down-at-heel.

In 2012, though, during a two-year (and €10.5 million) restoration, the demesne was entirely rejuvenated. The day-to-day management of the castle, gardens and new visitor centre was franchised to Shannon Heritage, a subsidiary of the government-owned Shannon Development company. Paths were relaid and added, the seven glasshouses were refurbished or replaced, and a programme of new planting was initiated. There are now around five thousand different varieties of plants. The devoted head gardener, Barbara Cunningham (who has worked here for over twenty years), and her excellent tiny team keep all things horticultural in tip-top shape, and with respect for Milo's legacy.

The 7th Baron began to garden here in 1950. He was an avid traveller, and collected seed and other plant material in South America, Mexico, Africa, India and Nepal, as well as in the Antipodes. He was a keen photographer too, leaving boxes containing 2,500 slides of his world travels. He was an obsessive note-taker, and his archive includes many notebooks and 6,000 index cards. The cards, recently scanned into a computer database, are a precious resource for gardeners and scholars. Using a fountain pen, and in graceful, italic English-public-school handwriting, Milo detailed the origins of his seeds or cuttings, propagation date, and the fate of the various seedlings. Many of the plants in the gardens today are his original accessions.

He conceived and sponsored the ambitious and important *Endemic Flora of Tasmania*, published by Ariel Press in London between 1967 and 1978. The six-volume work featured text by London-born Tasmanian botanist Winifred Curtis and illustrations by Margaret Stones, an Australian botanical artist based at Kew. Milo died before the final two volumes were finished, but Rose oversaw their completion and publication.

Although it is over four decades since Milo's death, his spirit permeates the demesne – especially in the intensively gardened 2-hectare (5-acre) walled enclosure and haggard to the east of the castle. In the haggard – the old farmyard – a state-of-the-art, climate-controlled glasshouse, with thermostatically controlled vents and automatic irrigation, was erected during the recent restoration. Known as the Cambridge House (after the manufacturer), it replaced the New Glasshouse, built in 1961 to shelter some of Milo's more tender collections. Among them is *Banksia serrata*, a protea from the coast of south-east Australia and northern Tasmania. It has tiny, shiny, elongated, saw-toothed leaves and beige bark, massively rumpled and obesely folded over on itself. This thick layer of cork-like armour protects the tree during bush fires.

There are several of Milo's bottlebrushes. According to the notations on his index cards, he collected the seed of one, *Beaufortia sparsa,* in Perth, and moved one of the seedlings into the New Glasshouse in July 1962. He found another, *Calliandra cumingii*, on the road to Puerto Angel in Mexico on 31 October 1965 at 2,286 metres (7,500 feet). He sowed its seed a month later, and the following year planted one of the five seedlings here. Seedlings were also sent to Kew Gardens and to his friend, Commander Tom Dorrien Smith at the Tresco Abbey Gardens in the Scilly Isles.

In the long Alpine Yard, one of the enclosures in the late eighteenth-century Walled Garden, Lord Talbot took a utilitarian approach to providing a congenial home for his plants. The south-facing wall was a hollow structure – an original 'hot wall' for fruit – containing a series of eight tiny fireplaces where fires could be lit in colder weather, so that the heat and smoke would keep frost at bay. But, despite having seventeen gardeners and groundsmen, the custodian of Malahide Castle was short of funds, and fires were out of the question. Instead, fussy about the soil here, he brought in tons of acid soil from the Howth peninsula and piled it at the base of the wall. He was unconcerned about covering up the fireplaces – features that another gardener might cherish for their architectural merit. The levels in the garden are often uneven, thanks to his adding topsoil here and there.

He also raised the height of the wall to increase the shelter it afforded. The breeze blocks (that's cinder blocks to American readers) that he used are still visible. His Tresco Wall, as this unlovely creation became known, was named for his friend's more clement garden in the Scilly Isles. The wall plantings suffered in the recent harsh winters, but one of the garden's rarest plants, a fern-leaved ironwood from the Channel Islands off southern California, is in fine fettle. *Lyonothamnus floribundus* subsp. *aspleniifolius* has evergreen, fern-like leaves and

OPPOSITE ABOVE The rare fern-leaved ironwood (*Lyonothamnus floribundus* subsp. *aspleniifolius*) overlooks the Alpine Yard.
OPPOSITE BELOW *Banksia serrata*, one of Lord Talbot's original collections.
ABOVE LEFT Bottlebrushes such as *Melaleuca lateritia* (top) and *Calliandra cumingii* (bottom) are plentiful at Talbot Botanic Gardens.
ABOVE RIGHT The eighteeenth-century dovecote, seen from the Alpine Yard.

fibrous, shredding bark that peels away to reveal fresh, cinnamon-coloured bark underneath.

Milo also used his breeze-block formula in the Chicken Yard, where an eighteenth-century dovecote dominates one corner with its grey and castellated presence. Fowl were once kept in the yard, but were banished long ago in favour of more precious botanical specimens. Among them is the coral plant (*Berberidopsis corallina*), an evergreen scrambler from Chile with pendant, bead-like flowers. Milo claimed to have introduced this plant to Ireland – and he may well have. Also here is the southern sassafras (*Atherosperma moschatum*) from New South Wales, Victoria and Tasmania, from high-altitude rainforests – the same habitat that favours *Nothofagus* or southern beeches (of which the demesne has plenty). It is sometimes called the Australian snowdrop tree, for its small white springtime inflorescences. Another snowdrop tree here is *Styrax redivivus* from California.

The Walled Garden is well furnished with glasshouses: the oldest, dating from 1901, is the Peach House in the north border. A meticulously trained red passion flower from Colombia, *Passiflora antioquiensis*, is strung along parallel wires. *Bomarea caldasii*, known as the climbing alstroemeria, is also from South America, and has clusters of funnel-shaped orange-and-yellow flowers. Nearby, in the Sunken House, the endangered, pink-flowered Majorcan *Paeonia cambessedesii* grows, along with the American *Clematis crispa* and a fierce gathering of spiny agaves.

In the Auricula House the air is filled with the seductive scent of lemons and honey, a blend which is peculiar to these historic primulas. There are hundreds of the little plants in clay pots, a collection that has been built up over the last fifteen years. The dainty flowers are in colour combinations that look like liquorice allsorts crossed with antique chintz. They are perfectly hardy, but are grown under glass to prevent the powdery farina washing off the petals.

OPPOSITE, CLOCKWISE FROM TOP LEFT
Berberidopsis corallina; *Bomarea caldasii*;
Passiflora antioquiensis; *P.* 'Amethyst'.
ABOVE *Passiflora antioquiensis* is carefully trained along the Peach House roof.
LEFT The Victoria House, salvaged from a convent in the south of County Dublin.

The grandest of the glasshouses is the high-domed Victoria House. Look at it closely and you'll see ornate cast-iron gutters affixed to the exterior, going nowhere. The house, which came originally from a convent in south County Dublin, is a composite of more than one building. Inside, a red-flowered *Corymbia ficifolia* (previously known as *Eucalyptus ficifolia*) from coastal western Australia towers over a multinational planting that includes *Tetrapanax papyrifer* from Taiwan, *Echium candicans* from Madeira and kangaroo paw (*Anigozanthos* spp.) from Australia. Outside, a turf-and-gravel parterre is based on the panelling in the castle's fifteenth-century Oak Room. The large beds around the glasshouse have been planted with nectar plants for butterflies and bees: *Buddleja* 'Nanho Purple', *Verbena bonariensis*, *Digitalis ferruginea*, and *Dierama* cultivars in plenty. Swathes of catmint are planted under groves of eucalyptus; the mingling of blues and greys gives a dusty, Antipodean air to the scene.

Outside the Walled Garden, a magnolia walk has been created, and beyond, a planting of forty tree ferns (*Dicksonia antarctica*) runs through a beech, ash, sycamore and yew woodland. Forty thousand bulbs were planted here during the recent restoration, so that a bright wash of flowers laps the edges of the path in spring. Among them are numerous heirloom varieties of daffodil, as well as Irish cultivars such as 'Tamar Lass', bred by Brian Duncan, and 'Tibet', bred by Guy Wilson. The Tasmanian cultivars, 'Indora' and 'Tasgem', bred by H.G. Cross, are also here. This area merges into the vast West Lawn, a 7.5-hectare (19-acre) expanse of flowing grass with plantations of shrubs, trees and perennials. Although Milo's aesthetic sense was somewhat doubtful in the Walled Garden, he was particular about maintaining vistas and lines here, especially when seen from the castle.

Forty *Dicksonia antarctica* have been planted recently in the woodland and are thriving in the dappled shade.

The Dillon Garden

DUBLIN

Just outside the Dillon Garden in Ranelagh, Sandford Road is rarely quiet. With the centre of Dublin only a few minutes away, there is usually traffic pouring along noisily. So it is a relief to turn into the short lane running parallel to the restless thoroughfare, and to crunch across the thick gravel inside the garden gate. To the left, broad steps, half-consumed by a low mound of creeping cotoneaster, lead to an expansive granite terrace in front of the smart Regency house.

Fifty birch trees line two sides of the perimeter, drawing a leafy curtain across the outside world. They are mostly *Betula utilis* 'Fascination' and *B.* 'White Light', both of which were bred in Ireland. In spring, hundreds of snowdrops glimmer at their feet, picking up the chalky tones of their bark. By summer, when the bulbs have retreated underground, their place has been taken by a shivering sheet of quaking grass (*Briza maxima*). This annual throws its seed around enthusiastically, so that tiny grasslings shoot up many metres away from the mother plants. Weeding out the unwanted volunteer plantlets from within clumps of bulbs and perennials is a laborious process, but it is characteristic of the level of intense attention that this place demands.

Such inch-by-inch management, in other hands, might lead to a fussy and strained space, but here the result is joyful, brave and proud. The garden, which is just less than half a hectare (about 1 acre), is widely acknowledged as one of the finest town gardens in the world. It has been made by Helen Dillon over the last four decades – with ample assistance from husband Val and other dedicated helpers, including Val's talented niece, Julie Dillon. Helen has written several books, which are full of the wisdom gained from nearly seventy years behind the trowel (she started gardening at a very young age). She travels widely giving lectures, and has been awarded the Royal Horticultural Society's Veitch Memorial Medal and the Massachusetts Horticultural Society's George Robert White Medal of Honor.

But let's get back to the front garden. The planting is shimmering and silvery, and accented with mainly blue and mauvish flowers. In summer, there are sea hollies in variety, including the lacy-ruffed *Eryngium* x *zabellii* 'Jos Eijking'; a tumble of palest lilac *Phlox paniculata* from North America; and clumps of South African

July in the Dillon Garden: the borders are crammed with repeating spires of purple loosestrife, clouds of pink meadowsweet, orange and yellow lilies and other extrovert plants.

ABOVE Planting in the front garden is light and shimmering and includes a mound of pale *Phlox paniculata* and arching sprays of *Dierama*.
RIGHT *Galanthus* 'S. Arnott', one of Helen Dillon's favourite snowdrops.
OPPOSITE Fifty birch trees create a miniature woodland, and are underplanted with snowdrops and other spring bulbs. In summer, *Aster divaricatus* blooms at their edge.
OVERLEAF Early August, and the reflective water of the canal makes a moment of quiet between the all-singing, all-dancing borders.

dierama slinging their fishing rods over the light-reflecting granite. From the same part of the Drakensberg Mountains as the dierama comes the curious and thistly daisy-flowered *Berkheya purpurea*. White wood aster (*A. divaricatus*) clusters in the shade under the birches. It is a tasteful gathering around the terrace, gleaming yet restrained.

Along the wall bordering the gravelled drive, however, the mood is noticeably brasher. In summer, hot-toned plants, including the scarlet-flowered *Geum* 'Mrs Bradshaw' and her amber-yellow relative 'Lady Stratheden', nod a jaunty welcome to visitors.

Their breezy radiance gives a foretaste of the garden that lies behind the house. There, Helen's current favourite colour strategy is spectacularly demonstrated by two borders that face each other across a narrow, 28-metre- (92-foot-) long, limestone-edged canal that bisects the garden. She is aiming for the effect of a 'box of Smarties – with all the colours dancing around, but completely free'.

This may sound scatty. The execution is anything but. Talented choreography is required to get those plants dancing together; as soon as one lot finishes blooming, another takes over. Helen augments the planting scheme with bulbs, perennials and woody things in huge, black plastic pots: black because it melts away into the shadows, unlike terracotta, which always attracts attention to itself. The containers are inserted into the borders when they are about to bloom, and are whisked away when they are spent or become tiresome. Regular candidates for the pot treatment here are tulips, alliums, sweet rocket, cornflower, lilies, cannas, dahlias, agapanthus and standard fuchsia. Of the last, Helen says: 'I know they are very unfashionable and considered quite naff today, but I am keen on them, as they give you interim height.' She especially likes 'Walz Jubelteen', with its slim, fidgety, shell-pink-and-rose ballerina flowers.

High summer is high dancing time for the borders. On the left-side stretch, a meticulously managed company

TOP Helen Dillon's main borders demonstrate her joyful 'box of Smarties' colour scheme. In the far border, leeks and runner beans add their flowers to the exuberant multitude; late June brings spires in plenty to the right-hand border, with delphiniums, white willowherb and foxgloves. In the foreground is one of the few roses in the garden, 'Rhapsody in Blue'.
ABOVE A Coade stone sphinx, one of a pair, gazes into the pool where papyrus and bulrushes grow; pots of *Verbena bonariensis* line the edge. The greenhouse in winter provides shelter for *Aeonium*, *Canna*, *Velthemia* and other tender plants.
OPPOSITE Tulips grown in dustbins make a spectacular display.

of candy-hued inflorescences shimmies ebulliently. The scheme is woven through with repeating clumps of purple loosestrife (including the native form, found in a ditch in Tipperary), wine-toned *Knautia macedonica* and *Persicaria amplexicaulis* 'Firetail'. Peach, yellow and orange lilies (*L. leichtlinii*, 'African Queen', Citronella Group and Golden Splendor Group) add their happily blazing trumpets. Tall alstroemerias display carrots-and-rubies flowers, while dahlias jump out in saturated, comic-book colours. Sunset-tinged clouds of the meadowsweet *Filipendula rubra* 'Venusta' float above the fray, while the occasional rose, including the pink 'Bonica' and the blood-red 'Florence Mary Morse', contribute their aristocratic blooms to the ensemble. Helen has 'edited out' from her garden nearly all the roses that need spraying, as she doesn't want to kill 'the nice bugs' (with which the garden is teeming). 'With the number of roses available, which is umpteen thousand, why not just grow the ones that can tolerate blackspot or that don't get it too badly? If they are going to be totally leafless by August, then I'm not interested.'

A paperbark maple (*Acer griseum*) stretches its dark copper, flaky trunk through the good-natured rumpus. It is one of a few carefully chosen trees in the back garden. Among the others are the golden-leaved honey locust (*Gleditsia triacanthos* 'Sunburst'), a variegated *Cornus mas*, and an old 'Bramley's Seedling' apple that was here when the Dillons arrived over four decades ago. The apple is given a smart haircut each year so that it looks as if an oversized, green umbrella is raised over the garden.

On the far side of the canal are a chunky Chusan palm (*Trachycarpus fortunei*) and *Crataegus orientalis*, a silvery-leaved hawthorn. The long border here is suffused with blues – in clear, singing tones. There are delphiniums en masse, their towers of flowers making bold, vertical strokes that counterbalance the strong, horizontal line of the canal. Some are Karl Foerster hybrids, while at least one is a cultivar bought at the Chelsea Flower Show in the 1970s from the Bristol breeders Blackmore and Langdon. Creamy foxgloves and the white-flowered rosebay willowherb (*Chamerion angustifolium* 'Album') also send their spires optimistically skywards. Alstroemeria, geum and knautia provide spots of brightness, while *Allium* 'Purple Sensation' and 'Globemaster' bring bouncing bass notes to the scheme. *Geranium* 'Rozanne' threads its pale-centred mauve blooms through the throng. Helen thinks this 'brilliant plant' has rendered certain other geraniums redundant. 'I used to have seven different forms of 'Johnson's Blue'. None of them were anything like each other: they were all different, and they were all rather boring.' One old geranium that she does love, though, is the double *G. pratense* 'Plenum Violaceum', which bears copious violet pompoms in summer.

The two 'Smarties' borders and the canal dominate the garden: the planting is clever, beautiful and vivacious; the Irish limestone morphs from silvery to dark depending on the light and moisture, and the water is infinitely mesmeric. It slides from one level to the next, in three muted cascades. The viscous surface is sometimes still and glassy, sometimes wind-wrinkled, and sometimes cut into a splashing V, as wild mallard fly in and ski to a halt. The ever-changing reflections add another dimension to the garden and lift it right out from between its granite walls. The theatrical water-and-borders centrepiece is so audacious that it immediately commands all one's attention, yet it takes up less than a quarter of the

space behind the house. Around it the garden is organized into sections, some loosely defined, others delineated by low walls, arches or hedges. Generous paved areas allow room for dozens of containers, with the plants in each in the pink of health. In recent years, Helen has been experimenting with using galvanized dustbins as containers. They are surprisingly effective, especially when inhabited by assertive occupants such as tulips: she crams seventy bulbs in three layers into each bin.

A heated glasshouse has a cool vestibule, originally for alpines, but now home to a collection of auriculas, pots of cuttings and tender plants being hardened off. Inside, the warmer part is essential for overwintering frost-vulnerable specimens such as *Aeonium arboreum* 'Zwartkop', canna, fuchsia and papyrus (which, in summer, lives in a deep pool at the end of the canal). Helen has been fond of pelargoniums since she was a teenager, when she was allowed to keep forty-two different varieties in the school greenhouse. Now she has just a handful, among them the blood-red and near-black 'Ardens' and the deep-purple-flowered *P. sidoides*. A white-star-strewn *Jasminum polyanthum* pumps its tropical scent into the warm, moist air in winter, while in summer it snakes its stems outside for an open-air performance.

Adjacent to the glasshouse, a terracotta-and-black-tiled enclosure is edged with raised beds of special plants needing sharp drainage, including spiny *Dasylirion acrotrichum* and blue-leaved and peach-spired *Beschorneria yuccoides*, both from Mexico; and *Buddleja agathosma*, with felted grey leaves and lilac flowers, from Yunnan in China. More treasures that require dry feet are at the far end of the garden in a circular raised bed: *Agave parryi*, with fat, blue leaves; *Trachycarpus wagnerianus*, also bluish (Helen loves glaucous foliage); and – blue-leaved again – the perennial nasturtium from Chile and Argentina, *Tropaeolum polyphyllum*.

Precious plants are cached all over, in places where they can be readily admired and easily tended. The sophisticated, lemon-yellow peony with the unpronounceable name, *Paeonia mlokosewitschii* (which everyone knows as 'Molly the Witch'), sits by one path edge. Not far away, in a north-facing border, is the Chatham Island forget-me-not (*Myosotidium hortensia*) with its blue-and-white porcelain flowers and shiny leaves, beloved of slugs and gardeners alike: there is a battle each spring as to whether molluscs or humans will lay claim to it. As the years go by, Helen has less patience with fussy prima donnas: 'I want plants to be happy. I don't want to be made to feel guilty. I want to be able to walk into the garden and say: "Now, are we happy? Yes! We're happy. Good. Because if you're not happy – out!"'

Helen is keen on the *Araliaceae* family, whose robust members are determinedly contented in her difficult soil – light and slightly limey and shot through with various plant-killing diseases. She has a small plantation of *Aralia elata* and *Pseudopanax crassifolius* in one area: their exaggerated leaf forms create a jungly and primeval effect.

She has even found room to grow food: ten or twelve raised vegetable beds are tucked into spare corners. They are productive all year round: even in the depths of winter oriental leaves, protected by cloches, are slowly ticking over. She grows greens too for her little colony of canaries and exotic finches in the aviary at the end of the garden. Their trilling and whistling gets louder whenever she approaches, making an ornate musical accompaniment to the canal's gently falling water.

The Dillon Garden is endlessly interesting, not just for its varied plants and supreme artistry, but also because it is in continual flux. At one time, it was famous for having one of the most exquisite lawns in the world – a preternaturally verdant, velveteen sward. Helen marked the millennium by digging it up and putting in the canal. Not long afterwards, she had the most perfect red border matched by a just-as-perfect blue border. Now these have been replaced by an exuberant carnival of colour. Change is constant here.

Helen pragmatically accepts that she and Val will not always be able to devote Herculean levels of energy to the garden, but she is excited, rather than daunted, at the idea of formulating a plan for the coming years.

'I'd leave the structure, the hardscape, because I think that it is quite strong. But I think I would like a field around it. Not a modern, fashionable meadow: I mean just a grassy field that might be covered in buttercups, or even dandelions. I think it would be peaceful and not anxious-making. The hand of man – of woman – has been laid on the garden. So the hand of nature would be laid back on top of it then.'

OPPOSITE, CLOCKWISE FROM TOP LEFT Two species of bumblebee and one hoverfly on a leek flower; *Aralia elata*; a canary takes a break from a broccoli dinner; *Agave parryi*; *Papaver orientale* 'Patty's Plum'; *Myosotidium hortensia*; the native purple loosestrife (*Lythrum salicaria*); *Paeonia mlokosewitschii*, known as Molly the Witch.

THE DILLON GARDEN

Hunting Brook

COUNTY WICKLOW

Hunting Brook, the garden of Jimi Blake, is 8 hectares (20 acres) of boisterousness and calm in west Wicklow, a yin-yang creation dictated partly by the landscape and partly by its maker. The land originally formed part of the Tinode estate near Blessington, which the Blake family bought in 1955 and sold again a few years ago. June Blake, Jimi's older sister, also gardens nearby, just 750 metres (half a mile) across the fields.

Jimi's domain is up a steep country lane, where his caramel-coloured timber house sits on high and enjoys a masterful view of the Wicklow Mountains. At 275 metres (900 feet) above sea level, the garden is slow to wake up in spring, but its sloping contours allow late frosts to flow harmlessly away. The land tumbles down on the south side through larch, oak and sycamore woodland and into a glaciated glen where beech trees ascend the far side. A lively little stream, Hunting Brook, flows over the stony floor, and gives the property its name.

Since Jimi started the garden in 2002, he has moved more plants through its soil than most gardeners handle in a lifetime. His borders are continually changing: not just the plants, but the style. At first, his planting was like an accomplished Oehme and van Sweden tribute, with throngs of grasses and perennials. But now, as the garden settles into its second decade, it is more individual, more assured and more rooted in the landscape. The remnants of two ringforts that probably date from the seventh century show that this parcel of land has been populated since ancient times. The circular earthworks once enclosed small settlements of a few wooden huts, and they are still visible as mossy ridges

within the woodland. Much later, during the nineteenth century, the precipitous valley at the edge of the garden was part of the ornamental demesne of Tinode House.

Jimi bravely admits that during his fiercely acquisitive period (a rite of passage in the development of many great plantsmen) his garden-making was fired by a desire 'to create this thing to show off in the summer'. His urge was to keep 'extending the garden, and get more and more plants'. But now he has learned to stay more still, to let the terrain and the history of the area have a say in what happens here. So while his patch is highly gardened in parts, in others it is wilder, in keeping with this corner of Wicklow and its layers of history and landscape.

The plot is most flamboyant around the house, but it has cohesiveness thanks to the repetition of key, structural plants. *Aralia echinocaulis* is Jimi's signature: a slender-trunked, ferociously spined small tree, a native of China. He collected the seed in 2002, when he joined a team from the National Botanic Gardens on an expedition to Sichuan and Hubei provinces. There are over two dozen of these prickly characters, including one that rises through the cantilevered deck that runs along one end of the house. The large, pinnate leaves make lightweight, dappled canopies over the planting below. Early in the year, the ground is painted a deep blue with hundreds of *Anemone coronaria* 'Mr Fokker'. As it fades, *Geranium* 'Mount Venus' takes over, a sterile cultivar of *G. psilostemon* that arose in the Dublin nursery of the same name. It flowers for months, animating the sloping bed with its dark-eyed, magenta blooms. It is joined by swathes of pink-torched *Persicaria amplexicaulis*, *Stipa gigantea* with its long-stemmed, frisky seed heads and an ever-changing parade of interesting perennials. An adjacent border has damp soil, which in late spring and early summer erupts into yellow and orange *Primula florindae* Keillour hybrids. The deep-maroon-leaved *Ligularia* 'Britt Marie Crawford' follows with its vivid orange daisies. The delicately-foliaged bamboos *Fargesia nitida* 'Eisenach' and *Thamnocalamus crassinodus* 'Merlyn' add their shimmery green presences to the concoction.

Along the perimeter of the garden, a south-facing border has a tropical air, with hot-coloured perennials and repeating woody specimens with evergreen, architectural foliage. These include the deeply-lobed *Kalopanax septemlobus*,

The Wicklow Mountains form the backdrop to Jimi Blake's garden at Hunting Brook.

and *Daphniphyllum macropodum*, which has leathery leaves and red petioles. *Euphorbia* x *pasteurii*, a cross between the Madeiran *E. mellifera* and the rare Azorean *E. stygiana*, is, according to Jimi, 'one of the very best evergreen shrubs', as it is hardy and 'keeps a lovely dome' – unlike its more popular parent, *E. mellifera*, which tends to get gangly and awkward as it ages. Early in the year, hellebores, primulas, pulmonarias and other plants that do not mind being smothered in summer clothe the ground. Later on, the large sedum 'Joyce Henderson', with dark stems and dusk-infused foliage, starts to produce its frothy flowers, while the pink-flowered *Geranium* 'Anne Thomson' crowds the edge of the border. The geranium, says Jimi, is a 'good one', but he concedes that 'in about four years' time I'll be tired of it'. He is a seeker – forever on the hunt for the new, the exciting, the impossibly perfect.

When the last frosts have passed, he drops in tender plants such as the wine-furred *Senecio cristobalensis* from Mexico, and dahlias in plenty, including the deep-pink, cactus-flowered 'Hillcrest Royal'. *Miscanthus* 'Hermann Müssel', which has warm beige silky inflorescences, held well above the foliage, forms one of the backbone plants for this jungly bed. Jimi used to collect *Miscanthus* and had amassed a hundred different varieties of the tall grass. Now he retains just a handful of cultivars. His ongoing quest for the most beautiful, hard-working and relatively trouble-free plants follows this model: acquire every possible worthy-looking variety of any given genus, trial them over a few years, and then keep only the very best. He runs a well-regarded plantsman's course each year, with the garden as his classroom and laboratory. His students end up with a greater understanding of plants than many experienced gardeners.

The most dazzling bed is an oval pool of airy perennials and grasses in front of the house. All the plants are fine and diaphanous, so when backlit in the morning and evening they glow with an incandescent light. Among the gauziest are the pink-frothed meadowsweet *Filipendula purpurea* 'Elegans'; the papery, shell-pink *Astrantia major* 'Bo-Ann'; a herd of different cow parsleys; and the grasses *Stipa tenuissima* and *Chionochloa rubra* (if you grow only one grass, says Jimi, it should be this swishy-swooshy New Zealander).

A view from Jimi Blake's tropical-themed border towards his timber house.

ABOVE *Aralia echinocaulis* (grown from seed collected in China in 2002) raises its sharply defined pinnate leaves over the planting. The refined pampas grass *Cortaderia richardii* waves its fluffy pinkish plumes. *Geranium* 'Rozanne' has since been replaced with 'Mount Venus', an Irish cultivar.
RIGHT *Primula florindae* Keillour hybrids and *Ligularia* 'Britt Marie Crawford' share a damp patch near the house with a quirky flower sculpture.
OPPOSITE *Filipendula purpurea* 'Elegans' throws a pink mist over a pool of see-through perennials and grasses.

As with all of Hunting Brook, this bed is liable to change from year to year. Early in the season this area comes alive with waves of small-flowered daffodils in cream and white.

As the garden moves under tree cover, the planting becomes gradually greener and quieter. But first, there is a last blast of horticultural swashbucklingness with a gathering of aristocratic woodlanders: pale and dandyish *Erythronium californicum* 'Harvington Snowgoose', peacockish *Meconopsis* 'Lingholm', sinister-looking arisaemas, beefy-leaved rodgersias, statuesque *Cardiocrinum giganteum*, and pink-flush-flowered *Podophyllum hexandrum,* its bronze and olive marbled leaves like creased umbrellas waiting for the rain to smooth them out. A large congregation of the yellow-and-wine-flowered Asian monkey orchid, *Calanthe tricarinata*, is happy here and is increasing yearly. The remains of the first of the ringforts is visible: a shallow ridge raised from the earth hundreds of years ago.

The path plunges precariously into the glen under old oak trees and then into a pillared treescape of sycamore and larch. There are timber-edged steps cut into the moist ground and handrails, but the damp air seeks to reclaim every wooden thing, coating its surface with moss and eating into its fibres. Your progress, therefore, must be careful and deliberate. Jimi has wrested years of brambles and laurel from the valley and in their place has added a few non-native plants such as Japanese maples, epimediums, Solomon's seal and the South American ferns *Lophosoria quadripinnata* and *Blechnum chilense*. But mostly, this is the preserve of indigenous species: toadstools, bluebells, wood sorrel and the ferns *Dryopteris filix-mas* and *Blechnum spicant*. After the busyness and urgency of the garden above, it is a place to pause and let the splashing of the stream work its soothing magic. Russet beech leaves cover the far slope, while the narrow flatness of an old road dog-legs down the gradient.

Work your way up the hill and yet another world opens up. A great wedge of meadow runs down to the second ringfort at the bottom of the property. Across the neighbouring fields, the horizon is worked by the Wicklow Mountains into a series of softly mounded peaks. After the tranquillizing balm of the valley the sense of space and light is spirit-freeing. As well as being a talented artist with plants, Jimi Blake is a skilful creator of therapeutic moods.

OPPOSITE, FROM LEFT *Meconopsis* 'Lingholm'; *Arisaema ciliatum*; *Erythronium californicum* 'Harvington Snowgoose'.
LEFT *Rodgersia podophylla*, primulas, ferns and other shade lovers carpet the edge of the woodland.
BELOW In the glen, moss gradually reclaims a table and seats made from Hunting Brook's own trees.

LOVELY DAY FOR A WALK
Rambles through the rare and spectacular

IN IRELAND, nearly every day is a day for walking. You might have to pack waterproof clothing in any month of the year, or get bundled into hat, scarf and gloves in winter or spring, but the outdoor life is possible no matter what the season in this largely benign climate. The gardens in this chapter offer the best of strolls, with interesting landscapes and satisfying views. All also offer exceptional trees: Kilmacurragh in County Wicklow, for example, is home to two dozen champions of Britain and Ireland, while Woodstock in County Kilkenny has two world-famous avenues and a host of champions. Tullynally in County Longford is where the remarkable Thomas Pakenham, the tree man, is still propagating and planting.

So, a characteristic of these gardens is that people with no partiality for plants can walk side by side with those who live and breathe horticulture – and everyone is happy and invigorated.

Before we take a stroll around the three mentioned above, I'd like to drift off for a brief spell to some other gardens that present excellent opportunities for walkers and plant lovers alike.

The demesne at Glin in County Limerick is a delightful fantasy of a landscape garden on the south side of the Shannon Estuary. It is overlooked by a large Georgian house that was theatrically dressed up with mullioned windows and battlements at the beginning of the nineteenth century. The gothicized Glin House was renamed Glin Castle by its owner, John Frauncels FitzGerald, the 25th Knight of Glin. As the holder of a mediaeval Anglo-Irish hereditary title, he felt it appropriate that his home should be a castle – albeit one that looked decidedly domestic under its crenellated hat. He also added battlements to the stable-yard, built an ornamental hermitage and installed gothic gate lodges at the entrances to the demesne. He built a little bathing lodge on the banks of the Shannon, done

PREVIOUS PAGES Daffodils and crocuses carpet the meadow under the old oaks at Kilmacurragh in Kilbride, County Wicklow.
OPPOSITE Glin Castle in County Limerick overlooks the Shannon Estuary and, across the water, County Clare.
BELOW The 25th Knight of Glin's bathing lodge, a miniature mock-fortress.

LOVELY DAY FOR A WALK | 195

ABOVE A snowstorm of wild garlic in the woodland at Glin.
RIGHT Limestone boulders at Glin form a late twentieth-century mystical stone circle in front of the early nineteenth-century hermitage.
OPPOSITE Bluebells bloom under the ancient oaks at Glin.

up as a pint-sized fortress, where make-believe men might monitor the river for invisible invaders.

The last and 29th Knight of Glin, Desmond FitzGerald, died in 2011, leaving no male heir, so the title has expired with him. Historian, writer, antiques expert and president of the Irish Georgian Society, he had as keen a sense of landscape drama as his great-great-grandfather, the 25th Knight. As Desmond's eldest daughter, Catherine FitzGerald (a landscape designer herself), says, he was interested in 'views and follies' and was 'like an eighteenth-century person setting out their demesne'.

The late knight and his wife, Olda, who has an eye for detail and a way with plants, made a formidable team. They refurbished and replanted the Walled Garden and restored the old follies, while adding a few of their own. A mystical circle of upright limestone boulders on the hill behind the castle has fooled many visitors. The totemic stones with their patina of moss and lichen are, in fact, leftovers from dynamiting operations for nearby roadworks that took place in the late 1990s. They lend a mock-ancient gravitas to the nineteenth-century hermitage next to them, while the great stone at the centre of the circle seems invested with a powerful force. The hill affords a vista of the mighty Shannon (the longest river in Ireland, longer than any river in Britain) pouring towards the Atlantic Ocean. Farther on, the walk continues through woodland that is luminescent with bulbs in springtime. The native wild garlic (*Allium ursinum*) lies like a late snow on the ground in April, while mature specimens of Japanese maples, *Drimys winteri* and *Crinodendron hookeri* – planted by the knight's mother and grandmother – salute the visitor. Gnarled oak trees are bedecked with ferns, including a generously spreading old-timer under which fritillaries, dog's-tooth violets and bluebells bloom in succession.

Fota House is on Fota Island, a chunk of land accessible by causeway in Cork Harbour, the estuary of the River Lee.

Fota or Foaty (as it was once known) is from the Irish *fód te*, meaning 'warm soil'. It is well named, as the climate is mild, and the soil is excellent for growing borderline plants. A fertile brown loam lies over a free-draining, gravelly, glacial layer. It is that coveted soil that gardening manuals always recommend (but that so few plots are blessed with): moist but well drained. Excess water also flows into a large, jungly pond – home to schools of fish, secretive moorhens and hunting herons – which drains via a sluice gate into the estuary.

The 47 hectares (116 acres) of parkland and gardens are a tree lover's dream, with an extensive collection of woody specimens. The house, originally an eighteenth-century hunting lodge, was expanded and grandified by John Smith Barry at the beginning of the nineteenth century, and it now sits importantly in its landscape park. His son, James Hugh, continued John Smith Barry's work, adding classical terraces, a walled garden and a kitchen garden. He also began the 11-hectare (27-acre) arboretum, planting the first saplings in the 1840s. His own son, Arthur Hugh, continued planting, and added an orangery and a frameyard. The last of the family to live here, Dorothy Bell, who died in 1975, was also a planter. By the time she inherited, the gardens and parkland were already well furnished with large trees, including three champion *Chamaecyparis* and a rare *Cryptomeria japonica* 'Spiralis', a puffy column of a tree that looks as if it has been cloud pruned by angels. Dorothy concentrated on smaller, more floriferous genera, such as *Cornus* and *Camellia*.

The historic house is now owned by the Irish Heritage Trust, while the gardens are managed by the Office of Public Works. Head gardener David O'Regan continues the tradition of planting, filling gaps with young specimens and hunting down suitable replacements for trees that are coming to the end of their mortal existence. Besides its extraordinary gathering of woody individuals, and its

restored walled garden, orangery and frameyard, Fota has a well-preserved Victorian fernery. This was constructed around 1888, at the height of pteridomania, when a fever for ferns gripped the people of Britain and Ireland. Every fashionable drawing room had its Wardian case of wild-collected species, and every country house of note had its fernery. In the decorative arts, filigreed motifs sprouted on carpets, curtains and clothing – and anywhere else where they could be engraved, carved, moulded or printed. At Fota, the fernery nestles under the outstretched boughs of a sweet chestnut tree. Moss-covered, river-worn rocks push up through a froth of native Irish ferns (including *Dryopteris filix-mas* and *Asplenium scolopendrium*), while above them tree ferns fan out their wheels of green plumage.

At Emo Court in County Laois, the house, which dates from 1790, was designed by James Gandon, who was responsible for the Custom House, the Four Courts and the King's Inns in Dublin. The squat, pillared and domed

OPPOSITE A varied treescape at Fota in County Cork: aged conifers and newer specimens, planted in recent years.
ABOVE, TOP LEFT The Orangery at Fota.
ABOVE, BOTTOM LEFT The Victorian fernery at Fota.
ABOVE, TOP RIGHT AND BOTTOM RIGHT The pond at Fota drains excess water from the gardens, and acts as a refuge for wildlife.

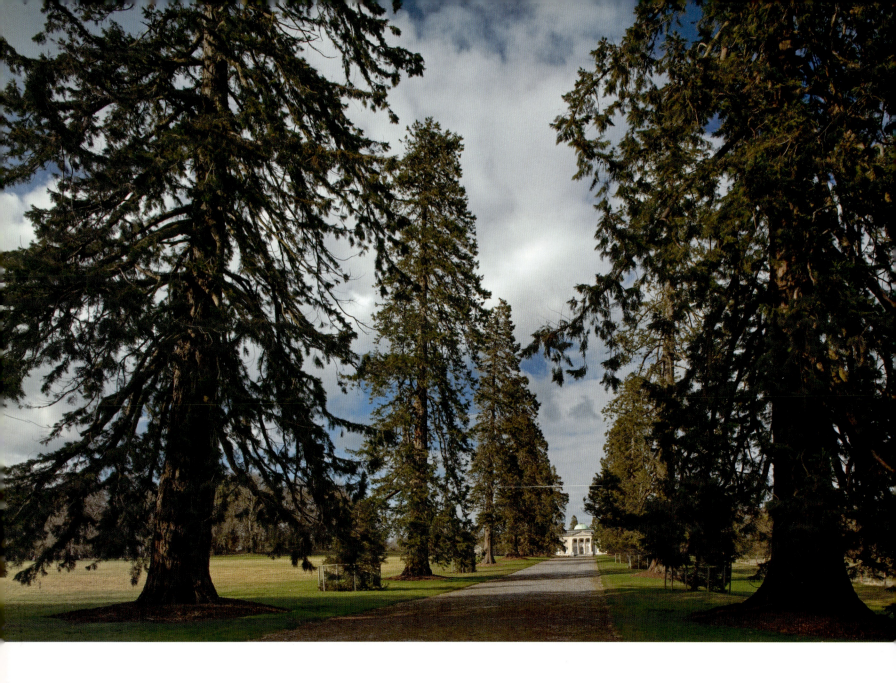

edifice is one of the neoclassical architect's few domestic residences. A brawny bulldog of a building, it is not pretty, but it has strength and solidity. It was designed for John Dawson, the 1st Earl of Portarlington, but it took the best part of a century to complete. It remained in the family until after the First World War, when it was sold to the Irish Land Commission.

The Jesuit Order purchased Emo Court in 1930, and substantially altered the building to accommodate a seminary. Walls were knocked down and ornamental elements were removed and put into storage. The next owner, Major Cholmeley Dering Cholmeley-Harrison, a London stockbroker, spared no expense in restoring the building to its former splendour and in refurbishing the demesne. He donated the property to the Irish state in 1994 and stayed on in the house until his death in 2008.

The massive grey building is surrounded by expansive lawns and parkland, while wooded walks, fringed with thousands of bulbs in springtime, lead to a 10-hectare (25-acre) lake. For me, the highlight of Emo is the mile-long Wellingtonia avenue, the longest run of *Sequoiadendron giganteum* in Ireland. The dark silhouettes can be seen for miles, a procession of giant tree-beings marching along the horizon. Their presence is rooted in a frenzied chapter in botanical history.

In 1853, William Lobb, a plant hunter for the British nursery Veitch, collected seed, cuttings and even seedlings of what he called 'the monarch of the Californian forest' in the Sierra Nevada. He did not know that the grove he saw on the slopes of the mountain range contained the largest living things on earth, but he knew they were unlike anything that Europeans had ever seen before. He reported that a recently felled tree was over three thousand years old, and was 300 feet (91 metres) in length, with a girth of 29 feet and 2 inches (9 metres). A section on show in San Francisco was so capacious that its interior contained a piano and seats for forty people. The *Gardeners' Chronicle* of 24 December 1853 was in raptures: 'What a tree is this! – of what portentous aspect and almost fabulous antiquity!'

The magnificent new species was named by John Lindley of the Horticultural Society in London: he chose *Wellingtonia gigantea*, after the Duke of Wellington, who had died the previous year. Lindley had beaten the Americans in the race to register a name, much to their chagrin, for they had intended to use *Washingtonia*, as a tribute to the first President of the United States.

The *Gardeners' Chronicle* was exultant as it divulged the appellation for this most supreme of trees: 'WELLINGTON stands as high above his contemporaries as the Californian tree above all the surrounding foresters. Let it then bear henceforward the name of WELLINGTONIA GIGANTEA. Emperors and kings and princes have their plants, and we must not forget to place in the highest rank among them our own great warrior.'

In time, it was discovered that another genus had already been named *Wellingtonia*, so the tree was restyled *Sequoiadendron*. But the common name of Wellingtonia has stuck (on the east side of the Atlantic at least), and I like to use it because of the story behind it.

In the decade after they arrived in Europe, the appetite for Wellingtonias was fierce, and they were planted in their thousands. The avenue at Emo Court is one of several that still exist, but it is touched with a melancholy impotence, as it no longer marks the main entrance to the demesne. The trees near the house are well maintained, and the gaps between them have been filled with youngsters. But as the double column of green giants leaves the formal gardens it wanders off, not through picturesque parkland, but alongside the industrial forestry and ploughed fields that have colonized the landscape. It is as if this triumphant parade of heroic veterans has lost its way, and forgotten what it was supposed to say.

OPPOSITE The Wellingtonia avenue at Emo is the longest run of *Sequoiadendron giganteum* in Ireland. The house was designed by James Gandon at the end of the eighteenth century, but its construction was a century-long affair.

LEFT The 10-hectare (25-acre) lake at Emo.

Woodstock

COUNTY KILKENNY

GAUNT AND ROOFLESS, the hollow shell of Woodstock House in Inistioge gazes sightlessly at four rectangular indentations in the lawn, the remnants of a famous winter garden. Ivy surges up the house's facade, and gangly elder seedlings spring from cracks, their lacy, exuberant flower heads at odds with its air of sadness. The great house was one of the many victims of the Irish Civil War, burnt out in 1922 by the Republicans after it was occupied by the Free State army and – before them – by the Black and Tans.

The five-bay, three-storey edifice was built between 1745 and 1747 by Sir William Fownes, 2nd Baronet of Woodstock. He had already been garden making for at least a decade at the Kilkenny estate on the banks of the River Nore, just south of the village of Inistioge. Correspondence from 1736 praises his cascade, 'so wild and natural that everybody of Taste must like it', and refers to an order of trees from nurseries in France: seventy-four dwarf peaches, four pomegranate trees, various vines and a pair of cypresses.

His cascade is long gone, as are nearly all his trees, but Woodstock is far from bare. The demesne is a tree-textured delight detailed in swirls of foliage and in heroic trunks and remarkable barks. Many of the proudest specimens were planted in the nineteenth century, newly acquired from the New World. Nurtured by the moist and mild Irish climate, they have grown into monumental woody beings. There are huge Monterey pines (*Pinus radiata*), found in California in 1833 by David Douglas, the plant hunter who was found dead in a pit trap, probably killed by the bull, who likewise tumbled in. Lofty Californian redwoods (*Sequoia sempervirens*), brought to Europe in the 1840s, are also here, as are their relatives, giant redwoods (*Sequoiadendron giganteum*), introduced in 1853. Christened Wellingtonia after the Duke who had died the previous year, they were planted in his honour in estates in Britain and Ireland. Nearby, multi-stemmed monsters – western red cedars (*Thuja plicata*) – rise from a carpet of russet-coloured leaf

OPPOSITE The famous Monkey Puzzle Avenue at Woodstock, planted in 1845.
ABOVE The hollow shell of Woodstock House; a grove of massive *Thuja plicata*, the western red cedar, introduced from North America by William Lobb in 1853.

litter. The bark on their low, looped limbs is worn smooth by a century and a half of bottoms.

The conifers were planted mostly during the time of William Frederick Fownes Tighe and his wife, Lady Louisa, whom he had married in 1825. She was the daughter of Charles Lennox, the 4th Duke of Richmond, erstwhile Lord Lieutenant of Ireland and Governor General of British North America. The latter post was the Duke's last, and it was cut short after he was bitten on the hand by a rabid fox. He died a few weeks later, aged fifty-four. His daughter (one of the fourteen children that his wife bore him) had a long life, dying at Woodstock in 1900, aged ninety-six.

The early years of Lady Louisa's marriage were tinged with sorrow, as her only child died when just a few months old. Perhaps she found some comfort by pouring her energy into the gardens, which were among the grandest in Ireland.

Louisa herself was said to have designed the flower terraces to the south-west of Woodstock's walled garden. The long box-outlined beds – in chain patterns of circles, diamonds and Ts – have been reinstated by the present owners, Kilkenny County Council, as part of a massive restoration that commenced in 1999. A circular, high-domed conservatory, designed by the innovative Dublin ironmonger Richard Turner, once stood at the end of the terrace, but it was demolished in the 1940s and sold for scrap. The pretty replacement, which stands on the original foundations, was made by Seamus and David Power from New Ross, in County Wexford.

The Walled Garden was once well supplied with glasshouses, which were heated by a Weeks tubular boiler. The warmth allowed the cultivation of flowers year round, as well as peaches and grapes, and delicacies such as pineapples. The last thrived under 'Hartley's rough plate glass', which – it was believed – allowed the passage of a greater number of beneficial light rays than clear glass. The glasshouses did not survive the decades, but the stepped,

urn-topped walls did, and the 0.8-hectare (1.9-acre) space inside has been refurbished to a simpler design than the nineteenth-century version. A double herbaceous border, featuring Victorian perennials, is managed by the head gardener, John Delaney, while the abundant vegetable beds around it are looked after by volunteers.

The Winter Garden, which was laid out in front of the house, was designed by the Tighes' Scots head gardener, Charles McDonald, a man described in 1863 in the weekly *Journal of Horticulture and Cottage Gardener* as possessing 'the enthusiasm of a poet, the eye of a painter, and the genius of the artist'. The raised terrace was 107 metres in length and 76 metres in breadth (350 feet by 250 feet) and was supported by expertly made granite retaining walls.

The terrace was a classic piece of Victorian design, with four sunken beds featuring evergreens (including dwarf Portugal laurels, laurustinus and yew) enclosed in scrollwork of box, and enhanced by coloured gravels. Today,

OPPOSITE Terraces designed by Lady Louisa Tighe in the 1850s and restored by Kilkenny County Council in recent times.
ABOVE Box-edged herbaceous borders, planted mainly with Victorian perennials.

the elevated terrace is still intact, but nothing remains of its elaborate contents except for the four depressions in the lawn – the last yews were dug out in 1978 to make way for the Scout Association of Ireland's Jamboree, an event attended by ten thousand Scouts from all over the world.

At the time of its creation, the Winter Garden was raised with cartloads of earth (10,704 cubic metres/14,000 cubic yards), hauled by the Tighes' tenants from a nearby area that was to become a rockery. It was an expensive operation which, according to head gardener McDonald, could have been done considerably more cheaply (by £200) if rails and wagons had been used instead of local men and their carts.

I suspect that the Scotsman was often at odds with the people of Inistioge. He was a man noted for his 'earnest self-denial and unremitting self-culture': in other words, he probably seemed po-faced to those of a more light-hearted temperament. All the same, it would be hard not to sympathize – a little – with him in this letter to the *Gardeners' Chronicle* published in 1863, where he bemoaned the perils of opening gardens to the 'working classes':

> A few years ago Colonel Tighe was induced to open his beautiful gardens on Sunday, but instead of that sweet recreation which they were to afford they have become a centre of vice. Parties arrived reeling drunk when the houses used to be open, and the plants were knocked about the passages in a manner no one would believe having seen it; plants were pulled out of the beds (and would be now except for rigid watching), and I was abused to the extreme for not allowing dancing to take place on the lawn. On Mondays the seats have to be cleaned of porter; in short everything wears a worse aspect than that of any tea garden I ever saw.

It was not just the working classes who displayed a casual attitude to the garden at Woodstock. According to the 1863 article in the *Journal of Horticulture and Cottage Gardener*, a party of 'what are termed as the upper classes' had 'kept merry at the Red House [one of the demesne's buildings] until the short hours of the morning'. When they attempted to leave, they discovered that the gates were locked, and instead of waiting for the gatekeeper to rise from his bed, they 'burst open the gates and took them from their hinges'.

Woodstock today is best known for its 550-metre- (1,805-foot-) long Monkey Puzzle Avenue: a double column of prehistoric-looking *Araucaria araucana* marching away from the house into a distant oak and beech wood. Thirty-one pairs of these Chilean natives were planted in 1845, just after they had been reintroduced to Europe by William Lobb. (Archibald Menzies had brought the first seeds in 1795, but they were a rarity until the second introduction.)

When Charles McDonald arrived at Woodstock in 1860, the monkey puzzles were ailing, having fallen foul of the poor drainage on the avenue. McDonald supervised the building of new drains, and the replanting of the trees (then between 1.25 and 4.25 metres/4 and 14 feet tall) after they had been scrubbed with soapy water and washed clean. Each was then planted on a mound of twelve loads of 'good mixed earth' over a layer of two to three loads of rough stone. They sprang back to life, 'fast becoming distinguished for green luxuriance, as they were previously marked by a sickly hue'.

Although some of its individuals have since succumbed to more drainage-related illnesses and have had to be replaced with new recruits, the avenue is still gothically impressive. The fat trunks push solidly from the ground, like giant elephant feet, while above their fissured and striated trunks, green branches spiral and swoop darkly.

Less celebrated than the Monkey Puzzle Avenue – and unfairly so, to my mind – is the Noble Fir Walk, which also radiates from the house. The forty-four pairs of steely blue conifers (*Abies procera* Glauca Group) grow strongly and confidently upwards, directing the gaze on a soaring journey into the sky. They were Colonel William Tighe's last big planting, made just before his death in 1878. What a supremely optimistic monument to leave behind!

Colonel William Tighe's swan song: the Noble Fir Walk, planted in the year of his death.

Tullynally Castle

COUNTY WESTMEATH

THERE IS NOT MUCH SIGN OF MODERN TIMES at Tullynally demesne in Castlepollard. The closely grazed parkland, with its picturesque clumps of trees and fine oak drive, throws you back a century or two. The castle, stretched proprietorially across the landscape, is a neo-Gothic-Tudoresque, grey gallimaufry of towers, pinnacles, crenellations, buttresses, arrow slits, hood-moulded windows and tall chimney stacks.

The present day touches it finally, in the form of a television aerial leaning companionably against the tallest turret. There is something disarming about this: it says that although this is the largest castellated house in Ireland, it is still a family home.

The gardens, which extend over 5 hectares (12 acres) of the 688-hectare (1,700-acre) estate, have a similar flavour about them. They are historic, sprawling, airy and idiosyncratic. They are gardens that take you on a ramble, where you are continually looking around the corner, in search of the next grotto or gazebo, sheltered niche or interesting group of trees. The personalities of the owners are all over them.

Thomas Pakenham, the 8th Earl of Longford (although he does not use the title), is an author, tree lover and plant hunter, while his wife, Valerie, is also a writer and a gardener. He, being a collector of seed – and hence a propagator of more

OPPOSITE Tullynally Castle, home of the Pakenhams, the Earls of Longford, is the largest castellated house in Ireland.
BELOW The oak-lined drive at Tullynally Castle.

ABOVE The Pakenhams' summer house, overwhelmed by roses.

RIGHT The nineteenth-century 'weeping pillar' cries eternally into its mossy plinth.

and more plants – has expansionist tendencies, and is forever carving out just another little clearing in the woods for his foreign treasures. She, meanwhile, is more concerned with maintaining control over the parts that have been reclaimed over the past few decades. Their differing views make for an interesting dynamic.

The estate, just outside Castlepollard, was originally called Pakenham Hall, and has been in the family since 1665, when the land was granted to Henry Pakenham, a captain in the Parliamentary Dragoons in Ireland. There was once a large water garden with canals, cascades and basins, but the formal geometry was cleared away around the middle of the eighteenth century to make way for a more romantic landscape park. This picturesque composition largely survives today: a hand-coloured aquatint come to life in this gently undulating county in the middle of Ireland.

A later Pakenham added the immense Walled Garden – now partially occupied by calves and a troupe of supercilious llamas. There were once at least a dozen glasshouses here, but nearly all have disappeared. Two peach houses survive, each wreathed in matching plantings of oriental poppies, verbascums, *Lysimachia ciliata* 'Firecracker', *Crocosmia* 'Lucifer' and other stalwart perennials. Next to them, a walk of paired Irish yews parades solemnly, with all the weighty dignity that comes from being two centuries old. They are escorted by a 'tapestry' hedge of yew, box and holly, the flat top of which erupts regularly into great blancmange-like domes.

The Flower Garden, nearby, is a cottagey tumble of campanulas, *Alchemilla mollis*, daylilies, phlox, sidalcea and galega. Old rambler roses, *Clematis viticella* and other climbers swarm convivially over a summer house that looks rather like a railway station (so this is what the family calls it). Across the path is the curious 'weeping pillar' dating from around 1830. This three-tiered fountain, encrusted with conch shells and water-worn rock, is coated with calcification and moss, and drips eternally into a lily pond surrounded by geraniums, native ferns and *Alchemilla mollis*.

Outside the Walled Garden, the Pleasure Ground and parkland are populated with venerable trees, including the two-and-a-half-century-old 'Squire's Walking Stick' – the loftiest oak in the Republic of Ireland, over 33 metres (109 feet) tall. The Tullynally beeches were planted two hundred years ago, but, cursed with the shallow roots of the species, they are coming to the end of their upright life. Fierce storms are waited out with bated breath in the Pakenham household. Thomas has been collecting their seed for years, and is cultivating their progeny, so their genes will live on.

The genes of an ancient sweet chestnut from Tortsworth in south Gloucestershire also survive here. The mother tree – celebrated by diarist John Evelyn in 1664, and by botanist John Claudius Loudon nearly two centuries later – is probably over a thousand years old; her baby is just fifteen, but elegantly shaped and vigorous. Thomas is eclectic in his seed collecting, as is demonstrated by the two walnuts grown from nuts harvested from the shelves of a Tesco supermarket. No one has planted trees in such abundance since his great-grandfather, who died in the 1880s. The present guardian of Tullynally is making up for the intervening treeless century by adding groves of hollies, magnolias, Japanese maples, oaks, cornus, rhododendron and other woody genera.

The spoils of three plant-hunting trips are gathered into two 'expedition' woodland gardens: the first with plants collected in Tibet in 1995, and the second with those found in the provinces of Yunnan and Sichuan in 1993 and 2005. (Thomas has a strict proviso that only plants grown from seed collected on these excursions can be used in these particular gardens.) A sprinkling of the yellow *Primula florindae* spreads out from the Tibetan Garden: they like it so much that they are seeding themselves uphill as well as down. Also here are berberis, white-berried sorbus, *Lindera triloba* with its eponymous lobed leaves and red stems, and unnamed roses with dark-pink flowers, glossy foliage and shapely hips.

In the second garden is a grove of Himalayan birch: each tree wears a slightly different shade of brown, peeling bark – shinier and more lustrous where it is stripped away. These are all *Betula utilis*, a tree that we are more used to seeing in its chalky and ghostly incarnation, var. *jacquemontii*. In its native land, the bark of the species ranges from chocolate-coloured to white, with the darker colours growing in the more easterly and damper regions. Other finds planted here are a rare oak, *Quercus aliena*, a native of Korea, Japan and China; the Chinese cork oak, *Q. variabilis*; a Chinese ash, *Fraxinus paxiana*; and an unusual alder, *Alnus nepalensis*. This last was collected by fellow plant hunter Brendan Parsons, Lord Rosse of Birr Castle, who was on one of the same trips as Thomas. 'Under my rules,' explains Thomas, 'I am allowed to have things from the trip – so if somebody else collects it, it's OK.'

The bright pink candelabra primula, *P. poissonii*, is one of the perennials that have happily set up home here. Others include the dusty rose *Anemone hupehensis*, one of the parents of the so-called Japanese anemone garden hybrids, and a gratifyingly tall and sturdy (needing no staking) form of meadow rue (*Thalictrum delavayi*).

A further 'little garden by a stream' has appeared in the woodland. Here Thomas has been entertaining himself by digging out interlinked channels, which are fed by a spring that bubbles up in the nearby pond. An American silver maple (*Acer saccharinum*) signals its approval by flushing scarlet and crimson in autumn. Although the garden-maker is an octogenarian, he shows no sign of stopping. The compulsion for continual progress runs in the family, and was remarked upon in 1832 by Maria Edgeworth. In a letter to her friend, Miss Ruxton, she wrote: 'When I congratulated Lord Longford on having done so much at Pakenham Hall, and upon having still something to do, he answered, "Oh yes, I never was intended for a finished gentleman!"'

OPPOSITE, CLOCKWISE FROM TOP LEFT *Primula florindae* crowd around the gazebo in the Tibetan garden; a surprising form of *Betula utilis* with chocolate-brown bark; *Anemone hupehensis*, grown from seed collected in Yunnan; the elegant *Primula poissonii* in the second of Thomas Pakenham's 'expedition gardens'.
ABOVE The American silver maple (*Acer saccharinum*) shows off its startling autumn foliage.

TULLYNALLY CASTLE

National Botanic Gardens, Kilmacurragh

COUNTY WICKLOW

At Kilmacurragh, Kilbride, in County Wicklow, the gardens resonate with the melancholic tones that emanate from the grim wreck of a once-beautiful house. The Queen Anne-style building, which was completed at the beginning of the eighteenth century, was the work of Sir William Robinson, the Surveyor General, who also designed the Royal Hospital in Kilmainham (see page 338), Marsh's Library and other important Dublin landmarks. Unusually for a country house of its calibre, it faces east, presumably to afford views of the sea – a thin sliver of water 7 kilometres (4½ miles) away, just visible across the sloping, rhomboid fields.

OPPOSITE The evening sun shines through Kilmacurragh's Broad Walk, planted by Janet Acton in the early 1870s.
BELOW In front of the gaunt remains of Kilmacurragh House the meadow is speckled with devil's bit scabious and yarrow.

The meadowy lawn in front increases in vibrancy every year as masses of *Crocus vernus*, planted over a century ago, reawaken and reseed, thanks to new methods of management, and crowd the grass with their purple goblets. Daffodils (including *Narcissus obvallaris* and pheasant's eye varieties), fritillaries, scillas, winter aconites and wood anemones also appear: some were here already, but tens of thousands have been planted in the last few years. Kilmacurragh's meadows contain 117 species of grasses and wildflowers – among them devil's bit scabious, ox-eye daisies, buttercup, heath spotted and common spotted orchids, and twayblade. The thriving abundance on the ground is in ironic contrast to the atrophying house above, where every storm fires another volley of slates earthwards, and loosens another seam of mortar in the crumbling walls. The gardens are part of a carefully conceived rescue mission. The house – alas! – is not. I hope that this will change, not just because it is ineffably sad to see such an elegant dwelling decaying day by day, but also because the building is pivotal to the garden, and is linked to so many of the vistas.

Since 1996, 21 hectares (52 acres) of the east Wicklow property have been owned by the Office of Public Works, and managed by the National Botanic Gardens. In June 2010 it was awarded botanical garden status in its own right. Its life during the previous century, like that of many Big House properties in Ireland, was full of upheaval.

The house was built by the Actons, a family of Cromwellian planters who were granted the lands – including the ruins of an abbey – and lived there for over two centuries. But three lots of death duties levied between 1908 and 1916 saw the Actons unable to stay at the estate. Over the next eight decades Kilmacurragh changed hands several times – sometimes being let, sometimes being sold, and at least twice provoking legal battles. During the 1930s, it became the Kilmacurra Park Hotel, run by the German Charles (or Karl) Budina, with dances, picnics and parties for young and old alike. Members of what the *Irish Times* referred to as the 'German colony', which included members of the Nazi Party, gathered here to celebrate national holidays. On May Day in 1939 they arrived to partake of luncheon, followed by 'various German national games ... under the direction of Mr. P. Trankner, who organises the "Health Through Joy" movement for Germans in Ireland'. After tea, 'the German colony band played traditional and other music, and the party joined in their national dances'. Four months later, as Europe plunged into the Second World War, Budina and fifty of his countrymen left Ireland for Germany, safe passage having been secured by then Taoiseach (Prime Minister) Éamon de Valera.

The estate's existence in the following decades was bumpy, and it slid into dereliction after further spells as a hotel and as an Irish college. The house caught fire on at least two occasions, and lost its roof. Rooks now flap darkly through the gaping spaces.

Budina's years in residence may have been the most sociable and lively, but few traces remain of his enterprise – except for a decrepit outdoor swimming pool (the first in Ireland). Instead, it is the legacy of the Actons that is apparent today.

The earliest elements of the historic garden are concurrent with the house, and reflect the contemporary interest in the formal Anglo-Dutch style of gardening. The axial vista from house to pond at the south end of the garden, the remains of canals and the so-called Monk's Walk date from this era. The last is a shady avenue of native yews (*Taxus baccata*) aligned with the pond. It salutes the site's earlier life as a monastic settlement. (Thomas Acton II tore down the abbey remains and reused the stone for his fine, new house.) The trees, sadly, have become infected with *Phytophthora* and are not long for this world. A replacement avenue will be planted soon, not with yews but with *Podocarpus salignus*, a Chilean evergreen with sombre, dark green leaves. Kilmacurragh has close links with the Royal Botanic Garden, Edinburgh, which operates the International Conifer Conservation Programme. A team from Edinburgh collected seeds from plants in the wild (where the species is endangered, because of habitat loss), and propagated them for the Irish garden. Kilmacurragh's head gardener, Seamus O'Brien, is minding fifty seedlings that will (in a few decades' time) grow up to be a twenty-first-century Monk's Walk.

There are a few other remnants from the garden's earliest days: a gothic gateway encrusted with ferns, the stubby remains of a bathhouse, and sundry stone pillars and ruins. Somewhat later elements also exist, most notably a wide oak avenue at the southern end of the property, planted around 1818 by Lieutenant Colonel William Acton. The avenue was

OPPOSITE, CLOCKWISE FROM TOP LEFT Swathes of *Crocus vernus* and *Narcissus obvallaris* in the meadow; *Narcissus* 'Actaea', the early pheasant's eye daffodil; a white mutation of *Crocus vernus* with very large flowers, special to Kilmacurragh; chequered purple and white snake's-head fritillaries (*Fritillaria meleagris*).
LEFT A ferny gateway: a gothic folly from the early eighteenth century.

PREVIOUS PAGES Early nineteenth century oak avenue: the plantings will eventually be restored with new *Quercus robur* seedlings.
ABOVE A specimen of *Podocarpus salignus* planted in the 1850s. It was grown from seed collected by William Lobb.
OPPOSITE, TOP *Rhododendron arboreum* subsp. *cinnamomeum* Campbelliae Group, grown from seed collected by Hooker in east Nepal.
OPPOSITE, BOTTOM *Rhododendron griffitheanum*.

once part of the medieval Dublin to Wexford road, where Oliver Cromwell and his troops (including, perhaps, the first Acton to live in Wicklow) marched in 1649. William Acton successfully petitioned to have the road moved, and was able to incorporate the original way into his garden. Many of the oaks are now as broken down as the house, and they present phantasmagoric silhouettes on a winter's day. The avenue's replanting is part of the garden's ongoing restoration plan.

Much of the Anglo-Dutch garden was summarily obliterated by the most famous Actons to live at Kilmacurragh. Thomas Acton (1826–1908) inherited the property in 1854, and lived here with his older sister, Janet (1824–1906); both remained unmarried. They embarked on a radical makeover – as extensive as it was expensive – expanding the gardens, making walks and avenues, and rebuilding gate lodges. And they planted. Oh, how they planted!

The Victorian era saw a sudden increase in the numbers of new plants coming into Great Britain and Ireland. It was the heyday of the British Empire and Britannia's merchant ships ruled the waves, carrying on trade with countries all over the world. Plant hunters were busier than ever, collecting seeds and other material in the Americas, Asia and the Antipodes. Thanks to the Actons' friendship with Dr David Moore and his son, Sir Frederick Moore, successive curators at Glasnevin's Royal Botanic Gardens, Kilmacurragh became an informal annex to the official institution.

At the Dublin botanic garden the shallow, alkaline soil was unsuitable for acid-loving plants, and the conditions were considerably colder and drier than at the Wicklow property. Kilmacurragh, with its deep layer of acidic, brown earth over basalt, its relatively mild temperatures and its above-average rainfall (now 1,118 millimetres/44 inches per annum), offered some of the best growing in the country. Moreover, the Actons were both expert gardeners, and had a well-trained staff, so the Moores knew that any acquisitions they passed on would be in safe hands.

Accordingly, Kilmacurragh provided a home to numerous precious specimens of wild-collected plants – via both Glasnevin and the Actons' own sources (they spared no expense on buying plants from the many nurseries of the day). A good number of their woody specimens are still alive, and have grown to champion proportions. Among them is the great hulk of a *Podocarpus salignus*, which looms impressively on the perimeter of the new car park. Grown from seed introduced by William Lobb in 1849, and planted here in the 1850s, it is the European champion. Lobb's *Crinodendron hookerianum*, with its dark leaves and fleshy crimson lanterns, not far from the old pond, is another champion. Usually a shrub, this behemoth is at least 15 metres (50 feet) tall. The Chilean native feels so at home here that its seedlings regularly germinate at its feet. Also from Chile is *Laureliopsis philippiana*, planted in 1878, and now the largest in the northern hemisphere. It came as a sapling, says Seamus O'Brien, from a 'famous nursery that everyone has forgotten: Messrs Rollisson of Tooting, near London. They were sending out plant hunters in the same way that Veitch Nurseries were.'

Another heroic Chilean, in the *Podocarpaceae* family, is the Prince Albert yew (*Saxegothaea conspicua*), grown from seed collected by William Lobb in 1847. Kilmacurragh is famous for its southern hemisphere conifers: from Tasmania comes the *Athrotaxis* genus, and – yes, predictably! – the garden has the European champions *A. cupressoides* (pencil pine) and *A. selaginoides*. The latter is known as the King Billy pine, after William Lanne, believed to be the last full-blooded Tasmanian Aborigine, and whose body after his death in 1869 was the subject of an unseemly battle between surgeons who wanted it for research. William Crowther, who subsequently became the premier of Tasmania, made the first move by surreptitiously removing the skull from the body while it was in the morgue.

The garden is also famous for its rhododendrons: their unrealistically bright blossoms light up the greenness from early springtime. Through David Moore, the Actons received material that Sir Joseph Hooker had collected in Sikkim, as well as Himalayan rhododendrons from other collectors, including Thomas Thomson, Hooker's Scots fellow collector.

F.W. Burbidge (curator of Trinity College Dublin's Botanic Gardens), writing in the *Gardeners' Chronicle* on 17 June 1893, enthused: 'The Rhododendrons alone would make the reputation of any one good garden, and they include one of the most complete series of the Sikkim and Bhotan and Nepalese species that is known. There is rarely a day in the whole year that one or other of them is not in flower. Nowhere else, not even in Devon or Cornwall, have we seen these Himalayan Rhododendrons so luxuriant in the open air.'

Despite the decades of neglect, many of the plant hunters' original seed-raised rhododendrons are still flourishing

at Kilmacurragh. Now given an annual mulch of nourishing compost, they are healthier than they have been in years.

The garden's most photographed scene – and rightly so, because it is magical – is the Broad Walk, an avenue of pink-blossomed R. 'Altaclarense', whose twisted, tilted trunks are interspersed with the near-black ovoids of Irish yews. As flowering progresses, the petals drift to the ground and lie in surreal crimson pools on the path. The more compact R. 'Cunningham's White' provides a later, snowy show.

The rhododendrons were propagated by Janet Acton: R. 'Altaclarense' is an early R. arboreum hybrid bred at Highclere in Hampshire. The yews are a later replacement for the original intermediary conifers, Chamaecyparis lawsoniana 'Kilmacurragh Variety', a slim variety that arose on the estate during the siblings' tenure, and which, during its juvenile years, looks like an Italian cypress. Another cultivar that appeared on the estate during this period was Cryptomeria japonica 'Kilmacurragh', a dome-shaped Japanese cedar with fasciated young foliage.

Roughly parallel to the Broad Walk, and also to the rear of the house, is a double border – which was likewise Janet's domain. It melted away during the derelict decades, but has been brought back to life. Seamus O'Brien's plan

OPPOSITE, TOP A *Rhododendron* 'Altaclarense' hybrid and the remains of the eighteenth-century bathhouse by the pond. The *Phytophthora*-stricken Monk's Walk can be seen behind, on the right.

OPPOSITE, BOTTOM *Rhododendron* 'Thomas Acton', a deliberate cross (between *R. campanulatum* and a white-flowered form of *R. arboreum*) raised in the 1880s by Sir Frederick Moore at the Botanic Gardens in Glasnevin.

ABOVE Double border: *Echium pininana* (on the right) are a testament to the mild climate. Opposite them is a mound of yellow-flowered *Patrinia heterophylla*, grown from seed collected in China in 2004.

LEFT Self-seeded myrtle (*Luma apiculata*) with *Dicksonia antarctica* underneath.

is to populate it with 'cool-temperate stuff, plants that people find difficult in the Dublin area: meconopsis, Asiatic primulas, cardiocriunum...' The worst weed, he complains, is Chilean myrtle (*Luma apiculata*), which germinates like mustard and cress in the deep, moist soil. Indeed, this area is full of mature, self-sown myrtles, and their rusty-brown trunks make an exotic backdrop to the scene. One of the most successful plants in the border is the herbaceous *Patrinia heterophylla*, a member of the valerian family, with tiny yellow flowers. It blooms from early July until the end of October. Its only character defect is that its foliage exudes the scent of malodorous tomcats. Its seed was collected from the wild during the 2004 Glasnevin Central China Expedition, and it is virtually unknown as a garden plant.

Modern plant-hunting expeditions continue to thus enrich the inventory at Kilmacurragh. An important acquisition, which came from Chile via the Royal Botanic Garden Edinburgh in 2001, is a pair of *Aextoxicon punctatum*, also known as *olivillo*, or *palo muerto* (the tree of death). The poisonous evergreen, which is dioecious (bearing male and female flowers on separate plants), is endangered in the wild and almost unknown in cultivation. Kilmacurragh's duo happily turned out to be of different sexes, and the female first bore fruit in 2012; it is the only known fruiting tree outside South America.

Thomas and Janet Acton also created a magnificent avenue into Kilmacurragh. The first three-quarters of its length were lined with *Abies alba* (silver firs, much admired by Burbidge in the *Gardeners' Chronicle*) and the last quarter with *Araucaria araucana* (monkey puzzles, which unaccountably he did not mention). The latter were probably grown from seed that was brought to Europe by William Lobb in 1845, when he reintroduced the species into cultivation. Only a handful of the original trees remain on the avenue, but the entire length will soon be replanted with sixty araucaria grown from seed harvested from these stalwarts. Additional trees will be placed on the hill in the neighbouring property, so that they stride off towards the horizon on the borrowed landscape.

Replanting with trees from native or heritage stock is part of Kilmacurragh's master plan. New oak woods will be created to replace those felled decades ago, and there are 2,500 saplings growing on in the nursery. Seed of *Quercus petraea* was collected in the wilds of Wicklow, while the parent for the *Q. robur* seedlings is one of the most impressive oaks in Ireland, the ramrod-straight and lofty Squire's Walking Stick at Tullynally Castle (see page 208).

It will take some time before this historic Wicklow garden heals after the years of neglect, but it is, nonetheless, a place of wonder, with its magnificent trees, ghostly shadows and parcels of intense horticulture. I shall leave you with some more of Burbidge's words from the *Gardeners' Chronicle* – which I have edited brutally, because he does go on:

After seeing a broad and beautiful old garden and domain of this kind, one feels an exaltation of the mind ... To thus see the cool lush grass, and the flowers, and the noble trees against the sky ... is ... to be assured in one's heart that there is something Arcadian left to us in the world after all.

OPPOSITE ABOVE *Picea orientalis*, planted by Thomas Acton.
OPPOSITE BELOW *Rhododendron* 'Altaclarense' with a wash of cerise petals on the Broad Walk; the rumpled foot of one of the garden's many monkey puzzles (*Araucaria araucana*).

NATIONAL BOTANIC GARDENS, KILMACURRAGH

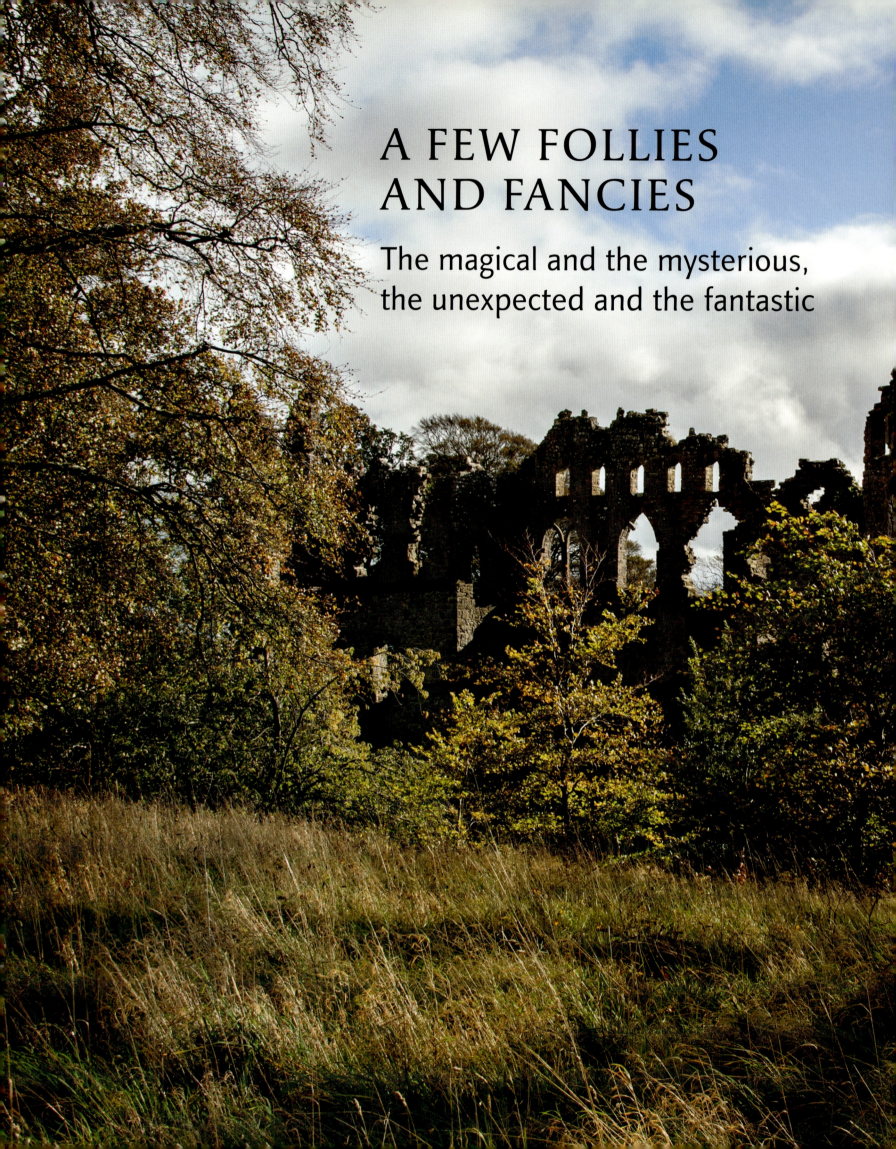

A FEW FOLLIES AND FANCIES

The magical and the mysterious, the unexpected and the fantastic

The landscape of Ireland is well peppered with follies – curious structures of exaggerated and romantic character that are monuments to their owners' whims or wealth (or both). Sham ruins and gothicky fantasies crop up in demesnes, as do intriguing arches and bridges, self-important obelisks and columns, secluded hermitages and grottoes, lonesome temples and ornate shell houses.

The eighteenth century was a fertile time for folly building, as members of the aristocracy returned from their grand tours of Europe with their minds full of ideas and their sketchbooks full of architectural gems. Skilled builders were able to improvise their own creations, while for those who required exact dimensions and drawings, pattern books supplied the plans for structures that ranged from simple rustic to high Palladian to unrestrained Gothick.

Some of the best-known eighteenth-century follies are those at Belvedere House in County Westmeath, erected by Robert Rochfort, the first Baron Belfield. Their austerity is in complete contrast to the bucolic thatched *cottage orné* at Kilfane in County Kilkenny, built about four decades later at the beginning of the nineteenth century. Folly building continues into the present day: among the more recent fanciful creations is the garden of Alfred Cochrane outside Bray with its seemingly ancient ruins (all created since 1980 from salvaged material) semi-shrouded in lush vegetation.

All the above are described further on in this chapter. I've also included the Japanese Gardens in County Kildare. The diminutive landscape is a curiosity left over from an intense and unrestrained period of 'Japanese fever' at the start of the twentieth century.

To the follies, fancies and fevers here, I've also added the fantastic. That last category includes the National Botanic Gardens in Glasnevin, which have some of the most splendid glasshouses in the world: remarkable feats of engineering in their day. Likewise, at the Botanic Gardens in Belfast, the Tropical Ravine and the Palm House are spectacular survivors of the Victorian era.

At Lismore Castle, overlooking the Blackwater in County Waterford, it is the collection of sculpture that makes the gardens exceptional. The owners, the Dukes of Devonshire, are lovers of contemporary art, and have converted one wing of the castle to a gallery hosting the work of international artists.

The walled Upper Garden, which dates from the beginning of the seventeenth century, was laid out by Richard Boyle, the 1st Earl of Cork (whose fourteenth child was Robert Boyle, father of modern chemistry and formulator of Boyle's Law). The 4th Earl's daughter, Lady Charlotte Boyle, brought the substantial Lismore estate as her inheritance when she married William Cavendish,

PREVIOUS PAGES A monumentally expensive way of hiding an unsavoury view: the eighteenth-century Jealous Wall at Belvedere, County Westmeath.
RIGHT The Upper Garden at Lismore Castle was first laid out in the seventeenth century.
OPPOSITE *Learning to Be I,* by Antony Gormley, at Lismore Castle.

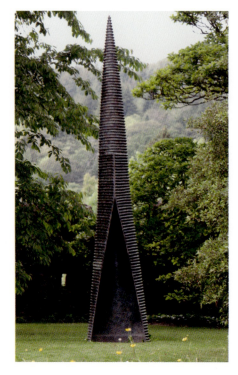

230 | THE IRISH GARDEN

the 4th Duke of Devonshire. In the steeply graded Upper Garden, the outer walls and formal terraces are original, while the plantings of herbaceous borders, vegetables and cut flowers reflect the tastes of today. Among the several sculptures here are two by Devon artist Bridget McCrum. *Poised Bird* is a simplified and gently rounded limestone passerine, and *Hunting* is a watchful bronze raptor, wings outstretched and curved as they hug an invisible updraft.

The Lower Garden is an informal pleasure ground with great lawns and fine trees, created by the 6th Duke in the 1850s. He brought in cartloads of mountain peat to provide the right conditions for the acid-loving rhododendrons and magnolias coming in from China during the latter half of that century. Irish artist Eilis O'Connell's *Over and Under Series IV* is a dark, corrugated spire positioned at the end of a double parade of huge *Eucryphia* x *intermedia* 'Rostrevor'. Her *Wrapt*, a blue-green, patinated bronze unfurling curve, sits quietly in a shrub border. David Nash, the Welsh-based sculptor, offers *Three Lismore Columns*, a lofty trio of totemic forms made from roughly worked oak.

Lismore's most popular sculpture is by Antony Gormley, who is best known for the *Angel of the North* at Gateshead in the north-east of England. His Lismore work, *Learning to Be I*, is a cast-iron mould of his own body. The vulnerable-looking form stands on tiptoe in the dappled shade of an aged yew walk, planted at the beginning of the eighteenth century.

Lismore's yews are the native species, *Taxus baccata*, which is commonly known as the English yew – although it is native to much of Europe, and parts of Africa and Asia. The Irish yew, *T. baccata* 'Fastigiata', is an upright variety: the sombre and fantastical yew of churchyards, which makes dark green and mournful punctuation marks among the graves. The first known Irish yew, which dates from around 1760, is still at Florence Court in County Fermanagh. It was found originally on the side of nearby Cuilcagh Mountain by George Willis, who was a farmer or gamekeeper (or both). The story is that he either found a pair of seedlings, or was able to divide a singleton into two; he planted one at his home, and gave the other to Lord Enniskillen, his landlord.

Willis's own yew has long since departed, but its companion at Florence Court (now owned by the National Trust) can still be seen today. It is a little bedraggled and a little misshapen, but the upright habit of its growth is still apparent. The tree is female, but the seeds come true extremely rarely, so the only reliable way to make a new Irish yew is to take cuttings from an existing one. This means that the Florence Court tree is the mother of millions of Irish yews. Almost all those in existence throughout the world were propagated from material that originated from it.

OPPOSTE ABOVE *Three Lismore Columns*, by David Nash.
OPPOSITE BELOW *Hunting*, by Bridget McCrum; Eilis O'Connell, *Over and Under Series IV*.
LEFT Mother of millions: the original Irish yew at Florence Court in County Fermanagh.

ABOVE, CLOCKWISE FROM TOP LEFT Blarney Castle in County Cork; in the Rock Close, the Wishing Steps, beyond the opening, are dated 1757 (walk up and down the steps backwards with your eyes closed, and your wish will be granted); more steps lead down to the Fern Garden, created recently in an erstwhile quarry; the oldest known yew in the gardens, believed to be six hundred years old.

OPPOSITE In the Rock Close, the roots of a yew grasp the entrance to the Witch's Kitchen.

There are more famous yews – at least fifty of them – at Blarney Castle, the home of the stone that endows those who kiss it with the gift of the gab. Blarney's yews are the non-fastigiate natives, *T. baccata*, and they were planted hundreds of years ago. About thirty or more are gathered in the Rock Close, a magical landscape created around 1767 by James St John Jefferyes, ancestor of the present owner of the County Cork estate, Sir Charles Colthurst. The spot, which was already strewn with great limestone boulders and rumpled with exposed bedrock, was said to have 'druidic' associations. Jefferyes enhanced its romantic character by adding a series of stone follies, including the Wishing Steps, a narrow staircase that burrows through the rock; and a cavern known as the Witch's Kitchen. The spooky entrance to the latter is embraced by a yew that looks as if it has been drawn by Arthur Rackham. Gnarled, bony, and pulsating with arboreal energy, its roots grasp the rock so closely and powerfully that the animate and the inanimate appear to be fused together.

Today, the lowest part of the Rock Close has been turned into a bog garden, luxuriant with big-leaved gunnera, skunk cabbage and bamboo. Water cascades, weeps and leaks from the rock face and adds its lachrymose presence to the melancholic ambience. On the upper, drier parts of the area is a pinetum: the

232 | THE IRISH GARDEN

oldest trees – among them an immensely tall Monterey pine (*Pinus radiata*) – date from sometime in the nineteenth century. Another lot was planted in the 1960s, after which brambles and sycamores claimed the ground for themselves. Recent clearance has given the conifers room to breathe again, and dozens of new specimens have been added. These include special plants such as *Pilgerodendron uviferum*, a rare member of the cypress family from Chile, and a grove of thirty *Podocarpus salignus*, also from Chile, where it is threatened by habitat loss.

On the far side of the castle in a patch of woodland is the equally atmospheric Fern Garden. The deep, rocky bowl, its sides clothed with ivy and native ferns, was once a quarry. Now, dozens of *Dicksonia antarctica* and other tree ferns (*D. squarrosa*, *Cyathea dealbata* and *C. tomentosissima* among them) populate the space with their massive, green, frondy wheels. Designed by head gardener Adam Whitbourn, the ferny plantation is only a few years old, but with the rampant growth here at the south end of the country, it is on its way to becoming a twenty-first-century Irish jungle.

Some of the most charming follies in Ireland are at Larchill Arcadian Garden, near Kilcock in County Kildare. The home of Micheal and Louisa de Las Casas offers 25 hectares (63 acres) of gardens, farmland, park, wetlands and lake. For most of the eighteenth century, the property was part of a much larger estate, Phepotstown, owned by the Prentices, a family of haberdashers from Dublin. This, their flax farm, was also their country retreat, where between 1740 and 1780 they created a *ferme ornée*, an ornamental farm set in a utopian landscape. Domestic animals which would normally have been accommodated in basic conditions were quartered in decorative gothic pens and houses. Beyond the farmyard, the landscape could have been a series of paintings by Gainsborough: contented livestock grazed among the well-placed trees, while artful prospects

ABOVE Gibraltar, at Larchill Arcadian Garden, where mock naval battles were fiercely fought.
LEFT The Greek temple is a primitive structure topped by eleven stone piers.

A FEW FOLLIES AND FANCIES

of garden buildings, water and statuary could be seen from various congenial vantage points.

The Prentices' country home was also a place for partaking in entertaining diversions of a more physical nature. A watery playground was made on and around a 3-hectare (7½-acre) lake which had been dug out of a low-lying field and lined with marl (one of three lakes on the estate). There, the family and their guests could play at naval battles, incorporating two small islands into the theatre of war. On one was a mini fortress, a chunky building with five towers and plenty of circular gun ports. This was known as Gibraltar, after the British crown colony that had been besieged by the Spanish in 1727 (and again from 1779–83). On the other island, a circular temple had an invigorating plunge pool at its centre.

Theirs wasn't the only mock Gibraltar. Indeed, there was another just a few miles away at Dangan Castle (now in sad ruins), the home of the Wellesleys, the Duke of Wellington's family. Dangan's lake was larger and its landscape was lavishly embellished with temples, grottoes, statues and obelisks. It is entirely possible that the Dublin haberdashers were making an effort to keep up with their grander neighbours.

At the end of the eighteenth century, the Prentices fell on hard times, and were forced to lease this part of the estate to a local family, the Watsons. They, it is believed, continued to maintain and enjoy the follies.

By the time Micheal and Louisa de Las Casas came here in the 1990s, the eighteenth-century garden had been nearly – but not quite – erased. Garden historian Paddy Bowe was able to tell from the few remaining clues that the landscape had indeed once included a *ferme ornée*, while architect James Howley had visited and documented the many follies in his book, *The Follies and Garden Buildings of Ireland*.

Micheal and Louisa restored the *ferme ornée* and its many follies with help from the EU-sponsored Great Gardens of Ireland Restoration Programme, the National Heritage Council and FÁS, the national training agency. Today, once again, cattle and sheep arrange themselves agreeably in romantic vistas, the lake has been cleared, and Gibraltar is fiercely defended – not by the men of the house, but by a pair of swans.

The Fox's Earth, said to be designed as a mausoleum-with-bolthole by Robert Watson, a keen hunter, who feared he would be reincarnated as a fox.

Belvedere

COUNTY WESTMEATH

Belvedere House, near Mullingar, County Westmeath, was built around 1740. Elegant and bow-ended, the two-storey villa was created as a place for men. The staircase that curves sinuously to the upper floor was just a little too narrow to allow free passage to the hooped and underskirted dresses of the time. The limestone house sits importantly on a rise, from whence it enjoys lordly views over the large, island-speckled Lough Ennell: a lake inhabited by quantities of particularly feisty trout and pugnacious pike. It was the perfect fishing lodge for Robert Rochfort, the first Baron Belfield, who later became Viscount Belfield, and finally the first Earl of Belvidere. ('Belvidere' was the original spelling of the house, and hence the title that was derived from its name.) The house, which has just two bedrooms, offered an escape from domestic matters at the family home at Gaulstown House a few miles away.

Robert's bolthole was designed by the architect of the moment, Richard Castle, whose many other buildings in Ireland included Powerscourt and Russborough in County Wicklow, and Leinster House and the Rotunda Hospital in Dublin. Its situation met with the unqualified approval of the eighteenth-century travel writer Arthur Young (although he didn't think much of the nearest town). In his *A Tour in Ireland, 1776–1779*, he wrote: 'Left Mullingar, which is a dirty ugly town, and . . . stopped at Lord Belvidere's, with which place I was as much struck as with any I had ever seen. The house is perched on the crown of a very beautiful little hill, half surrounded with others, variegated and melting into one another. It is one of the most singular places that is anywhere to be seen, and spreading to the eye a beautiful lawn of undulating ground margined with wood . . . Lake Ennel, many miles in length, and two or three broad, flows beneath the windows. It is spotted with islets, a promontory of rock fringed with trees shoots into it, and the whole is bounded by distant hills. Greater and more magnificent scenes are often met with, but nowhere a more beautiful or a more singular one.'

Interestingly, there is no mention of the demesne's famous and unmissable Gothic Revival follies, which were added to the landscape by its owner around 1760. Today, the limestone structures have a powerful presence, their mystical vibrations echoing across the centuries. The current owner, Westmeath County Council, has imposed a Narnia trail (based on the films of C.S. Lewis's novels) onto the demesne's historic fabric – complete with signage and statuettes. The

The Gothic Arch, built to a design by Durham-born Thomas Wright.

ABOVE Belvedere House, built around 1740, with incompatible terraces added a century later.
OPPOSITE Light filters through the woodland of beech, oak and Scots pine.

Earl of Belvidere may well be writhing with irritation in his grave. He might also be baffled and slightly hurt, because his own story is as gothic as his follies, and does not deserve to be pushed aside by a movie franchise.

Robert Rochfort lost his first wife to smallpox less than six months after they were married, when he was just twenty-four years old. Four years later, and shortly before he was created Baron Belfield, he married the sixteen-year-old Lady Mary Molesworth, daughter of Richard, 3rd Viscount Molesworth, a military officer and later Commander-in-Chief of the British forces in Ireland. After several years, and four children (including the necessary male heir – plus two spares), it all went horribly wrong. Robert was rarely home, having a grand time in Dublin and London – and down the road at his Belvedere refuge.

On one of his rare visits home, he accused his wife of adultery with his younger brother, Arthur. The accusation was said to be false – by some sources. Perhaps he was tired of her, and longed to be rid of her. Mary admitted the charge, perhaps because she was subjected to force, or perhaps because she was advised to (time has inserted 'perhaps' into every turn of the story). Or perhaps she was guilty.

In any case, the outcome was not good for the young wife: she was imprisoned at the family seat at Gaulstown for over thirty years, and Arthur fled to England

with his wife and children. Upon his return, many years later, he was successfully sued for adultery by his aggrieved brother. Unable to pay the fine of £20,000, Arthur landed in prison, where he ended his days. Mary engineered a brief escape from Gaulstown, but her father sent her back, and she was locked up again until the Earl's death in 1774.

During his wife's incarceration, the Earl of Belvidere was having a whale of a time and spending money as if it were water. He made the fishing lodge his principal home and spared no expense in beautifying it inside and out. He laid out a classic eighteenth-century landscape park, and built several follies on the gently rising and falling ground. Among them is the largest sham ruin in Ireland, now known as the Jealous Wall. Three storeys tall and 55 metres (180 feet) long, the dark limestone edifice is a wonderfully gloomy imitation of the facade of a decaying, mediaeval priory. It is pierced with many windows in a mixum-gatherum of architectural styles: simple rectangles, round-topped Romanesque and pointed Gothic. Its top makes an exaggeratedly jagged silhouette against the sky, and its forbidding appearance is helped considerably by the darkly sinister rooks which gather among its desolate stones, cawing dolefully.

The Earl had jumped spectacularly on the bandwagon of current fashion, when 'gothick' follies were a sign of a gentleman's wealth and sophistication. 'Ruinated' buildings not only enhanced the designed landscape, they also offered opportunities for melancholy ponderings on the impermanence of life and such like. Robert's giant folly had another rather ignoble and sour-grapeish purpose: it was intended to screen the large house built by his second brother, George, with whom he had fallen out. The seven-bay, three-storey Rochfort House, later renamed Tudenham Park, was also designed by Richard Castle.

An article in the *Gardeners' Chronicle* of 1901 reports that the Earl's wall was erected at a cost of £10,000 – no small sum in the middle of the eighteenth century. It was restored around 2000 by Westmeath County Council, when it was cleaned up, and its fabric invisibly pinned together with hundreds of stainless steel rods. The cost of that operation, which has made the wall safe for the foreseeable future, was £265,000. The house it was meant to screen is now a romantic shambles. Its last use was as a military hospital during the First World War. It was de-roofed and gutted in 1957.

The Earl's remaining follies include a red brick and limestone gazebo. The octagonal building, which has ogival arched openings, sits on a plinth which affords glimpses of Lough Ennell through the surrounding trees. It also offers a place to stop and draw breath on the way to what is – to my mind – the most beautifully phantasmic folly in Ireland. Belvedere's Gothic Arch was built to a design by the Durham-born mystic and astronomer, Thomas Wright, who visited Ireland from August 1746 until June 1747. The lichen-encrusted limestone creation, which looks wrought rather than built, stands forlornly on a small hillock, its dark arch making a perpetual silent howl. A central oriel window protrudes above the arch and is embellished with river-worn, wormy-looking limestone. The walls are perforated with roughly fashioned geometric openings, while snaggle-toothed castellations crown the top. The picturesquely grotesque structure is backed by a dark stand of woodland which concentrates its aura and ties it to this earth.

The first Earl of Belvidere left behind a remarkable set of follies and a gem of a house. He emptied the family's coffers in the process, and bequeathed a substantial packet of debt to his eldest son and heir, George Augustus Rochfort. The second Earl of Belvidere, although married twice, died childless, and the titles became extinct. The estate passed to his sister, who inherited it at the age of seventy-seven. Her grandson became the next owner, followed by his cousin, Charles Brinsley Marlay. Marlay constructed a walled garden in the 1850s, and added a series of grand – but incongruous – terraces to the front of the house.

Next in line was Lieutenant-Colonel Charles Kenneth Howard-Bury, military man, botanist and explorer. He gained some fame as the leader of the 1921 reconnaissance expedition to Everest. His name is honoured in the little *Primula buryana*, a native of Nepal and south Tibet. After his death in 1963, his friend, Rex Beaumont, inherited Belvedere. Finally, in 1982, Westmeath County Council bought the 73-hectare (180-acre) property. In 2000, the council completed a £5.7 million project, £700,000 of which was spent restoring the garden and landscape, including the Arcadian lakeside and woodland walks.

ABOVE The Gazebo is built of limestone and is lined with red brick.

LEFT The Earl of Belvidere's Jealous Wall, the largest sham ruin in Ireland, cuts a mournful figure on an autumn evening.

Kilfane Glen and Waterfall

COUNTY KILKENNY

In August 1986, Hurricane Charley, a storm that was born along the Florida Panhandle, tore across Ireland, dumping record quantities of rain on the island. Rivers burst their banks, houses were flooded, roads were damaged, trees were uprooted and crops were destroyed. And, in a woodland above a secret glen in County Kilkenny, a forgotten late eighteenth-century canal – its narrow width blocked by decades of debris – began to fill up. The water gathered strength and gradually surged through the accumulated leaf-mould, branches and other detritus. Finally, it launched itself over a sheer 9-metre (29-foot) rock face, first as a trickle, and then as a joyous cascade, falling noisily into the valley below.

The sudden appearance of this (literally) marvellous waterfall presented the owners, potter Nicholas Mosse and his wife Susan, with an exhilarating clue to an earlier decorative function of the little dell. They had bought their property, two miles north of Thomastown, a few years previously. Their house, built in the first half of the nineteenth century, had served in turn as the gamekeeper's cottage, land agent's residence, and dower house for the large estate at nearby Kilfane – one-time home of various aristocratic Kilkenny families. With the purchase came a parcel of 8 hectares (20 acres) of overgrown gardens and woodland, part of the original Kilfane demesne.

After the miraculous manifestation of the tumbling waters, the Mosses, spurred on by their friend Jim Reynolds (then of Butterstream Gardens in County Meath), embarked on finding out as much as they could about the glen. One day they heard from Jeremy Williams, an architect and historian, that he had seen an interesting set of drawings, dating from 1804, in the Royal Society of Antiquaries in Dublin. Early the next morning, Nicholas drove up from Kilkenny, found the sketches and watercolours, and had them photocopied. They depicted the little wooded dell, with its crashing waterfall, and, standing on a tiny lawn – oh joy! – a fairytale thatched house.

When they searched the glen, long since choked with laurel and *Rhododendron ponticum*, the Mosses found the remnants of three walls in exactly the right place. These were the ruins of the thatched building. It had been a *cottage orné*, a Georgian folly of the kind that was then fashionable among landowners of means and taste. Perfectly situated to afford a view of the cataract plummeting

Kilfane's *cottage orné* offered the ladies of the house and their guests a little place of refuge in the woodland glen.

The Powers of Kilfane

John Power was born around the middle of the eighteenth century at Tullamaine Castle in County Tipperary. His father had served as aide-de-camp to Lord Clive, commander in chief of the Anglo-Indian Army at the Battle of Plassey in 1757 — the conflict that led to the annexing of Bengal by the East India Company. John Power was partial to a bit of military activity himself, and got together a company of local yeomen to fight the United Irishmen during the 1798 Rebellion. That was an eventful year for Captain Power (as he was then known), on the domestic front as well, as his wife, Harriet, presented him with twin boys.

Around the same time, he took out a perpetual lease on the estate at Kilfane, owned by Henry Amias Bushe, Harriet's brother. John's own brother, Richard, who had a house in Dublin, often lived here with the family. A man of culture, he founded the Private Theatre of Kilkenny, where the performances raised thousands of pounds for charity during its seventeen-year lifespan.

John Power was a famous huntsman, and a founder of the Kilkenny Hunt. The February and November club dinners were convivial affairs, according to the anonymous *Memoir of the Kilkenny Hunt* (published in 1897):

> 'The dinners held at night were famous for good wine and good fellowship. Sneyd's claret, largely "fortified" with Hermitage, and old port were the liquids. Mr Power was not himself one of the three-bottle men, but he was a very pleasant companion, clever and well read and could talk on a variety of subjects besides hunting.'

theatrically from the ledge high above, it offered a fanciful place of refuge for the ladies of the house and their guests at the end of a long walk. The servants, of course, would have been sent along beforehand to prepare tea or a meal, and to light the fire.

At that time landscape design had moved away from the gentle, pastoral style of Capability Brown and his peers, and was taking on a more dramatic flavour. Instead of imitating art in carefully constructed painterly tableaux, it found its inspiration in nature – and the more wild and rugged the better (within reason, of course, to allow the ladies to negotiate it in their long and gauzy garments).

The Mosses, with help from several experts, set about rediscovering and then remaking the walk that meandered thrillingly through a 4-hectare (10-acre) patch of landscape, and that culminated in the glen with its welcoming, thatched house. Above the waterfall, the canal, a mile-long feat of engineering, and still largely intact, was cleared and repaired. At the time of its creation at the end of the eighteenth century, the owners were John and Harriet Power, pillars of Kilkenny society (he was later awarded a baronetcy, becoming the first baronet of Kilfane). Harriet, it is believed, had a major hand in the landscape. William Robertson, an architect who had also worked for the Tighes at nearby Woodstock, was employed to design the cottage. Its faithful reconstruction in the 1990s was overseen by architect David Sheehan, while the late Sybil Connolly, doyenne of Irish fashion and design, also advised.

Today, the visitor to Kilfane is offered two very different gardens: the Powers' historic glen and walk, and a more contemporary upper garden. The latter is a classic 'garden of rooms', with a recurring theme in the thoughtfully placed pieces of sculpture. Susan, a Missourian with a degree in fine art from New York's Cooper Union, is deeply interested in the proper siting of artworks outdoors. 'Outside, the whole sense of scale opens up, so things that look big in a gallery or garden centre can shrivel to pea size when you get them home.' Light, background and 'the amount of air around a piece' are crucial to how it is viewed.

You meet the first sculptures in the ivy-and-fern-floored oak woods near the garden's entrance. *Descending Vessel Kilfane* is a totemic piece carved from a still-standing oak tree by David Nash; and Bill Woodrow's bronze *Rut* is a wheel and a basket forever unravelling and ravelling into each other. The never-ending inscription 'work to make it just to make it work to make it just to make it work...' travels around the rim of the wheel. The dappled, chartreuse light and the column-like trees make the woodlands a complementary setting for these graphic sculptures.

The most exciting of the Mosses' artworks is a short stomp through the woods. James Turrell's *Air Mass* is, quite simply, a corrugated metal box, the size of a small barn, sitting in an open space. Enter, settle onto the bench that hugs the walls and gaze upwards at the rectangular opening in the roof. The resulting experience, as the light changes and envelops your soul, is meditative and sublime.

Back in the woodland, two sandstone pillars mark the start of the more formal garden near the house. An orchard of cherries, plums and crabapples leads into a peaceful area outlined by clipped laurel hedges and dominated by a lily pond where goldfish dart among the water weeds. Beyond is Susan's Moon Garden, which glows with chalky blooms – including campanulas, foxgloves, white delphiniums and daisies – and ghostly, grey and glaucous foliage: quilted hostas, woolly *Stachys lanata* and verbascum. Adjoining it, American environmental artist Richard Fleischner has contributed an untitled work: a plain, green rectangular garden – the sort of thing that drives critics of contemporary art mad. A huge stone sphere, peeking through a bite in the laurel hedge, is Susan's own welcome addition.

Running alongside this garden and the Moon Garden is a Victorian fern walk which terminates in an entertainingly wobbly mirror, the work of Dublin-based engineer Sean Mulcahy. A little farther along is British sculptor William Pye's *Vessel*, a great chalice where the water slides ever and elegantly into a central cavity.

More woodland beckons here, and soon you are on the path to the *cottage orné*. The interactions with the sculptures have already honed your vision and imagination, so it is easy to enter into the spirit of adventure that the excursion requires. Eyes are open, ears are pricked and senses are all a-tingle. The sound of running water draws you onward to a stream strewn with moss-coated boulders and overhung with beeches. The uneven ground underfoot is sprinkled with ferns. A stone bridge, also abundantly furred with moss, transports you over the tumbling flow. The path narrows and travels upwards; beech, laurel and ancient rhododendrons crowd in from both sides. The air is damp: moss and moisture drip from every surface. The noise of water – not the rush of the stream, but a more energetic

ABOVE, FROM TOP TO BOTTOM *Rut*, by British sculptor Bill Woodrow; *Bird of Peace* was bought from a salvage company and once adorned a building in Belfast – the disproportionately large head is evidence that it was positioned high up on a tall building; a salvaged stone sphere peeps through a laurel hedge.

clatter – gets nearer, and then you catch a tantalizing glimpse of the silvery waterfall across the little valley.

Soon after, the thatch of the little cottage appears below. Moss and seedlings of beech, bracken and rosebay willowherb have rooted in its reeds. It is an unintentional green roof, conferred by nature. The glen, when you finally make your way down to it, is overpoweringly romantic, all verdant and picturesque. The waterfall throws sheets of water into a pool, and a gentle stream winds along the valley floor. A grotto next to the cascade is a rough and gloomy place – lacking only a wise and tattered hermit.

The planting is natural and ingenuous: ferns, foxgloves, primulas and – in spring – daffodils and bluebells. The cottage, a poem of bucolic bliss, is clothed in honeysuckle, jasmine and the old roses 'Noisette Carnée' and *Rosa x odorata* 'Pallida'. The Mosses received a grant from the European Union Cultural Commission in 1993, which helped with the restoration of the glen and the paths. The condition that the planting had to be period-correct has worked well here.

You can leave the glen – reluctantly – by climbing to the top of the waterfall, where a mist is thrown into your face by the water cascading over the rocks. And then, you retreat into the woods and gradually return to the reality of the present day. But not before saluting John and Harriet Power, who conceived this diversion, and Nicholas and Susan Mosse, who brought it back to life. Hurricane Charley, too, must have a share of the laurels.

OPPOSITE The Orchard offers a transition between the wildness of the woodland and the formality of the gardens near the house.
ABOVE The nineteenth-century waterfall flows anew after its choked waterways were opened up in 1986 by the force of huge volumes of rain.
LEFT An undulating path bridges the little stream in the woodland.

Corke Lodge

COUNTY WICKLOW

Green, green, all is green in the garden at Corke Lodge on the borders of counties Dublin and Wicklow. When you walk through the little wooden gate at the side of the Regency house, you enter a world that could be under water. The light – filtered by a woodland canopy above, and gently radiated back by a near-monochrome, leafy planting – is soft, mystical and emerald. To the west, a circular parterre of box fights its corner at the edge of the encroaching greenwood. Down a narrow grass path, crowded by the vast fronds of tree ferns, a statuesque and ornate granite arch stands, a lonesome fragment nearly engulfed by the dark laurels around it. Other arches and columns stand forlornly around the perimeter of the 0.8-hectare (2-acre) garden, like the abandoned remnants of an earlier, grander era.

Further into the woods, cloudy mounds of box billow up from the ivy-clad ground. With the look of deep-green thunder-heads, they could be portents of some impending storm, or perhaps the residue of a past tempest. If there were a soundtrack for this garden it would be heavy with cellos and kettle drums. Instead, there is the chinking alarm call of a blackbird, the loud polemic of the wren and the occasional rusty screechings of pheasants. The whoosh of distant traffic sounds an unexpected note, for although the last century has not seemed to impinge on Corke Lodge, this dreamlike place is minutes from modernity, sandwiched between the town of Bray and the village of Shankill, both expanding. A buffer of farmland and golf course keeps the hurly-burly of suburbia at bay.

The garden is a fantasy, an invention, a theatrical amusement. In its present incarnation it was created by the architect and furniture designer Alfred Cochrane, whose great-uncle Sir Stanley Cochrane bought the property in 1905. Stanley, then living at the adjoining estate, Woodbrook, was one of the heirs to the Cantrell & Cochrane mineral water business. He bought the neighbouring house because its lands would give him the scope to construct a proper golf course for his inamorato, a champion golfer. The resulting eighteen holes, which are bounded by the sea to the east, must be the only golf course in Ireland built for love.

When Alfred inherited the property in 1980, the house had been lying empty for years, and the garden was 'swamped by laurels'. In their midst, various imposing and distinguished trees planted over a hundred years earlier survived, unperturbed by the laurels nipping at their ankles. Evergreen oak (*Quercus ilex*), American cedar

Stonework salvaged from the demolished Tudor Revival wing of Glendalough House in Annamoe now lives on in folly form in Alfred Cochrane's delightfully theatrical garden.

ABOVE AND RIGHT Corke Lodge's cork oak is a benign monster of a tree with fantastically crooked limbs; the evergreen chain fern, with its elaborately filigreed fronds, makes a decorative companion.
OPPOSITE A granite doorway emerges from the dark laurels at the west end of the garden.

(*Thuja* spp.), giant redwood (*Sequoiadendron giganteum*) and yew (*Taxus baccata*) had all been put in by the well-to-do Magan family from County Meath. They had owned the estate – then around 80 hectares (200 acres) – during the previous century, and had refashioned the house into a hunting or sea-bathing lodge. The grandest of the Magans' specimens, a huge cork oak (*Quercus suber*), is now the undisputed king of the garden. It squats centre stage, an immense beast of a tree with massive, low-slung, fissured and rumpled branches. At its feet, a planting of *Woodwardia radicans* makes a suitably ceremonial frill with its intricate filigreed 2-metre (6½-foot) fronds. Native to southern Europe, this evergreen chain fern is evidence of the mild climate here.

The name of the property, which has been variously Corke Little (the townland's appellation), Corke Farm and Corke Lodge, has nothing to do with the massive tree in the heart of the garden. It comes from the Irish word 'corcach', meaning marsh. The land here was originally waterlogged and boggy, but at some time in the past, it was laboriously improved. When Alfred dug up the garden recently to deal with the drains, he discovered many artificial layers of soil, gravel and sand, put in hundreds of years ago, he thinks. This vintage stratification has served the garden well, and has allowed the Mediterranean cork tree to thrive in what was once an Irish bog. Thanks to the underlying peat, though, there are streaks of acid soil, which allow azaleas to grow – and self-seed.

When Alfred embarked upon his re-creation of the garden, he went at it with the eye of an architect and the enthusiasm of an amateur. His influences were international: he has spent much time in Lebanon (his mother is Lebanese), and he was at university in Italy. Taking the existing woodland as his starting point, he designed the space to look as if there was a much more ancient and classically formal garden being consumed by the rampant trees. Hence the episodes of box hedging – some nearly submerged, others crisply clipped – and the masonry oddments mournfully clinging to the landscape, like the elements in a Piranesi etching. The granite stonework came from Glendalough House in Annamoe, County Wicklow, where the Victorian mock-Tudor wing had been demolished in the 1970s.

Alfred chose his plants only for visual effect: bold-foliaged phormium, bamboo, gunnera and ferns; and showy-barked trees such as chalky-stemmed birch, cinnamon-toned myrtle (*Luma apiculata*) and raggedy paperbark maple (*Acer griseum*). Some of his choices were considered questionable by certain gardening acquaintances: 'I was a naïve gardener,' he says. 'A lot of the plants I used were considered to be incredibly naff.' One friend, a garden historian, was aghast when he heard that the neophyte was putting in a small avenue of cordylines. The result of this wrongdoing is rather effective now – and looks like a guard of fierce and bristling warriors lined up to protect the back entrance to the house. 'The last straw', says Alfred, 'was when I put in *Lonicera nitida*' – the small-leaved, dusty shrub beloved of suburban gardeners. But an even greater crime was to follow when he planted a screen of Leyland's cypress at the end of the garden, 'Castlewellan Gold' no less, the hedging plant that sticks out like a jaundiced thumb in rural Irish gardens.

He gets away with this though, and other perceived planting misdemeanours, because his vision is always clear. The acreage, which was designed in relation to the house, has strong lines of view, and its plants – although some may be incongruous to the over-tutored eye – all work harmoniously together. The cast of strange characters and the superb lighting effects make Corke Lodge a singular and bravura performing landscape.

Mounds of box leak out from the woodland and, beyond a tumbling sea of lush foliage, a pair of Italian cypresses shelters along the west-facing wall of Corke Lodge.

THE IRISH GARDEN

The Japanese Gardens

COUNTY KILDARE

IN THE EARLY NINETEEN HUNDREDS, Britain and Ireland were gripped by 'Japanese fever'. Interest in the eastern country had been building since it opened to trade in 1854, after having been sequestered from the rest of the world for over two hundred years. The beginning of the twentieth century saw the signing of the Anglo-Japanese Alliance and the formation of the Japan-British Society. In 1910, the enormous Japan-British Exhibition in London was attended by over eight million visitors. Among its many attractions were examples of Japanese gardens.

But opinions were divided on their worthiness, and their aesthetic caused some confusion. In its 'Garden Notes' column on 11 June 1910, the *Irish Times* reported of one of them that a 'friend' had been 'utterly disappointed with this Oriental creation. We fear from the glowing accounts published during its making he expected too much and found too little.' The writer went on to instruct: 'An old willow pattern plate should give anyone a good outline of a Japanese garden, and with a barrow load of stones, a bucket of water, and a little imagination, there is no reason why one should not concoct a sample of Japanese gardening . . .'

At Tully in County Kildare, however, businessman, Conservative MP and horse-breeder Col. William Hall-Walker had gone much further than mere willow-pattern-plate-copying in the construction of his own specimen of Oriental garden artistry. He persuaded London-based, Yokohama native, Saburo Eida (who had arrived in England in 1893), to come to Ireland in 1906 with his English wife and two young boys to make a garden. Although Eida is widely described as a 'gardener' or 'gardener-artist' in contemporary accounts, he was, in fact, a well-known dealer of Japanese antiquities and art, with a business based in Conduit Street in Mayfair and – prior to his marriage – chambers in Piccadilly. His brother, who was still in Japan, was responsible for collecting the antiques and artworks for the London business, and for shipping them to England.

How Eida became a 'gardener' is a bit of a mystery, but because he came from a cultured background (his father had been a surgeon in Yokohama), it is likely that he was well able to contrive a Japanese garden that would keep westerners happy. And with a ready source of authentic lanterns, statues and 'pigmy trees' – as bonsai were known at the time – he could conveniently be both artist and supplier.

A tea house, shipped in from Japan, adds an authentic note to the County Kildare garden made for Colonel Hall-Walker at the beginning of the twentieth century.

The garden at Tully was ambitious, taking four years to complete, and demanding the work of forty labourers. A boggy area was chosen, and the water was channelled into ponds, rivulets and lakes. Hundreds of tons of rock were brought in from Ballyknockan in west Wicklow, and mature Scots pines, some weighing as much as 8 tons, were dug up and hauled from Dunmurry, several miles to the north. Stepping stones, steep stairways and a shiny red lacquer bridge guided the visitor along a journey symbolizing the uneven and often arduous path of man from the cradle to the grave.

The miniature landscape was liberally furnished with stone lanterns, statues, mature bonsai and a tea house, all shipped in from Japan. The 'less is more' concept of the true Japanese garden was eschewed in favour of a 'more is more' Edwardian approach. This, after all, was still the golden age of curio-collecting, and with an entire garden in which to display his oriental acquisitions, Hall-Walker saw no need for restraint.

Moreover, the craze for Japanese gardens coincided with the new fashion in alpine plants. To some western eyes, an orientalesque landscape was a glorified rockery crying out for swathes of colourful alpines. Tully's Japanese garden was garnished with fine specimens of rockery plants, including, according to the *Gardeners' Chronicle* of 1910, 'Saxifraga 'Guildford Beauty' – a mass about 7 feet through – and other lovely gems of the Alpine flora'.

At Tully, there was an endless source of alpine plants, for Hall-Walker – a man who did nothing by halves – had just started an immense 30-acre (12-hectare) nursery, where alpines and other plants, including gladioli and 'Saint Bridgid's Anemones', were raised by the thousands. The nursery manager, Mr W.H. Paine, was also in charge of the Japanese garden, and as the *Gardeners' Chronicle* reported, he had 'caught the "Japanese dwarfing fever" ' and was 'successfully operating upon many of the trees'.

Some visitors to the garden were puzzled, including members of a forty-strong contingent of the Irish Gardeners'

ABOVE The garden has a large collection of bonsai, or 'pigmy trees'. Some, such as the *Chamaecyparis obtusa* (top) were imported from Japan by Saburo Eida.

OPPOSITE, ABOVE The symbolic Bridge of Life, leading to the Garden of Peace and Contentment, where life slows down to a leisurely pace.

OPPOSITE, BELOW Japanese stone lanterns and figures were among the many antiquities acquired for the garden when it was first created.

Association: 'It is all so very different from our western notions of what a garden ought to be, that it is difficult to say whether one really likes it or not,' wrote one of their number in *Irish Gardening* in 1910. Over in the *Irish Times*, however, the garden got a thumbs up: 'To console those who cannot visit the Japanese garden at the Jap-British Exhibition in London, the opinion of those qualified to give it is that it is but a poor thing, and quite disappointing. We can still flatter ourselves that *we* have the finest specimen outside Japan in the Japanese garden at Tully, Kildare' (17 September 1910).

The 'finest specimen outside Japan' line had become inseparable from the Tully garden, and was often repeated in the *Irish Times* and elsewhere.

The Japanese family didn't stay long in Ireland, returning to London in 1910. Saburo Eida, who had heart problems, was in poor health, and died in 1911. His legacy in Ireland included not just the remarkable gardens, but also his son's namesake, a famous racehorse, Minoru. The bay stallion was named by Hall-Walker after Eida's elder son, and while leased to Edward VII, he won the 1909 Epsom Derby – the first time a reigning British monarch had won a Derby.

In 1915, Col. Hall-Walker gave the entire property at Tully, including the gardens and the stud farm (along with eighty-three horses), to the British Crown. He had owned the Kildare acreage only since 1900, but his horsebreeding techniques had made it an important place for raising winners. It operated as the British National Stud until 1943 when it was handed over to the Irish government.

The Irish National Stud now runs the stud farm and gardens. A water and rock garden was created in 1999 by Martin Hallinan and named after St Fiachra, the patron saint of gardeners.

Saint Fiachra's Garden, designed by Martin Hallinan, is a naturalistic and flowing landscape meant to evoke the simple spirituality of early monasticism. The water-worn limestone – across which ancient stumps of bog pine splay – was brought from land near the border of Clare and Galway that had been reclaimed for farming.

National Botanic Gardens, Glasnevin

DUBLIN

IN 1795, the Dublin Society, an organization devoted to the promotion of agriculture, arts, industry and science, founded a botanic garden at Glasnevin. The 11-hectare (27-acre) estate alongside the Tolka River had previously belonged to the widow of Thomas Tickell, secretary to the Lords Justices of Ireland. Tickell was also a poet; his best-known offering was the rambling 'Kensington Gardens', with its endearing description of snowdrops as 'vegetable snow'. His patron was Joseph Addison, co-founder of the *Spectator*, and secretary to the Lord Lieutenant of Ireland. Addison's Walk still exists from the original garden – a sloping path lined with thirty-one yew trees. Their brown trunks are unexpectedly slim and sinewy, with the dense wiriness of the long distance runner. Tickell's house, now enlarged, is the residence of directors of the National Botanic Gardens, and today is the home of Dr Matthew Jebb, the present director.

The Irish Parliament had given funds to the Dublin Society (later known as the Royal Dublin Society) to establish the gardens with the specific aim of promoting the science of agriculture. And while the early gardens contained many exotic and ornamental species – some sheltered in hothouses – the space was mainly occupied by more useful plants. An Esculent Garden contained root vegetables, peas, brassicas, fruits and other produce, while the Cattle Garden was devoted to forage plants for pigs, horses, cattle, goats and sheep. Harmful species were presented in adjacent beds. Plants for cereals, pasture, meadows, sand-binding, dyeing, medicinal purposes and other practical applications were likewise on display.

In time, and under the curatorship of David Moore (who was appointed in 1838), the range of plants expanded greatly. There were tree ferns from the Antipodes, cacti and succulents from the Americas and Africa, orchids and palms from tropical regions, proteas from Australia and the Cape, conifers and alpines from the northern hemisphere,

OPPOSITE The Victorian Palm House, built for less than £800 in 1884, and restored 120 years later at a cost of €14,167,000.
ABOVE Addison's Walk is one of the oldest parts of the National Botanic Gardens.

and much more. In 1864 the Irish gardener and writer, William Robinson, described the Glasnevin gardens as 'the Kew of Hibernia'. In his fulsome piece in the *Gardeners' Chronicle*, he pointed out in logorrhoeic detail (one sentence was 479 words long) the pleasures that the Glasnevin gardens afforded on Sunday afternoons to 'the "intelligent workman" – a type of great rarity in many places, but not by any means so in Dublin'.

His reference to Sundays and enlightened working men may have been a dig at members of the Royal Dublin Society who had fought and lost the battle three years earlier to keep the public out on the Sabbath day. The *Spectator* of 4 May 1861 reported that the society's Dr Gayer had argued that such an action would 'demoralize the working man' and that 'the surrounding country would become a focus of whisky-shops and tea-gardens'. When asked was it not better to have the people enjoying themselves in the gardens than drinking in a public house, he replied, '"I admit that; but let us not recognise small vices to avoid greater. You might as well advocate concubinage to prevent adultery."'

When it had originally opened in 1800, after five years of development, the Dublin plot was the largest publicly funded botanic garden in Europe. For the first year, everyone was freely admitted, but because 'idle persons and particularly children' had 'done considerable mischief' (according to notices in local papers), entry was then restricted to members of the Dublin Society, those with special tickets, and those who sought admission from the head gardener. It was another fifty years before the requirements were relaxed to allow weekday entry for all, with Saturday and Sunday opening eventually following.

Two men dominated the gardens' early history: father and son David and Frederick Moore. David, a Scotsman, had moved to Ireland in 1828 to take up the position of foreman at Trinity College Botanic Garden. Ten years later he was appointed curator at Glasnevin. Upon his death in 1879, Frederick was elected his successor and remained in the job until 1922. Between them, the Moores managed the gardens for 84 years, making Glasnevin into one of the world's important botanical institutions. They fostered relations with other gardens, both public and private, and used several Irish demesnes as informal annexes to Glasnevin. In the Dublin plot, conditions were nowhere near as favourable as those in many of the country's famous gardens. The soil was shallow and alkaline, rainfall (now at 724 millimetres/28.5 inches) was at the lower end of the Irish scale, and the winter often brought killing freezes that wiped out precious plants. So, there was a steady stream of material going to gardens such as Kilmacurragh and Mount Usher in County Wicklow, Headford in County Meath and Fota in County Cork.

David Moore had worked as a botanist with the Ordnance Survey immediately before taking up the post at the gardens, and while here he continued his work with the flora of Ireland. He also expanded the arboretum and dramatically increased the numbers of non-native plants. Pampas grass (*Cortaderia selloana*) was introduced to cultivation via seeds received from a Scots collector in the Argentine, John Tweedie. When it flowered in 1842 (the first time in Europe), Moore was delighted with its immensely tall, plumed inflorescences. One can't help wondering what he would think of this luminously swishy native of the South American plains becoming the cliché of suburban front lawns of a certain era.

Another first for Glasnevin was in the cultivation of tropical orchids. Between 1844 and 1849, four species were raised from seed and brought to flower, a feat never before achieved in a botanical garden. David Moore also oversaw collections of insectivorous plants: he grew and hybridized *Sarracenia*, and was very successful with *Nepenthes*. William Robinson praised the 'finely grown' rarer species and noted that 'The collection of Pitcher plants is in fact almost unique for a botanic garden.'

In 1845, a mysterious blight began to affect potatoes in Ireland. The disease, which went on to devastate the crops for several years, was one of the factors in the Great Famine. Moore was one of the first to promote the idea that the cause was a fungal pathogen, and not excessive amounts of atmospheric electricity, as was believed by many at the time.

In 1878, the year before David Moore's death, the gardens were taken over by the state. Frederick Moore, although he had just turned twenty-two, succeeded his father. He continued the work with orchids and insectivorous plants, and was also involved in hybridizing *Nerine*, *Lachenalia* and rhododendrons. During his time, the gardens were further extended, a new rockery was made, and a pinetum (now known as Pine Hill) was planted. He was a keen gardener, as interested in plants for their garden merit as for their botanical value. He was a friend of William Robinson and

embraced his principles of naturalistic gardening. In a letter to Robinson in 1916, he writes: 'I have a clear recollection of your grand fights in the eighties for Nature development in the garden, which appeals to me immensely . . . I have tried to keep formality of every sort out of Glasnevin, and think the lower part of the garden about the pond, rock work, etc, would please even as severe a critic as you are.' In 1911, Frederick Moore was knighted by King George V for services to horticulture.

Today, the joint legacy of the father and son is most obvious in the magnificent glasshouses, the undisputed glory of the gardens. Accordingly, I have chosen to give them the lion's share of these few pages.

The Curvilinear Range, over 100 metres (328 feet) long and 12 metres (39 feet) tall at its highest point, is one of the finest such structures in the world. It was built in three phases between 1843 and 1868 and is largely the work of Richard Turner, the Dublin iron master. Turner, whose family had been in ironwork for generations, was involved in constructing glasshouses at Belfast, Kew and Regent's Park. His Hammersmith works (in Ballsbridge in Dublin) also manufactured workaday items such as boilers and bedsteads, and gates and railings. The well-known boundary railings of Trinity College in Dublin were manufactured at his foundry.

The glasshouse at Glasnevin used new techniques: most of the iron was wrought rather than cast (as had been the norm). Turner's bars could be stretched thinner than those of his contemporaries, allowing a more lightweight and taller structure. Even now, in an era of digital technology and materials, the house's airy elegance is remarkable.

In 1990, after well over a century of service, the great glasshouse was feeling its age. In the humid warmth, corrosion had galloped along at four times the normal outdoor pace, while the structure as a whole had gradually become less stable. Panes of glass were being shucked from the flaking and spavined iron at the rate of 300 per year. The building was closed to the public, and over the next few years underwent a complete and faithful restoration. All the components were tagged, dismantled and cleaned,

ABOVE, LEFT TO RIGHT Glasnevin has a long and successful history of growing orchids and insectivorous plants: *Arpophyllum giganteum* is native to Central and South America; the slipper orchid *Phragmipedium* Cleola is a very old cross between *P. reticulatum* and *P. schlimii*, registered by Veitch in 1891; the cobra lily, *Darlingtonia californica*, is from boggy habitats in the north-west of the United States.
OVERLEAF The first Chusan palm planted outdoors in Ireland nestles in a sheltered corner outside Turner's Curvilinear Range.

and those that were unsalvageable (just 13 per cent) were replaced with material from Turner's glasshouse at Kew, which had been superseded by a stainless steel replica. In 1995, in time for the bicentenary of the gardens' founding, the reborn Curvilinear Range opened, having been rebuilt piece by piece, and refitted with 8,427 panes of glass.

Inside, it is divided into three main areas: a Mediterranean east wing, a tropical west wing, and a central part filled with useful plants. In the first, species from South Africa, Australia and South America – regions with poor soil, hot, dry summers and winter rainfall – crowd the central beds and perimeter planters. Among them are Cape heaths, the showy cousins of Ireland's bogland plants; proteas and banksias with complicated, highly crafted flowers like Victorian desserts; pelargoniums with leaves that emit the fragrance of lemons, roses and peppermint. The giant spear lily (*Doryanthes palmeri*), a monocotyledon from the west coast of Australia, turns visitors into Lilliputians with its 3-metre- (10-foot-) long, pleated leaves and scapes of blood-red flowers that can reach over 5 metres (16 feet). The *Puya* genus, terrestrial bromeliads from the Andes, also bear metres-high flower spikes, and leaves armed with sinister barbs that can entangle birds and even sheep.

In an adjoining segment of the glasshouse is *Abutilon pitcairnense*, from Pitcairn Island, the scrap of land in the South Pacific settled by the mutineers from HMS *Bounty*. The lanky, pale-yellow-flowered shrub is currently extinct in the wild, and is the subject of a safeguarding and reintroduction project by conservation botanist Dr Noeleen Smyth. Conservation and research work are now of great importance at the gardens.

The lofty central house hosts a gathering of useful plants from warmer regions: avocado, tapioca, olive, rice, sugar cane, ginger, plantain, coffee, tea and various herbs and spices. Tobacco (*Nicotiana tabacum*) is here too, its hairy, floppy leaves topped with a flourish of pretty, pale pink

trumpets. Its innocent appearance is at odds with its role as the single greatest cause of preventable death in the world.

Outside the range, in a sheltered nook, is an altogether more positive exhibit: the first Chusan palm (*Trachycarpus fortunei*) planted outdoors in Ireland. It was one of a pair planted by David Moore in 1870 to test the species' hardiness (its mate, behind the director's house, lasted about 125 years). Also here, and planted by Moore at around the same time, is his namesake, *Crinum moorei*, the pink-flowered Natal lily. It was grown and successfully flowered from seed sent to Glasnevin by a Captain Webb, then serving in South Africa. This south-facing border holds a collection of other plants indigenous to that country, among them *Agapanthus*, *Dierama*, *Eucomis* and *Kniphofia*.

The west wing of the Curvilinear Range is inhabited by plants from the mountains of South East Asia – from Java to New Guinea. The warm and moist space is dominated by rhododendrons of the Vireya subgenus, donated by the

OPPOSITE The east wing of the Curvilinear Range is devoted to a Mediterranean-type flora including restios, pelargoniums and strelitzias from South Africa.

ABOVE, CLOCKWISE FROM TOP LEFT *Abutilon pitcairnense* from Pitcairn Island; *Tecomanthe volubilis* subsp. *volubilis* from New Guinea; *Rhododendron javanicum*, one of the Vireya rhododendrons; *Protea eximia* from South Africa.

ABOVE The Palm House in early spring: in the foreground the gardens' collection of grasses has been neatly barbered.

RIGHT The cactus and succulent wing of the Palm House.

Royal Botanic Garden Edinburgh, which holds the National Collection. Australian tree ferns (*Dicksonia antarctica*) mimic Asian species, while epiphytic orchids and pitcher plants, and indeed epiphytic rhododendrons, nestle in woody and mossy crevices.

Climbers, including *Jasminum polyanthum* (a Chinese native) and the silky, pink-belled *Tecomanthe volubilis* subsp. *volubilis* (from New Guinea) scramble into the roof trusses.

The gardens have several other glasshouses open to the public, including an alpine house and a teak conservatory. The Victoria Regia House, now awaiting restoration, was built in 1854 to hold the giant water lily (*Victoria amazonica*), a species that had flowered at Chatsworth five years earlier for the first time away from the Amazon river basin. The Dublin house was half-funded by a horticultural fête, which raised £260. In 1855, in the stovehouse's second year, the great lilies bloomed. Current estimates to restore the building and the adjacent, later Cactus and Succulent House are around €5 million.

But the most prominent glass building here is the Palm House: 22 metres tall, 24 wide, and 30 long (72 by 79 by 98 feet), it thrusts itself into the garden like the prow of a great glassy boat. Built in 1884, it replaced a timber glasshouse that had lasted only two precarious decades before it had to be taken down. William Robinson had slung many insults at the angular, unlovely form of the doomed house: it was 'barnilinear' to Turner's curvilinear, a dodo to his dove, and a 'hideous gutta-percha faced Amazon of Dahomey' to his 'Gibson's Venus'. Its replacement, which was restored in 2004, is as curvaceous as a jelly mould or, indeed, John Gibson's opulent *Tinted Venus*.

Inside, it is hot and steamy, a green multi-textured complexity of tropical plants. Periodically the irrigation system shoots out clouds of micro-droplets that bead every leaf-hair and cobweb with water. Generations of Dublin children have rightly called this the 'jungle house'. Among the plants in the dense Glasnevin rainforest

ABOVE The Palm House, restored in 2004 and replanted the following year, lives up to its 'jungle house' nickname.
OPPOSITE ABOVE The very rare cycad *Encephalartos woodii*, which is extinct in the wild.
OPPOSITE BELOW An infant specimen of the endangered Madagascan palm, *Tahina spectabilis*.

are species of great rarity. The recently discovered Madagascan palm, *Tahina spectabilis*, numbers less than a hundred individuals in the wild, while the cycad *Encephalartos woodii* is extinct except in cultivation. The latter was found only once, in 1895, when an all-male colony was discovered in KwaZulu-Natal. The gardens' specimen was bought in 1905 for one guinea, and is considered the best in Europe. It is one of several superior cycads, massed together under a canopy of palms.

There are useful plants here too, among them *Carludovica palmata*, which provides the fibre for Panama hats, and *Bambusa vulgaris,* which supplies edible shoots as well as material for basketry and boatbuilding. The seeds of *Strophanthus kombe* produce a neurotoxin, once used by Africans to stun their prey. The planthunter and physician John Kirk, who travelled with David Livingstone, inadvertently discovered its use as a heart medicine when seeds he had stored in his wash-bag tainted his toothbrush. His angina was instantly calmed each time he brushed his teeth. It is one of the many vines that scurry up the pillars and trunks to flower above the leafy canopy.

There are two wings off the Palm House – one a xeric habitat filled with cacti and succulents, while the other contains orchids. Belizean species are a speciality

of the gardens' orchid expert, Brendan Sayers, who has worked with the Belize Botanic Gardens to find and record that country's native orchids. Some, such as members of the *Platystele* and *Pleurothallis* genera, can be seen here, but you must look closely, as they are like tiny flies pirhouetting on wires. They are just a few of the 17,000 species and cultivars living in the gardens. In the herbarium building another 750,000 dried specimens are neatly filed.

Tropical Ravine and Palm House

BOTANIC GARDENS, BELFAST, COUNTY ANTRIM

THE BOTANIST Samuel Alexander Stewart, in the introduction to *A Flora of the North-East of Ireland* (published in 1888), is decidedly snippy about the Botanic Gardens in Belfast. They 'were formed with the avowed object of affording opportunities for the cultivation of botanical science, and providing a desirable place of recreation', he says, and then goes on to carp, 'That the society has succeeded in the latter object cannot be questioned, but the former purpose is at present in abeyance.'

Later, while decrying the various 'so-called Botanic Gardens' that were dependent on voluntary support and needed to raise money through public events, he has another go at Belfast, which must 'compete with the Circus in tight-rope performances' and 'have the grounds injured by the crowds brought together to witness balloon ascents, or displays of fireworks'.

Reading this today, I can't help wondering what Charles McKimm – then curator of the Gardens for eleven years – must have thought of these remarks. However, because he was at the time preoccupied with erecting one of the Gardens' most spectacular and enduring creations, it probably annoyed him no more than the fungus flies hovering over the compost in his seedling pots.

McKimm, who was renowned for his prowess with plants, was, with the help of his gardeners, building the 'Glen', now known as the Tropical Ravine. The new house, which opened in 1889, was a fine example of High Victorian horticulture, and was used chiefly for ferns – the subject of a long-lasting fashion during the nineteenth century. The red brick structure, with large windows and a glass roof, was 33.5 metres long and 13.7 wide (110 by 45 feet). It contained a sunken glen furnished with soft sandstone rocks, and with portions of limestone for particular plants. Visitors entered through a door that opened onto a narrow walkway overlooking the chasm below, and were treated to a lushly spectacular view of rare ferns, cycads, palms, bamboos, mosses and other species. There were grottoes and pools, and a cascade operated by a chain pull.

Frederick William Burbidge, curator of Trinity College Botanic Gardens in Dublin, writing in the *Gardeners' Chronicle* in 1898,

> was especially taken by 'a dense green bank of "Killarney Fern" measuring about 9 feet long and 3 feet broad'. He went on to surmise: 'I suspect that Mr McKimm has more *Trichomanes radicans* now growing in the Belfast Garden than could now be found in Killarney.'

He was probably right: the little filmy fern has been almost eradicated in the wild by souvenir hunters.

McKimm's fernery was all the more remarkable and surreal because it was in '"the cold black north" of Ireland' in a 'city of towering chimneys and whirring looms surrounded by Flax-fields and bleach-greens'. The population, as described by Burbidge, bears no resemblance to Samuel Alexander Stewart's unruly crowds. Instead, he sees them with a benign (and wince-makingly paternalistic) eye: 'the workers in the factories and dockyards of Belfast are alive now to the gentle spirit of the garden, and ... flock here with their children and their wives to see the flowers, or to stroll on the green turf under the trees, or to meander quietly through the conservatories, and to peep into what is certainly one of the finest and most artistically arranged of all the Fern-houses in Europe, or in the world.'

The fern house was still impressive six years later in 1904 when the British fern expert, Charles T. Druery, wrote about it, also in the *Gardeners' Chronicle*. It had been extended by

Tree ferns, aspidistras and palms surge up from the lowest level of Belfast's Tropical Ravine.

another 23 metres (75 feet) to accommodate a separate stovehouse section, with large water tanks over the boiler, in which grew the giant water lily, *Victoria amazonica*, as well as 'a strange-looking colony of the floating Pontederias ... like huge green vegetable bubbles which have developed leaves'. Druery was in awe of the bananas, mainly the inedible *Ensete ventricosum,* which in a single season grew '20 to 30 feet high, with leaves 10 or 12 feet long . . . towering juveniles, which would seem to have been fed with Mr H.G. Wells' "Food of the Gods"' – a reference to the novel *du jour*, published that same year.

Now, more than a century later, there is still something fantastical about the Tropical Ravine, with its barely contained exuberant growth and its moist air torn by the loud calls of the birds that sneak in to forage in its artificial jungle. The atmosphere is pungent with a complicated aroma, a mixture of rubber, turf and other indefinables – the gentle decay of the tropics. Energetic plants – including some of the original cycads so admired by the Victorians – push up urgently from the moss-covered base of the glen. Orchids and monkey cups (*Nepenthes* spp.) surge out of hanging baskets, while bougainvillea and Indian clock vine (*Thunbergia mysorensis*) clamber and dangle overhead, with the latter stringing a bead curtain of yellow and red flowers across the walkway. Spanish moss (*Tillandsia usneoides*) is draped across the building's stays, like giant skeins of ghost-coloured wool. The red brickwork sprouts a dense green fuzz of maidenhair ferns (*Adiantum* spp.). Everywhere that a root can push, or that a tendril can curl, plants have colonized the space. If you listen hard you might hear a banana unfurling a leaf or a fern crozier uncoiling.

The Gardens' other Victorian pride is the Palm House, designed by Belfast-based architect Charles Lanyon. The elegant glasshouse has two matching wings, each 19.5 metres (64 feet) long and about 6 metres (20 feet) in width and height. They splay out from either side of a soaring, central dome, which is 11 metres (36 feet) tall and has an oval footing of 13.7 by 20.3 metres (45 by 66½ feet). The Dublin iron founder Richard Turner, who had perfected the use of curved iron ribs in glasshouses, constructed the wings. They are the first known examples of his work, and were finished in 1840, a year after the foundation stone for the Palm House was laid by the Marquess of Donegall. Turner's attention was then diverted elsewhere, to other monumental glasshouses: to the famous Curvilinear Range at Glasnevin, the Palm House at Kew and the Winter Garden in Regent's Park. Eventually, the great central dome at Belfast was constructed by Charles D. Young & Co. of Edinburgh, and completed in 1852. The two phases of the construction cost £2,400. The funds were raised privately by the entities that owned the Gardens: the Belfast Botanic and Horticultural Society, and latterly, the Belfast Botanic and Horticultural Company (Limited), which replaced the society in 1860.

Over a century and a half later, and after a complete restoration in the 1970s and 1980s, the Palm House still cuts a noble figure in the Gardens (now owned by Belfast City Council). Its planting, especially in the cool west wing, is a set piece of Victorian staging. Here, half-hardy plants – *Scaevola*, flowering tobacco, *Osteospermum*, *Bidens* and others – are packed into colourful banks under a canopy of *Puya*, *Cordyline terminalis*, *Dodonaea viscosa* 'Purpurea' and acacia. In spring, their place is taken by hundreds of hyacinths and daffodils.

Across in the east wing, a warm and waxy smell rises from the throngs of stovehouse plants, among them striped crotons, purple *Tradescantia pallida* and big, paddle-leaved *Strelitzia nicolai*. In the central section of the Palm House, the dome, with its great arched ribs, rises up loftily. Beside the eponymous palms, there are pine-like *Araucaria cunninghamii* and flame-flowered *Brachychiton acerifolius* from Australia, glossy-leaved *Corynocarpus laevigata* from New Zealand, and a forest of other woody plants from warmer climates. Around the outer perimeter, succulents, among them *Crassula*, *Aeonium*, *Kalanchoe*, aloes and agaves, take up the sunnier half. And in the shadier rear, dozens of different ferns are overhung by the antlers of vast staghorn ferns, like strange vegetable trophies.

OPPOSITE ABOVE Fruiting banana plant; monkey cups or pitcher plant; Indian clock vine.
OPPOSITE BELOW The cool west wing of the Palm House is spectacularly crammed with tiers of half-hardy plants.

TROPICAL RAVINE AND PALM HOUSE | 277

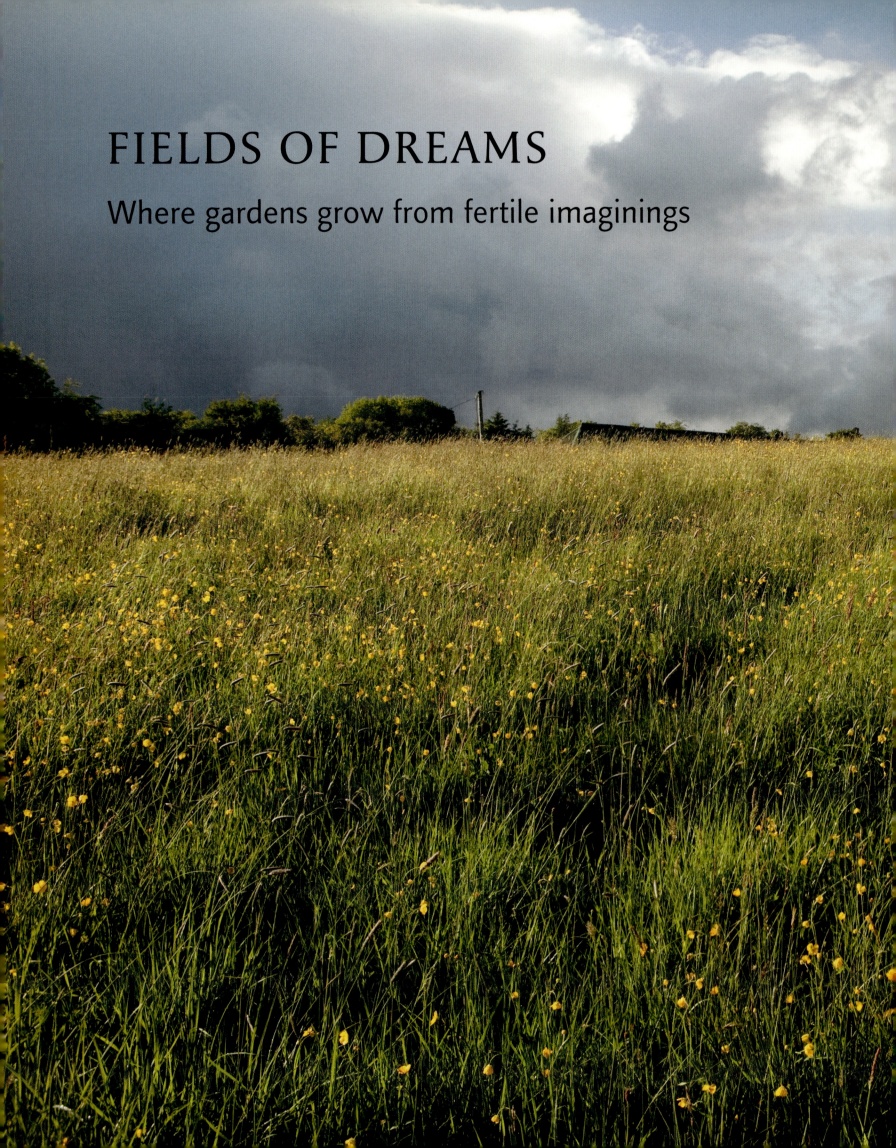

FIELDS OF DREAMS
Where gardens grow from fertile imaginings

THE GARDENS IN THIS CHAPTER are completely different from each other, but they share one characteristic. All are privately owned, and although they are open to visitors, they were conceived as personal rather than public places. They are suffused with intense concentrations of the owners' personalities. These are idealistic gardens powered by fantasies and by strange late-night impulses that demand to be set in train at dawn the next day. Their owners are gardeners through and through, from their grimed skin to their creaking spines to their nurturing hearts.

Some of these patches have the advantage of being on good soil. For instance, the Bay, home of Frances and Iain MacDonald, is on fertile Wexford clay, while Brian and Rose Cross's Lakemount, above Cork city, is on rich land that was once a poultry farm. But others are not on such favourable terrain: Lorna MacMahon's Ardcarraig is on unyielding rock and spongy bog on the edge of Connemara. Its existence is a tribute to the power of one woman with a pickaxe and an unusual determination. At Salthill House, on the edge of Donegal Bay, Elizabeth Temple contends with salt-heavy westerlies off the Atlantic Ocean, and some of the highest rainfall in Ireland.

June Blake's garden, meanwhile, is on granite-laced ground on the weather-beaten side of the Wicklow Hills. The rainfall is lavish and the winters are among the coldest and longest in Ireland. Despite these hardships, her garden is – to my mind – the most exciting of those that have recently been created in this country.

There are other gardens that I must mention here, before we explore the five above. Lakeview, near Mullagh in County Cavan, is the home of Daphne and Jonathan Shackleton, and has been in her family since 1666. The lands, which include an organic farm, have a feeling of settledness and continuity, and are anchored by nineteenth-century plantings of beech trees. The house is fronted by an idyllic hay meadow that rolls down toward Mullagh Lake. The grass has never been

fertilized artificially, and is daintily embroidered with clover, ox-eye daisy, buttercup, bluebell, yellow rattle, plantain, selfheal and other meadow species.

The ornamental garden, at the side of the house, was laid out in the 1930s, but by the time the Shackletons inherited sixty years later, the garden was thick with briars and saplings. They uncovered paths and divisions, and restored the pavery and stone terraces that emerged. Apple, rhododendron, Japanese maple and other specimen trees were given space to breathe once again. Daphne, who is an artist and garden consultant, has brought a painterly eye to the plantings. Hostas and other leafy plants are used as broad green brush-strokes to delineate the paths. Above them, well-chosen perennials bloom expansively in the clay soil that rarely dries out. Some, such as the variously toned *Iris sibirica*, were rescued from Daphne's and Jonathan's erstwhile home, Beech Park in Clonsilla, County Dublin, where his late father, David Shackleton, had a famous

PREVIOUS PAGES Meadow sweeps up to the eighteenth-century Salthill House, Donegal home of the Temple family.
OPPOSITE Lakeview in County Cavan has been in Daphne Shackleton's family for nearly three hundred and fifty years.
ABOVE The unnamed *Iris sibirica*, in strong blue tones, bridges the gap between spring and summer in the borders.

garden. (The silvery-leaved *Celmisia* 'David Shackleton', which the plantsman discovered in a bed at the National Botanic Gardens in Glasnevin, was named in his honour.)

In the moist conditions, Daphne's plantings have matured, while moss and ferns have obligingly recolonized the crevices in the grey Silurian stone. The garden looks as if its incumbency here has been long and uninterrupted.

Continuity is also a characteristic of Warble Bank in Newtownmountkennedy, County Wicklow. As you enter, choice trees such as the Chilean *Podocarpus salignus* and *Nothofagus dombeyi* and the Californian *Sequoiadendron giganteum* tell you that this has been the home of plant lovers for a very long time. Anne Condell's family have owned the eighteenth-century farmhouse and land since 1900, and it has been gardened constantly since then. She follows in the carefully placed footsteps of her mother, grandmother and great-grandmother in the garden.

Behind the oatmeal-coloured house, the plot has evolved naturally over the years, and is a happy fusion of productivity and prettiness. There is no clear division between the ornamental and the edible plants: roses ramble up stout old apple trees, while annuals and perennials are threaded through the fruit bushes and vegetables. Some of the herbaceous plants have been here since Anne's mother's time and have been divided again and again – and sent off to other gardens. Phlox, goldenrod, geranium, shasta daisy and other cottagey types mingle enthusiastically. Anne has refined and added to a herbaceous border that her mother put in some decades ago. It has a strong blue cast: with monkshoods (both early and late), herbaceous clematis, campanulas, veronica and asters. The informal profusion adds an exhilarating fizz to this gratifyingly solid and atmospheric garden.

At Rathmichael Lodge in Shankill, County Dublin, the exuberance is nearly overwhelming. Roses pile themselves over pergolas and up the back of the house, herbaceous perennials heave sensuously out of the borders, and frothy *Alchemilla mollis* and hardy geraniums form lacy frills wherever they can. The 2.5-hectare (6-acre) garden of Corinne and Richard Hewat is almost comical in its

The garden at Warble Bank in County Wicklow, home of Anne Condell, is an egalitarian gathering of flowers, herbs and vegetables.

FIELDS OF DREAMS

ABOVE At Rathmichael Lodge in County Dublin, eager ornamentals invade the vegetable garden.

OPPOSITE Turkish hazels form an orderly procession to the summer house at Rathmichael; roses, hardy geraniums and other high-summer plants crowd the path.

voluptuousness. It is a great big tipsy party, awash with good humour and playfulness. Even the kitchen garden, mock-primly enclosed in a picture-book picket fence, is having a laugh: the sensible broad beans and chard have been invaded by rogue foxgloves and sugary sweet peas.

But this is a clever garden too, where moments of exquisite calmness contrast with the hurly-burly. A grassy avenue of Turkish hazels offers a corridor of green coolness, while next to it an elegant and watchful horse grazes peacefully in a paddock. Like the others in this chapter, Rathmichael Lodge is a garden that is comfortable in its skin while being intensely charismatic.

284 | THE IRISH GARDEN

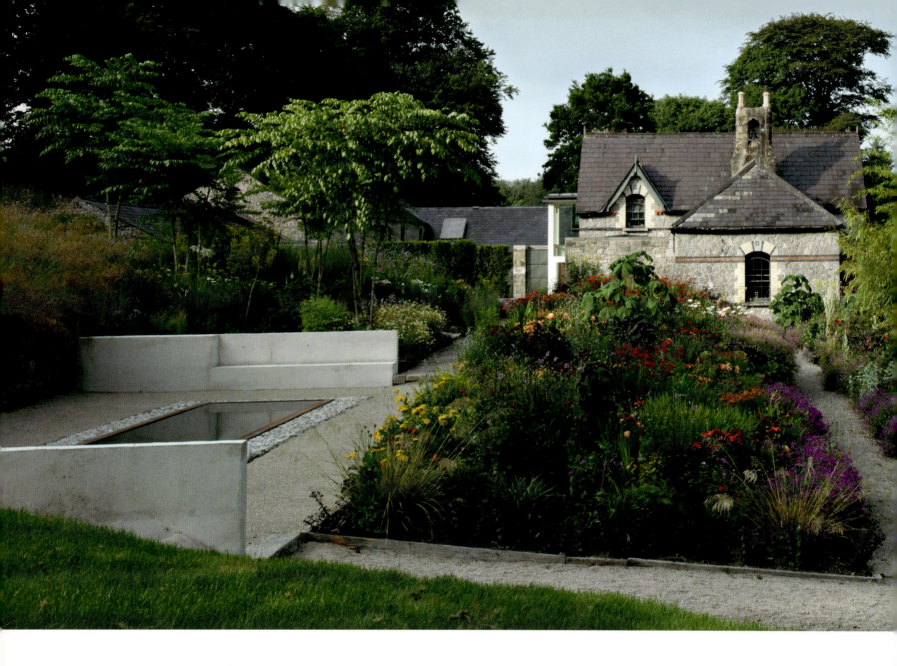

June Blake's Garden

COUNTY WICKLOW

SEEFIN, Seefingan, Kippure and Mullaghcleevaun: the mountains to the south-east of June Blake's garden dictate the climate and way of life in this part of west Wicklow. On Jacob Nevill's map of the county, published in 1760, the cartographer inscribed across the depictions of the obdurate granite masses and the intervening barren moorland: 'This Vast Tract of Mountains and Bogs is Uninhabited.' Two and a half centuries later, it still is, for the most part – even though the centre of Dublin city is less than an hour away. The rocky, peaty ground supports the occasional swathe of coniferous forestry, but little else.

The mountains hold the clouds along their inland flanks, so although they are only a mile or two from June's garden, they are often invisible. Rain is frequent and plentiful, more plentiful than in the town of Blessington, just 6 kilometres (4 miles) to the south. Snow falls most winters, sometimes

staying for days. Spring is always late, and summers are cooler than elsewhere in Ireland. In June's 1.25-hectare (3-acre) patch, the base soil is acidic, poor and stony. The adjoining fields support little more than a few head of sheep. It is hard and ungiving land.

So, it is remarkable to find a good garden here, but it is all the more remarkable to find one that is so abundant and exuberant. And yet, it is a garden that is intensely connected to the place, with a strong and good-looking framework that feels utterly right in its setting.

The immediate surroundings are charming: the property was once part of the estate of Tinode House, a Victorian granite pile on the hill above, built in the 1860s for William Henry Ford Cogan, a Liberal MP. June's home – originally the steward's cottage – was built a few years later. Cogan employed the prolific Arts and Crafts architect George Coppinger Ashlin to design the little house and stable-yard. Among the designer's many other commissions were the Round Room in Dublin's Mansion House and work on churches all over Ireland, including the Pro-Cathedral in Dublin.

The ruins of a much older building appeared recently in a corner of the garden, when June was doing some earth-moving. It is shown on old maps as Horseshoe House, a coaching inn. Until around 1820 (when it was moved a few hundred metres away), the main road to Dublin was the narrow lane which is now June's private drive. The erstwhile importance of the unpaved way is no longer clear,

A strong framework of paths and beds brings a sense of order to the densely planted space that is June Blake's garden.

JUNE BLAKE'S GARDEN | 287

as it appears to be no more than a tributary shooting off Tinode House's drive – an impressive avenue of moss-covered beeches straddling dry-stone walls.

June has lived in the area all her life, and has gardened since she was a girl – although she took it up seriously (very seriously!) only a decade and a half ago. Her early adult life was spent as a jewellery designer, after which she turned to sheep farming and raising her family. But after twenty years of the gruelling work and endless bureaucracy that the sheep offered, she returned to the garden. At first she ran a small nursery, but within a year or two she found that she was her own best customer, filling up ever-expanding beds with choice plants that somehow never made it to the sales benches. *Arisaema, Cardiocrinum, Saruma henryi* (discovered by the Irish plant hunter Augustine Henry) and other floral luxuries were inexorably sidetracked into the woodland plantings along her drive. Before long, the plant display area and car park were banished to a less obvious position, and a grand transformation began.

Where once sensible pots of plants were lined out, there is now a grid of wide walkways and large beds. Tons of topsoil were brought in from a nearby quarry. It was gritty, open, acid mountain soil – black and beautiful, but low in nutrients. June amended it with heavy applications of manure from her own and neighbours' farms, and planted a mixture of grasses and perennials. For structure, she has added well-placed blocks of hornbeam and yew hedging, and a few trees and shrubs – including the big-leaved *Paulownia tomentosa* and the thorny-stemmed, light-canopied *Aralia echinocaulis*.

More paths and rectangles – including an oblong reflecting pool – create a pleasingly ordered system throughout the garden. The more you examine it, the more satisfying it is, for it gradually becomes apparent that none of the lines are accidental. This one is aligned with the edge of the cottage,

that one terminates at the main window, while another relates to the central gable of Tinode House just beyond the north-west boundary. All the paths, which are surfaced in granite gravel, are 2 metres (6 feet) wide.

June's choice of hard landscaping adds another element of gratifying appropriateness. The bones of the garden – the walls and walkways – are all made from materials salvaged from the property, or found locally. Walls have been built using stone from tumbled-down outbuildings, from the farm fields, and from a quarry a mile away, while the granite chippings for the paths also came from nearby. The paving outside her front door once floored a cattle shed, while the steel beams which she has used to outline some of the paths came from a huge hay shed that she dismantled. The use of materials that are all local, and the way that the spaces relate to their surroundings, give this garden an intensely indigenous quality.

OPPOSITE The base and sides of the shallow pool are painted black to act as a mirror, and to contrast with the pale granite gravel.
BELOW The old wall has been exposed to display its carefully laid stones. It is topped with a light-catching line of giant oat grass (*Stipa gigantea*).
OVERLEAF June's house was once a steward's cottage; beyond, the Wicklow Hills, often obscured by cloud, are visible today.

ABOVE High summer profusion in the borders; at the end of the garden an upended tree trunk makes a mock-solemn totemic statement.
OPPOSITE, ABOVE *Echinacea* 'Rubinstern' and *E.* 'White Swan' mingle with *Angelica sylvestris* 'Ebony', *Persicaria amplexicaulis* 'Rosea' and other lanky plants.
OPPOSITE, BELOW LEFT The seed heads of *Geum triflorum* are like exquisitely elegant curls of smoke.
OPPOSITE, BELOW RIGHT The white tails of *Sanguisorba tenuifolia* var. *alba* waggle engagingly among *Persicaria amplexicaulis* 'Firetail' and two forms of *Angelica sylvestris*.

The inner structure is all rectangles and formality, softened by supremely artful planting (more on that shortly), but the outer perimeter of the garden is informal and flowing. June, with the help of Ned Maguire (a man who can do wondrous things with a mini-digger), has created various landforms along the margins. The smooth slope to the north-west is interrupted by a number of horizontal ripples, which are echoed by the long, low roofs of farm buildings in the nearby stable-yard. The grassy undulations play tricks with perspective, diminishing the dominance of Tinode House beyond, making it distant and benign instead of proprietorially omnipresent.

Along the south-west margin, a serpentine path raises itself above the meadowy grass and glides sinuously downhill, to merge into a woodland walk at the lower end of the garden. The visitor is elevated for much of this journey around the boundary, and is able to gaze down on the formal geometry of the garden below, and through the

JUNE BLAKE'S GARDEN | 293

ABOVE The gravel paths are carefully aligned with the house.
RIGHT *Geranium* 'Anne Thomson' is planted en masse along a central path.
OPPOSITE Layered planting in the hot border: big-leaved *Paulownia tomentosa* and red-foliaged *Cotinus* 'Grace' rise above fiery characters including *Lilium lancifolium* and *Crocosmia* 'Malabar'.

ABOVE A curiously toned mauve and peach *Primula florindae*, and *Pulmonaria* 'Blake's Silver'.
OPPOSITE The lily-flowered tulip 'Aladdin' is planted in between the zigzags of a low box hedge.

trees onto the gentle curves of the shadowy mountains. It is an exhilarating and spirit-freeing experience. And entirely different from being inside the garden's grid, for there, as you walk the paths or pause to sit on the drystone walls that enclose the beds, you are engulfed in plants. Although the slow springs mean that the garden is reluctant to get moving, by late summer it is in full swing. The season of profusion goes on and on, helped by the cooler temperatures and the abundance of rain.

Because almost all the beds are raised, and because June favours tall perennials – 'I have a dread of small plants, *little* things' – leaves, stems and flowers are delivered at eye level or higher. It makes for an intimate involvement with hundreds of species, both floral and faunal. You are nose to proboscis with the bees and butterflies that populate this pollen- and nectar-rich patch. Two beds filled with airy, lacy plants are especially popular with insects, which enjoy the umbellifers, *Angelica sylvestris* and its very dark cultivar 'Ebony', as well as the cone-topped echinaceas 'Rubinstern', 'Magnus' and 'White Swan', and the pink and mauve pincushions of *Knautia macedonica* and *K. arvensis*. Among the many other lanky perennials here are *Persicaria amplexicaulis* 'Firetail' and *P. a.* 'Rosea', and *Rudbeckia laciniata*.

Nearby are June's 'hot' beds where fiery-toned plants are gathered. The flaming crocosmias 'Dakar' and 'Malabar' (bred by Irishman John Joe Costin) are calmed down by the plum-leaved smokebush, *Cotinus* 'Grace'. *Euphorbia griffithii* 'Dixter', which is 'too much of a runner to let loose', is curtailed in big pots sunk into the soil. It provides 'fabulously clashy colour', and its rust-tinged foliage and screaming inflorescences clang off the tissue-paper petals of an old, scarlet oriental poppy. The latter is cut back at the base after flowering, leaves and all. 'I treat them very badly, because you can,' says June, pragmatically. 'I need them for May and June.' Later, from high summer onwards, the beds are spangled with the orange tiger lily, *Lilium lancifolium*. Its copper-dusted, velvety stamens are beloved of the pollen-crunching marmalade hoverfly (*Episyrphus balteatus*). June often teams this feisty lily with the angry-red *Crocosmia* 'Lucifer', so there is a spirited interchange between the two. The dark-foliaged and pale-spired bugbane, *Actaea simplex* (Atropurpurea Group) 'Brunette' adds a pacifying note to the dialogue.

This last is one of June's favourite plants, and she uses it a lot, including in one particularly damp bed, where it is joined by giant plants of *Gunnera manicata*, *Rheum palmatum*, about five different varieties of *Ligularia*, and other moisture-lovers. Another favourite is *Datisca cannibina*, a stately perennial – which never needs staking – with elegant foliage and drooping chains of tiny greeny-white flowers. Hardy geraniums are also put to good use. The central path is lined on either side with the magenta-flowered 'Anne Thomson' along one section, while the industrious, mauvy-blue 'Rozanne' fringes the next.

Since making the garden, June has been refining the planting, using only what works in her relatively cold and moist climate. Chances are, by the time you are reading this, her palette will have adapted further. Two fierce winters saw off the tender salvias and dahlias and most of the tree ferns. *Dicksonia squarrosa* and *D. fibrosa* bit the dust, but she still has a handful of *D. antarctica* that are overwintered in the polytunnel. These are planted each year in the tranquil and leafy enclosure that she has dedicated to the late John O'Donohue (1956–2008), the poet-philosopher from County Clare whose work she admires. Monumental boulders skirted with more ferns and mantled in moss form the backdrop to this contemplative space under the trees. Plants that enjoy a cool root-run are happy here: trilliums (*T. albidum* and *T. recurvatum*), woodland anemones and the mayapples, with their broad parasols of leaves, including *Podophyllum delavayi*, *P. pleianthum* and the brown-freckled 'Spotty Dotty'. *Deinanthe bifida*, a delicate white-flowered hydrangea relative from Japan, is here, as are the giant helleborine from North America (*Epipactis gigantea*) and the pleated-leaved *Veratrum album* and *V. nigrum*.

A river of *Primula florindae* flows in midsummer – blood-red at this end, and diluting itself to terracotta and yellow as it moves into the adjacent rectangle of woodland garden. June uses a lungwort, *Pulmonaria* 'Blake's Silver', as a leafy foil for the primulas. The plant, which has springtime, rose-pink flowers (with a small amount of blueing as they age), appeared as a chance seedling in the garden of June's mother, Kathleen, when she lived in Tinode House. The leaves are almost completely silver, and are robust and long-lasting. Another plant with great longevity – in the flowering department – is the little cowslip *Primula* 'June Blake'. Deep yellow and highly scented, it arose in a batch of seedlings over a decade ago in June's old glasshouse. The plant is sterile, so the flowers set no seed, and bloom for at least three months from February.

Because the winters are long and cold here, June treasures her early spring flowers. Hellebores, in slaty blues, plummy reds and other swanky colours are gathered near the front door. A trio of larches, bent into arches and angles by the wind, act as interesting frames for various tableaux. June trims them of excess foliage (from atop a cherry picker) to keep their figures lissome and svelte. Likewise, an ancient box tree, probably as old as the house, is pruned into green clouds, exposing the antique, buff bark – as smooth and precious as vellum. There is more box: a low hedge that pursues a swooping, zigzag course through the nearby bed. In late spring, hundreds of tulips light up the ground here with their jewel-coloured goblets. Eight sheaves of the evergreen (or ever-rusty) grass *Chionochloa rubra* ensure that there is constant movement as they shimmy with the breeze. Even in winter, there is energy here.

This is a garden to which I return constantly, not just because it is one of the most handsome in Ireland, but because it is always gives me the best kind of mental exercise. June Blake has created something like a piece of poetry in homage to her home place. It is deeply integrated in the landscape, rooted in its history, and immensely satisfying.

Aruncus dioicus var. *kamtschaticus* and self-seeding campanulas fill a corner of the garden dedicated to the late poet-philosopher John O'Donohue.

Salthill House

COUNTY DONEGAL

SALTHILL HOUSE was built in the middle of the eighteenth century for the land agent who looked after the Conyngham estate at Mountcharles, in County Donegal. The salt works that were based in the area gave their name to the demesne. Now the home of the Temple family (owners of the Donegal tweed business, Magee), the tall and masculine building sits proudly on a slight rise overlooking the crushed horseshoe of Donegal Bay. The sea is just a couple of hundred metres away.

The house is surrounded by its own undulating sea of meadow grasses. In summer, red clover, golden buttercup and bouncing, kinetic drumsticks of plantain swim among the green waves, making a merry counterpoint to the handsome and stern dwelling. The meadows are, in turn, bounded by a mixed woodland, which gives some shelter from the salt-laden winds that whip in off the Atlantic.

It is lovely to wander along the paths that are mown through the grass and that duck into the woods, where they are lined with a frill of cow parsley and ferns. But it is lovelier still to creep into the walled garden behind the house and its outbuildings, and to be greeted by the loud hum of bumblebees and the many fragrances that float on the air. There is the sugary aroma of sweetpeas and the sensuous smell of lilies, but mostly, the heady scent of roses. The nineteenth-century kinds grow especially well here, and their numbers include the white alba 'Mme Legras de St Germaine' and the magenta centifolia 'Tour de Malakoff'. They thrive in the shelter of the walled garden, and have plenty of room to stretch their thorny stems. Pale 'Paul's Himalayan Musk' scales a north-facing wall, while pinky-mauve 'May Queen', creamy 'Sander's White Rambler' and the golden-bossed, ivory *Rosa mulliganii* ease themselves over arches, creating perfumed portals for the visitor to pass through.

The 0.5-hectare (1¼-acre) enclosure has that delightful feeling of privacy and mystery that is particular to old walled gardens. Paths – some gravelled, some grassed – saunter around the perimeter and ramble through the interior, passing great gatherings of herbaceous plants amid mature shrubs and noteworthy trees. Easygoing, cottage-type perennials look perfectly at home here. There are spangled crowds of old-fashioned shasta daisies, bunches of tansy with yellow scattershot inflorescences and ranks of satisfyingly geometric, spiny lollipops of a white-flowered form of globe thistle (*Echinops*). Throngs of the orange-red *Crocosmia*

Salthill House is on the edge of Donegal Bay and at the mercy of its changeable weather.

ABOVE The inquisitive heads of a white-flowered *Echinops* pop up along the edge of the oval lawn.
OPPOSITE Paths meander through the walled garden; and *Crocosmia pottsii* stretches out from the border.

pottsii crane their elegant necks over the path: this South African native is one of the parents of *C.* x *crocosmiiflora*, the orange montbretia which has naturalized in ditches and hedgerows over so much of Ireland.

Rose-clad arches lead to an oval lawn that is embraced by yet more herbaceous plantings. The borders are remarkably packed, but convivially rather than uncomfortably. This is one of Elizabeth Temple's approaches to keeping weeds down: with such dense planting, there is no room for interlopers. She gardens largely using organic principles, and uses no weedkillers. She doesn't spray her roses either: 'Any rose that gets black spot, I just cut it right back, and let it grow again.'

Throughout the garden, the eye is continually led upwards by interesting trees: among them are slow-growing Japanese hornbeam (*Carpinus japonica*), with glossy, elongated foliage; shiny-barked *Prunus serrula*; *Fagus sylvatica* 'Cockleshell' with prettily-rounded leaves; variegated

myrtle with its cinnamon-coloured bark; and *Cornus mas*, which produces shiny red fruits, beloved of the many birds that inhabit this protected space.

A winding grass path is lined with peonies, irises and opium poppies during the first half of summer. Later, two dozen kinds of daylily open their brassy horns here, and blast forth in all tones of yellow, orange, red and wine. In the long greenhouse nearby, highly scented trumpet lilies pump out a powerful perfume. Hidden among them are the ragged-flowered *Hedychium*, *Cautelya* and *Roscoea*, exotic members of the ginger family.

The nearby potting shed – complete with working fireplace – was added by Elizabeth and her husband, Lynn Temple, but it has a settled look, and sits well within the old walls.

The earliest part of the garden enclosure is the same age as the house, while the newer walls were erected sometime before 1830. But when the Temples came in 1984, Salthill House had been used by the previous owners as a summer home, so there was little growing inside the venerable walls except for lawn and some fruit. There was a lot of work to be done.

Elizabeth was prepared for the challenge. The daughter of a clergyman, she had led a nomadic childhood moving from one rectory to the next. Wherever

they landed, her mother, who was a strong Quaker, would immediately set about making a garden. Elizabeth inherited her work ethic and solid determination, and – of course – her love of gardening. Over the years she gradually transformed the unremarkable acre enclosed behind the house. As her children grew up and fled the nest, her dedication and confidence increased, and the garden is now an intensely personal and lively place. You recognize this as soon as you step inside the gate: the space contained within these old walls vibrates with industry, charm and character.

The soil – limey and dense – was 'good soil waiting to be broken up' when the Temples arrived. So, over a number of years, they planted potatoes to break up the heavy clay, and regularly added manure and seaweed for fertility. Now, the soil is beautifully black and fertile. The vegetable patches, which line parts of the north- and south-facing walls, are managed as traditional Donegal ridges. In an area where the rainfall is anywhere between 1,500 and 1,800 millimetres per year (59–71 inches), these raised beds are essential for drainage. At present, local man Sean Gillespie digs and shapes them each year. Crops are planted in the broad, raised ribs (the '*iomairí*'), while the troughs (the 'sheughs') are mulched with seaweed.

ABOVE AND OPPOSITE, ABOVE Traditional Donegal ridges are crafted every year in the walled garden.

OPPOSITE, BELOW *Hedychium* cultivars and other members of the ginger family shelter in the greenhouse.

SALTHILL HOUSE | 305

The vernacular earthworks are an important part of this Donegal garden. Elizabeth has had a stone arch built onto the south-facing wall that backs one of the vegetable areas, so that you can sit in the shallow alcove and admire the dark, sumptuous corduroy of the ridges on either side.

Stone arches are a recurring theme here. Folly-building is in Elizabeth's blood: her great-grandfather's garden in Aghalee in County Antrim was filled with quirky stonework and other entertainments, including a waterwheel and a shell house. Following in her ancestor's footsteps, Elizabeth has embellished the fireplace in the potting shed with floral motifs made from mussels and razor shells. And in a warm and sheltered courtyard annex that acts as an ante-room to the main walled garden, scallop shells encrust the underside of a stone arch.

It is mostly a gardener's garden though: where many of the plants have a story, and where most have been grown from seed or cuttings. The beech hedges, for example, and an intriguing, rectangular beech room were grown from saplings transplanted from the Temples' woods above the garden. The unexpected moments of formality (such as the beech room) and the strong lines of the walls and paths keep some order among the joyously relaxed planting. But Elizabeth had no master plan when she came. 'I remember standing at the gate when we came to live here, I thought, right, I'm just going to start here, and it will all work out.'

A full moon rises over Donegal Bay.

The Bay Garden

COUNTY WEXFORD

WHEN GARDENERS Frances and Iain MacDonald were looking for a house in County Wexford, Frances had a particular wish: 'I always wanted to live in the country, but with a bus going by that says "Dublin" on the front.' Which is exactly what they got in 1989, just a mile south of the village of Camolin. The busy Wexford to Dublin road flies by the nineteenth-century farmhouse, but on the far side of the thoroughfare are fields, while more farmland surrounds the garden along almost the entire perimeter.

They also got acid, free-draining loam over a marl and shale base: the kind of soil that gardeners dream about. And, as this is the so-called 'sunny-southeast' of Ireland, the skies are bluer and drier than over most parts of the country. Annual rainfall is around 810 millimetres (32 inches). Frosts, though, are harder and more prolonged than in some areas, especially since the garden is in a chilly dip formed by the River Bann, which meanders through the landscape two fields away.

The house had lain empty for the best part of the previous eighteen years, and parts of the 0.5-hectare (1¼-acre) plot were waist-high in weeds. There was little evidence of horticulture, except for a badly decayed orchard (too far gone to rescue), a laurel hedge (now smartly rehabilitated) and, in front of the house, a big old holly tree. Frances and Iain minded this last very carefully, in deference to the Irish and British tradition that it is bad luck to take out holly. The tree is reputed to protect houses from both lightning and witchcraft. Holly was also classified in early mediaeval Ireland as one of the *airig fedo* or 'nobles of the wood', with its timber being used for chariots and spears, and its foliage for fodder. The fine for the unlawful removal of a single branch was a one-year-old heifer.

The MacDonalds found themselves observing another tradition when an unknown woman arrived in the gate one day with: 'Are you moving in? Keep that door yellow. It's always been yellow!' So, the front door, watched over by the holly, remains canary-coloured to this day. In early summer, it is enveloped in a tasselled blue shawl of *Wisteria floribunda*. The tiny cottage garden in front is filled with roses, fuchsias and herbaceous perennials, and is dominated by a great plum pudding of box – so corpulent that birds nest in it. In autumn a line of *Nerine bowdenii* hugs the sheltered space at the foot of the house wall and hoists up candy-pink, spidery blooms. In winter and early spring a substantial shrub of *Sarcococca hookeriana* var. *humilis* perfumes the air with its tiny, tufted white flowers.

At the side of the house, where the old orchard once was, is the Serpentine Garden, with its abundantly furnished curvaceous beds swooping sinuously through the lawn. There is much herbaceous stuff here, including campanula, geranium, penstemon, thalictrum and lilies in summer,

OPPOSITE Mauve *Wisteria floribunda* cascades over the yellow-painted front door.
LEFT Some of Frances's hosta collection, with Tom, the shadowy cat (who matches the 'Queen of Night' tulips).

TOP ROW, LEFT TO RIGHT *Clematis* 'Multi Blue'; *C.* x *durandii*; *Phuopsis stylosa*.

ABOVE *Pelargonium* 'Lord Bute'

OPPOSITE, LEFT TO RIGHT *Phlomis tuberosa*; a garden hybrid of the orchid *Dactylorhiza*; one of the Bay Garden's own candelabra primula seedlings.

OVERLEAF In the Barn Garden in early autumn, the low sun provides dramatic backlighting for *Miscanthus* and *Calamagrostis* grasses. In the foreground, the delicate pampas grass *Cortaderia richardii* waves its plumes. Behind, autumn-red sumach (*Rhus typhina* 'Dissecta') adds jaunty splashes of colour.

as well as that excellent, but underused edging plant with its balls of pink mist, *Phuopsis stylosa*. In autumn, asters – 'Little Carlow' and x *frikartii* 'Mönch' – and sedums create a sombre rose and purple glow. There is also a strong presence of trees and shrubs: 'You have to have shrubs and trees for structure,' says Frances. 'Everyone has gone mad on herbaceous. But you don't have a winter garden if you don't have shrubs. You don't have a good spring garden or autumn garden either.' As if in agreement, a purple-leaved *Berberis thunbergii* f. *atropurpurea* 'Helmond Pillar' makes a solid (if bristly) exclamation mark at her side. Each of the beds is punctuated with eye-catching woody specimens. Among the many other trees and shrubs lending coherence to this part of the garden are the pale-barked Swedish birch *Betula pendula* 'Dalecarlica'; *Cornus kousa* 'China Girl', with its beauteous, snowy bracts; and *Parrotia persica*, which lights up the autumn with its blazing foliage.

The MacDonalds make good use of climbers on the walls of their house and outbuildings. Iain is expert at the arts of pruning and training, so that there are never unruly tangles of growth. Particularly satisfying is the combination of *Vitis vinifera* 'Purpurea' and *Clematis* 'Perle D'Azur' on the south-facing wall of a workshop. The wine-soaked, decorative leaves of the grapevine make a sumptuous backdrop for the thunder-cloud-toned blooms.

The garden wraps around the house in a series of 'rooms'. Just off the Serpentine Garden is a geometric box garden, populated by fragrant roses and froths of cosmos and *Alchemilla mollis* in summer, and enclosed by high hedges of *Thuja plicata*. The fruity, resinous smell of the coniferous plant, says Frances, is an easy way of distinguishing it from the largely unwelcome beast, Leyland's cypress. And unlike that plant, *Thuja* can be clipped back hard and it will regrow. This enclosure is an ante-room to the Funereal Border and the Hot Border, which glower at each other across a cooling patch of lawn. The former, Frances's creation, is a solemn gathering of dark-hued plants. Permanent residents include the shrubby *Physocarpus opulifolius* 'Diabolo', *Sambucus nigra* f. *porphyrophylla* 'Black Lace' and a particularly dusky form of *Berberis* 'Helmond Pillar', as well as the perennials *Geranium phaeum* and *Ophiopogon planiscapus* 'Nigrescens'. In summer, the shiny, maroon succulent, *Aeonium* 'Zwartkop', and the deep and velvety *Pelargonium* 'Lord Bute' are bedded in, as are the annual cornflower 'Black Ball', sweet pea 'Midnight' and black pansies.

The Hot Border, in contrast, is zinging with flame-coloured perennials: dahlias, perennial sunflowers, *Rudbeckia fulgida* var. *sullivantii* 'Goldsturm', *Crocosmia* 'Mrs Geoffrey Howard' and annual calendulas and Spanish flag – the little scrambling *Ipomoea lobata*. The deep scarlet floribunda rose 'Florence Mary Morse', introduced by Kordes in 1951, puts on a show for many months. (This, apparently, was the only rose that Christopher Lloyd left intact when he dug up his late mother's rose garden to make his famous exotic planting at Great Dixter.)

After all the show-off plants in this section, the Pool Garden, with its softly billowing, matching borders of silvery and grey-foliaged plants, offers a place to sit and relax for a minute. Double white water lilies push out of the pool, while pond skaters skim the surface and water boatmen scull manfully among the lily pads.

My favourite part of the garden, and indeed one of my favourite patches in Ireland, is concealed behind an old stone-and-brick farm building. The Barn Garden is a 150-metre- (492-foot-) square expanse of swaying perennials and grasses that sweeps gently downhill at the back of the property and overlooks a broad field on the neighbouring farm. In the years when the farmer plants grain, the ground is pleasantly dotted with straw bales by late summer. These add considerably to the charm of the view, as does the Wexford train thrumming by on the field's far margin. A 70-metre- (230-foot-) long path, in the shape of a cursive 'M', snakes through the naturalistic planting, so that the visitor may converse with the swathes of sturdy perennials – and the bees and butterflies that work among their nectar- and pollen-rich blooms.

The soil here, according to Iain, was 'mostly marly subsoil'. The building had been a threshing shed in a previous life, and the adjacent area had been stripped of topsoil and layered with rubble to provide a stable surface for machinery. Starved and compacted, the land grew nothing but weeds and rocks. Iain had to break up the ground with a pickaxe, and cart off tons of stone. At planting time, he gave each plant a bucket of compost, but did not otherwise amend the soil. The lean diet has been good for these citizens of the prairies and steppes. All are self-supporting, and require no staking.

The foundation fabric of the Barn Garden is woven from grasses. They swing and shimmy in the breeze, and hold the light in their fuzzy plumes and tails, making this an always moving, ever-changing picture. The upright *Calamagrostis* x *acutiflora* 'Karl Foerster' and *C.* x *a.* 'Overdam', the wispy ponytail grass *Stipa tenuissima*, and the fluffy *Pennisetum villosum* – with its hairy caterpillars on stalks – perform in midsummer. In August, the *Miscanthus* tribe unfastens its massed feathery inflorescences to reveal cascades of silver and gold, and lustrous pink and wine.

Among the first of the perennials are *Digitalis parviflora* with its spears of rusty-orange, tubular flowers, and *Phlomis russeliana*, which has knobbly beads of yellow flower threaded onto square stalks. Both are well-engineered plants that look just as satisfying dead as alive. They are joined by the sprawly pink geraniums, 'Patricia' and 'Anne Thomson'. Midsummer brings into flower the metallic blue *Eryngium planum* 'Blaukappe'; yellow-hatted *Helenium* 'The Bishop'; *Knautia macedonica*, with its deep-red pin cushions; purple *Verbena hastata* and it taller brother, *V. bonariensis* (which seeds freely in the path, providing an endless supply of new recruits after a hard winter).

In late summer and autumn, the Americans – Joe Pye weed (*Eupatorium purpureum*) and many coneflowers (*Echinacea* spp.) – make an appearance. Mounds of *Sedum* 'Herbstfreude' and clouds of purple asters combine with the buff and rust-coloured grasses to create a deep and sonorous end-of-season swan song. A miniature grove of sumach (*Rhus typhina* 'Dissecta') hoists it tattered blood-red flags into the cool air.

The Barn Garden dies gracefully, leaving its skeletons to rattle in the winter winds. In February, when it is looking a bit weary, Iain puts it out of its misery with a hedge trimmer, shearing the sere plant matter to the ground, and depositing it on the compost heap. Later on, he fills in the few gaps that have arisen, weeds the paths, and walks away. This light-filled and kinetic plant community needs no more maintenance for the rest of the year.

Which is just as well, because there is one part of the garden that absorbs a large amount of Iain's attention. Two years after acquiring the house, the MacDonalds bought a steeply sloping field of about a third of a hectare (just under an acre) at the north-east end of the property. It is now called the Woodland – although it is more like a mini-arboretum. The lower end dips into very damp ground – with a stream on one side and an alder-speckled marsh on the other. A wooden walkway through the soggy hollow leads to a gazebo, and offers a place to contemplate the abundant moisture-lovers in residence. A clump of giant *Gunnera manicata*, all bristles and business, lurks behind the lattice-work of the shelter, like something from *The Little Shop of Horrors*.

Primulas in plenty – *P. bulleyana*, *P. japonica* and *P. pulverulenta* – make up a luminously pointillistic composition of yellow, orange, pink and purple, at its best in midsummer. A little later, a host of *Iris ensata* hybrids unfurl their yellow-embroidered flags of mauve and violet. Among them are 'Ruffled Dimity', 'Eden's Charm', 'Eden's Paintbrush' and 'Flying Tiger'. Adding their elaborate leaves to the planting scheme are damp-loving ferns, including *Osmunda regalis*, *Athyrium filix-femina* and *Dryopteris cycadina*. Bold-foliaged hostas make a foil to the baroquely decorative ferns. The ruffle-edged 'Niagara Falls' is the largest of the twenty or so varieties here. (Up at the house, Frances grows another twenty kinds outside the back door).

The Woodland is home to dozens of different woody plants, far too many to mention – but they keep Iain busy: 'I do a lot of looking and checking when I am in that part of the garden.' Where possible, trees are planted as very small specimens, and without being staked, a practice that he believes makes them grow sturdy and straight. The huge, pool-like beds are underplanted with bulbs, *Pulmonaria*, *Epimedium* and other spring flowers. Hybrids of *Rhododendron yakushimanum* – which make compact, floriferous domes – are happy on the moist, acid slope. Iain's collection of magnolias (at least a dozen and a half) is here, as is most of his growing bevy of *Cornus* varieties.

Back near the house, and at the entrance to the garden, beds of healthy vegetables and a plant sales area adjoin a little cottage tearoom. Inside its doors await a welcome cup of tea and homemade biscuits.

ABOVE At the damper end of the Woodland, primulas, orchids and *Gunnera* congregate.

LEFT The Woodland is home to Iain's growing collection of trees.

Lakemount

COUNTY CORK

There is nothing subtle about the colour of the vegetation at Lakemount, the garden of Brian and Rose Cross. You won't see carefully graded borders, or ruminations on twelve tones of mauve here. Instead, the 1-hectare (2½-acre) patch in Glanmire, a few kilometres north-east of Cork city, is a lusty celebration of full-bodied colour – in petal, leaf and bark.

Fire-engine-red alstroemerias fight it out with burning orange crocosmias while violet phloxes stand coolly by. And in the foliage department, a catalogue of impertinences is blithely perpetrated. Around a grey Liscannor flagstone terrace, white and green variegated shrubs – including a splashy-dashy, speckled pittosporum – rub shoulders with the yellow-striated grass, *Hakonechloa macra* 'Aureola'. A gold-washed Irish yew, a red-leaved Japanese maple, a blue-boughed fir and other leafy characters compete for attention. Who would imagine that foliage could have such kaleidoscopic qualities?

This free-spirited disregard for the usual niceties of colour management is entirely intentional, and is mainly the work of Brian Cross, who has gardened here all his life. His early years were spent under the tutelage of his late mother, Peggy, who died in 1997. She was a good gardener from a long line of good gardeners, and she began to work the soil here in the 1950s. It was excellent soil: acid and fertile (the land had at one time been a poultry farm), and plants established quickly in the damp climate. Now, Brian is not sure what the annual rainfall is, other than 'too bloody much' – but I'd guess that it's probably around 1,100 millimetres per annum (43 inches).

The garden wraps sinuously around the low house, with each section flowing easily into the next. Massed plantings of mophead hydrangeas appear again and again, and help tie the different areas together. Most were planted by Peggy long ago, and their names are long forgotten or lost. The acid soil has conferred on them a range of colours – clearest cerulean blue, purple and lavender – that makes their blooms swim glowingly through the milky Cork light.

Hostas are also threaded through the garden, where they grow sumptuous and fat. Luxuriant cultivars such as 'Sum and Substance' have tropical lushness: surely a magnet for molluscs? 'They have the best of soil and they are treated like children: they get plenty of slug-killer,' says Brian. Great pots of them guard the steps to the plant house, a shed that was magicked into a conservatory by adding glazing to the roof and sides. A big-leaved crimson glory vine (*Vitis coignetiae*) rushes up alongside the door and garlands the top with its floppy and furry foliage. The steamy interior is populated by jungly looking individuals: fine-fronded asparagus ferns, purple-leaved bananas, silvery *Plectranthus*

OPPOSITE Foliage of every shape and hue gathers around a small pond. The punctured vase is by Australian ceramicist Tim Goodman.

FAR LEFT *Crocosmia* and *Alstroemeria* cultivars come together with a loud clash at Lakemount.

LEFT The tender golden polypody (*Phlebodium aureum*) thrives in the shelter of the plant house.

and sky-blue-flowered *Plumbago*. The Indian *Rhododendron dalhousiae* var. *rhabdotum* bears creamy yellow trumpets nattily outlined with red pinstripes, while the climbing *Lapageria rosea* has improbable blooms that seem to be moulded from pink bubblegum.

Rose, who came to Lakemount after marrying Brian about a dozen years ago, has her own domain here, entered through a gate with a nameplate cheekily inscribed 'Rosemount'. Her plantings, described by her husband as 'very feminine', are cottagey and charming. They change from year to year, but always demonstrate her enjoyment of cascading peals of colour. The perennial wallflower *Erysimum* 'Bowles's Mauve' chimes against royal blue delphiniums, bright pink poppies, plum-coloured lupins and other harmonious flowers.

Lakemount is well known for its expertly shaped small trees: among them, rhododendrons, birches, maples and an especially elegant *Heptacodium miconioides* from China. Brian is a master of 'pruning up' where lower limbs are removed and the tree's structure is opened. By lessening the shade underneath, it allows for dense underplanting. It also gives each tree a sculptural, consequential presence which perfectly suits this super-realistic and stagey garden.

OPPOSITE The plant house that was once a shed is luxuriantly draped in *Vitis coignetiae*.
LEFT Mophead hydrangeas produce flower clusters in all shades of blue.
BELOW Rose Cross's corner of Lakemount, known as 'Rosemount', is a relaxed tumble of annuals and perennials.

Ardcarraig

COUNTY GALWAY

Ardcarraig, just south of the downward-hanging tail of Lough Corrib, is the hardest-won garden in this book. The 2-hectare (5-acre) parcel of land has a thin skim of poor, acidic soil over glacial granite. In the lower parts, the plot dips into spongy bog, which regularly oozes and floods, thanks to the 1,750–1,825 millimetres (69–72 inches) of rain per year. Boulders and rocks are scattered everywhere, some partially buried, some perched on the surface. I've visited other Irish gardens with more challenging terrain, but none that has seen such determined hard labour from a single person.

That person is Lorna MacMahon, who singlehandedly coaxed the garden out of the tough Connaught ground. Since she started her work in 1971, the pickaxe has been her most essential tool. The new bungalow that she and her late husband, Harry, bought came with an acre of land, windswept and barren, just west of Galway city, and on the edge of Connemara. She came to an agreement with Harry, a busy doctor: 'I would dig and pickaxe every square inch myself, provided he gave me the amount of topsoil I needed.'

Thirty-four loads of soil later, she managed to sow a lawn and to plant a heather and conifer garden artfully punctuated with granite outcrops. But something was wrong: her new garden seemed sickly. She sent a soil sample for analysis. The results showed that her imported topsoil was the highest in lime and the lowest in nutrients that the lab had ever seen. She addressed the deficiencies with a feeding regime, and things began to improve.

The 'dwarf' conifers, which she had been sold by unscrupulous nurserymen, shot up into great strapping lumps, shading everything around them. She has kept a few, but over the years she has happily seen off the others with her chainsaw (a gift from one of her sons). Her optimism is impressive: if a plant needs removing, she can't wait to fill its place with something else. In spring of 2011, after two harsh winters with prolonged periods of sub-zero temperatures (and a low of -15°C/5°F), she was marvellously sanguine. She saw the wreckage of the myrtles, phormiums, Chilean hard ferns (*Blechnum chilense*), South African restios and other borderline species as a series of planting opportunities, and – in some cases – firewood. She is a model of positivity and energy – qualities that have kept her continually creating and moving onward when another gardener might have said 'Enough'.

Bluebells, moss and ferns spring lavishly in Lorna MacMahon's hazel woodland.

THE IRISH GARDEN

When Lorna had turned her unpromising acre into a garden, she directed her attention to the land behind the house, which belonged to the farmer next door. In contrast to the bleak terrain that she had been working with, some of this was squelchy bog, but most was woodland, predominantly hazel, probably planted in the nineteenth century or a little later, to be coppiced for wood. Native trees such as holly, birch, willow, hawthorn and blackthorn had spread through the hazel.

Harry arranged to buy an acre and a half, but when Lorna went to inspect it, she found a little stream just outside the new boundary. 'So, I went to the farmer and negotiated another three yards on the far side of the stream. He thought I was absolutely daft, but he wanted to see what I was going to do.' It was the beginning of a prolific trading partnership: over the years, the MacMahons bought six lots of land from their neighbour.

This back area is a place of assured artistry, where wild and cultivated meet in a series of gardens threaded through the woodland. Paths dip and ramble through the trees. The ground is clad in moss and ivy, and speckled with ferns, woodruff, wild arum and wild garlic, and – in spring – hazed with a shimmer of bluebells and wood anemones. Moss-fleeced granite boulders are tumbled all over: on the path edges, along the stream, and through the woodland. Foxes have a den in a particularly dense cluster most years, which can make things difficult for the pheasants that have found refuge here from a local gun club. Ardcarraig is abundant in wildlife: herons fish for trout in the stream, frogs help keep the mollusc population under control, and at dusk the air is busy with night-flying moths and bats.

Just over ten years ago, Lorna herself moved into the woods, into a newly built house: all glass and steel and stone, and very discreet. Its cantilevered deck flies over the garden, and offers a glimpse of the waters of Lough Corrib.

There are about a dozen gardens in strategic clearings among the hazel trees. Some are named for special people: the Mary O'Conor Garden is a tribute to an exceptional gardening friend, the Madden Garden is named for friends Mary Joe and Charlie Madden, and Harry's Garden commemorates Lorna's husband, who died in 1996.

The visitor goes on a magical journey from one to the next, from the darkness among the trees to the brightness of the planted glades. Water is everywhere, not just in the little stream that splashes among the boulders, but in many still and silent pools. It is hard to believe that each of these naturalistic-looking gardens has been hacked out of the rocky ground by one woman and her pickaxe. Lorna excavated cavities for the trees, shrubs and ponds, using the rock to build paths, and saving the

RIGHT The cantilevered deck offers one of the best views in Galway.
OPPOSITE Lorna found the antique *yukimi-doro* (snow-viewing lantern) for her hill-and-pool garden just a few miles away, in Oughterard. A miniature Mount Fuji is just out of shot.

meagre soil for the planting holes. Despite the challenging conditions – including the presence of honey fungus, which attacks woody plants – Ardcarraig is peppered with interesting trees and shrubs. Among them are porcelain-flowered magnolias, scores of Japanese maples, the ancient *Ginkgo biloba,* the snowdrop tree (*Halesia monticola*), and *Cercis* 'Forest Pansy' with its liver-coloured, heart-shaped leaves.

One of the more important trees is a unprepossessing conifer that you could be forgiven for passing without pausing. *Athrotaxis selaginoides* is threatened by bush-fires and logging in its native Tasmania and Australia. Harry picked it up many years ago at the 'connoisseurs' corner' at the now defunct Marlfield Nurseries in County Dublin. Neither he nor Lorna knew of its rarity until they received a visit from a gardener who had the only other specimen in Ireland at that time. Now, a couple of decades later, it is still only occasionally for sale.

From late spring candelabra primulas spread like floral wildfire across the gardens. Lorna has many kinds, and they have seeded about in the damp, acid soil, especially around the stream and pools. Each proudly upright flower stem is a feat of engineering, with circular tiers of vivid flowers neatly spaced along its length. *Primula pulverulenta*, with its shocking pink flowers and mealy stems, is the first to bloom, in April. The western China native has made itself at home, flinging its seeds in a frenzy of colonization into every patch of empty ground near the water. The books give its maximum height as 90 centimetres (3 feet), but in the moist hollows nestling in the shelter of the woodland, it can grow to 1.5 metres (5 feet) or more. Also here are many variations of *P. japonica*. This species is half the height of the mammoth *P. pulverulenta*, and has no dusting of farina. Among Lorna's named cultivars are 'Miller's Crimson', 'Postford White', 'Valley Red' and 'Red Hugh'.

One of her favourite members of the genus is the diminutive Japanese *P. sieboldii*, which has crinkled leaves with neatly lobed edges. In its homeland, there are societies dedicated to the species and its cultivars – which number in the hundreds. The flowers, in tones of white, pink and mauve, have delicately lacy petals, as if they have been carefully cut from fine paper. Lorna grows hers in a Japanese-style section in one of the clearings. The hill-and-pool garden is dominated by a large granite *yukimi-doro* (snow-viewing lantern). She was prepared to go to the ends of the earth to get one, but as luck would have it, she found this antique specimen just a few miles away, in Oughterard. Luck remained with her while she was uncovering a promising-looking rock that was to provide a balancing focal point. When it emerged from the bracken and ivy, it revealed itself to be a near-perfect miniature Mount Fuji. A cut-leaved Japanese maple (*Acer palmatum* var. *dissectum* Dissectum Atropurpureum Group) makes a wine-coloured cascade next to the lantern.

There are azaleas here also – and all over the garden – bought en masse thirty or forty years ago from the famous nursery at Mount Congreve in Waterford. Their names have long since been lost, but their flamboyant flowers – in sherbetty pinks, yellow and orange – are as startlingly vibrant as the primulas. Blue Himalayan poppies (*Meconopsis grandis*, *M. betonicifolia* and 'Lingholm') add a final note of incomparable purity to the range of flower colour.

Lorna collects hostas, and has seventy or eighty varieties. She divides them yearly, potting up dozens that she sells at her annual open days. Visitors queue for plump specimens of popular cultivars such as the stately 'Sum and Substance' and the steely blue 'Halcyon', as well as more special kinds such as the incandescent 'Moonlight'.

The open days are important events on the Galway calendar – with thousands of people attending. All the garden entrance fees and the proceeds from the plant sales go to the Galway Mental Health Association – an organization that Lorna has supported for decades. In 2006, Galway's National University of Ireland conferred an honorary Master of Arts for her services to horticulture and to charity.

OPPOSITE The little stream originally belonged to the neighbouring farmer, but its watery course is now an important part of the garden; blue poppies (*Meconopsis*) are happy in Ardcarraig's damp acid soil, as are the many hostas and primulas.
ABOVE There are Japanese maples throughout the garden; the dainty *Primula sieboldii* has naturalized in the hill-and-pool garden.

PARADISES REINVENTED

Old gardens carefully reawoken from the slumbers of gentle dereliction

PREVIOUS PAGES The nineteenth-century yew enclosure at Glenarm Castle in County Antrim was one of the few elements remaining in the walled garden before its recent restoration.
ABOVE At Oakfield Park in Donegal, the restorations included building the classically inspired Nymphaeum.
OPPOSITE, CLOCKWISE FROM TOP LEFT The Master's Garden at the Royal Hospital in Kilmainham, Dublin; a modern mound at Glenarm Castle; Lutyens's oval garden at Heywood in County Laois; rhododendrons, Japanese maples and laburnums add splashes of colour to the Ladies' Garden at Kells Bay in County Kerry.

Nothing disappears more quickly than an abandoned Irish garden. The mild and moist climate ensures that nature's hand moves swiftly, bountifully distributing moss, weeds and saplings over man's horticultural work. A year or two of neglect, and a garden is decidedly rough around the edges, but give it a decade, and it is all but lost. Well-built structures survive, albeit invaded by ivy and damp; but lawns, borders, paths, waterways and vistas are overwhelmed by mutinous vegetation.

Two world wars, and Ireland's own difficulties as it achieved nationhood, meant that many estates and gardens fell into neglect in the twentieth century. In some cases, erstwhile well-furnished estates were stripped of their assets. For instance, at both Lissadell in County Sligo (see page 366) and at Oakfield Park in County Donegal (see page 330) timber was cavalierly felled and sold in a grim period between the 1940s and 1960s. At Lissadell, because then-owner Sir Michael Gore-Booth was mentally ill and

unable to manage, the estate was administered by the Solicitor-General for Wards and Minors. During the state's management of Lissadell, woodlands were felled without being replanted and the timber was not properly accounted for. It was a sad chapter in Irish history.

In the 1990s, Irish gardens got a boost when the Great Gardens of Ireland Restoration Programme was initiated, with funding from the European Union administered by the Irish tourist board, Bord Fáilte (now Fáilte Ireland). Twenty-six gardens received financial help and expertise for restoration and conservation projects. During the main period of the scheme – 1994 to 1999 – there was much optimism and energy as derelict or neglected gardens were brought back to life. Now, nearly two decades after the programme's inception, a few of the gardens – Killruddery in County Wicklow and Birr in County Offaly, for example – have continued to blossom, as it were. But others have fallen upon hard times: head gardeners have been let go,

and owners are once again struggling with upkeep. Some are no longer open to the public. Visitors, perhaps, are concentrated in too few areas in Ireland, making it difficult for gardens in less travelled regions to survive.

Yet, in the last decade or so, other gardens have risen from the weeds and abandonment. In this section, you can read about the enthusiastic and careful restorations at Oakfield Park in County Donegal, at Glenarm in County Antrim and at the Royal Hospital in Dublin. I've written too about Kells Bay, on the Ring of Kerry, where Billy Alexander is tirelessly recreating a subtropical landscape, and about Heywood in County Laois, where the restoration has been in stop-start mode for the last couple of decades.

Oakfield Park

COUNTY DONEGAL

The first thing that you notice at Oakfield Park, just east of Raphoe in County Donegal, is the grass: lavish expanses of striped lawn, sweeping over the gently swelling ground. It is like a vast green bedspread laid out to dry on some Brobdingnagian washing day. Above the emerald-banded fabric sits the grand Georgian house, built in the eighteenth century for the dean of the Anglican parish of Raphoe. Its many windows gaze approvingly at the picturesque landscape all around. Venerable trees – cedar of Lebanon, lime, chestnut – rise up proudly, strong woody personages that draw the eye and colonize the views.

From the house, your eye bowls down the grass, stops briefly at a tree-fringed man-made lake with a little temple – the Nymphaeum – before rising up again, gliding across a paddock and soaring off into the distance where it is directed by a long ride onto the far-off mound of Croaghan Hill.

330 | THE IRISH GARDEN

This is a softly lumpy part of Donegal, with a more subdued topography than the more northerly and savage end of the county. In an invisible crease in the scene, traffic flows along the public road that separates the Upper Gardens from the Lower Gardens. Together, the two parts make up about 42 hectares (102 acres), much of which is managed as parkland, in varying degrees of wildness.

The vistas are many and impressive, creating pleasing connections between the house and other carefully placed elements. There are several follies, including the Nymphaeum, while in the Lower Gardens, a miniature castle presides over a 1.5-hectare (4-acre) lake. There are other eyecatchers too, and meadows, and well placed copses and *allées* of trees. The perspectives are as elegantly choreographed as an eighteenth-century minuet, with each subject dipping and bowing airily and with infinite appreciation to the others.

The elegant body of water at Oakfield Park was once part of a flax-retting operation. A few ancient trees remain in the grounds of the Georgian deanery, although many were felled for timber during the last century. The deanery was built in 1739, but the beautifully striped lawns are the product of sophisticated modern mowers.

The Deanery of Raphoe
The deanery, which was completed in 1739, cost £1,680 to construct, and was attached to the Anglican parish of Raphoe. It was built during the tenure of William Cotterell, an English cleric who had come to Ireland as a newly ordained young man, one of three chaplains brought over by the viceroy, Lord Carteret. The practice of settling many of the best ecclesiastical positions on English clergymen caused some unhappiness among the Irish Protestant community. Among them was Dean Jonathan Swift, a staunch champion of his fellow Irishmen. After the appointments of Cotterell to the deanship of Raphoe (worth a substantial £1,000 a year) and of his fellow chaplain William Burscough to the bishopric of Limerick, he noted with barely disguised sourness in a letter to Lord Carteret: 'Since your Excellency has had an opportunity so early in your government of gratifying your English dependents by a bishopric, and the best deanery in the kingdom, I cannot but hope that the clergy of Ireland will have their share in your patronage.'

When Cotterell was later promoted to the bishopric of Ferns and Leighlin, his successor at Raphoe was indeed an Irishman, Arthur Smyth. But he was far from homegrown – he landed the position through the patronage of the powerful Cavendish family, the Dukes of Devonshire, for whom he had worked as a tutor. Smyth eventually went on to become Archbishop of Dublin. The Deans of Raphoe took themselves seriously: a later incumbent, James King, had his portrait painted by Sir Joshua Reynolds. Oakfield Park was sold by the church in 1869, and had several owners before it was bought by the Robinsons.

This picturesque landscape, worthy of Humphry Repton or one of his peers, was, in fact, largely created recently, during a period of around ten years starting at the end of the 1990s. Businessman and broadcaster Sir Gerry Robinson and his wife, Heather, bought the old house in 1996 and embarked on a complete and sensitive renovation of the entire property, which had been indiscriminately developed over the centuries. The estate had also suffered some degradation: in the 1940s Oakfield Park was bought by a timber merchant who harvested almost all the eponymous oaks before reselling the property. Such asset-stripping was a not uncommon occurrence in the then cash-strapped Ireland.

The Robinsons have replanted trees by the tens of thousands, including at least 160 varieties of oak. Sir Gerry, whose father was a carpenter, is devoted to trees, and is keen for the demesne to live up to its Oakfield name once again. He has inherited his father's woodworking skills, and has made numerous constructions around the gardens, including a summer house, a boathouse, various bridges, and all the boardwalks that run over the wetlands and water.

The Robinsons worked with Belfast-based conservation architects and garden designers A & E Wright, who restored the house to its graceful Palladian lines, and enabled it to strike up a perfect and delightful relationship with its gardens and parkland, and with the wider rural landscape. The result is quite a grand demesne, which the original residents of the house would no doubt applaud.

Although the layout of the demesne is in the eighteenth-century landscape style, there are many contemporary elements – which are deftly assimilated into the grand scheme. The most surprising of the modern additions is the Difflin Lake Railway. This miniature train, with its teeny carriages and pint-sized engines (including the steam-powered Duchess of Difflin), rumbles along 4 kilometres (2.5 miles) of narrow-gauge track through the Lower Gardens. It is an entertaining way to see this part of the estate. Garden purists might frown on this unseemly playfulness, but I'll bet that earlier owners – including the Deans of Raphoe – and their many guests would have had a whale of a time on it. The deanery, in times past, was a place of conviviality, as is evidenced by its well-inscribed visitors' book – whose signatures include that of songwriter and painter Percy French.

LEFT The little Duchess of Difflin engine pulls her dainty carriages along the narrow-gauge Difflin Lake Railway in the Lower Gardens.

BELOW The Nymphaeum was built in 2008, but the adjacent planting is restricted to native species or those introduced to Ireland by the middle of the eighteenth century. Among them are Portugal laurel (*Prunus lusitanica*), strawberry tree (*Arbutus unedo*), holm oak (*Quercus ilex*), royal fern (*Osmunda regalis*) and Irish ivy (*Hedera hibernica*).

The little train takes a circuitous route, crossing and recrossing the old coach road to Strabane, which bisects the Lower Gardens. It offers all the thrills of a real railway excursion compressed into a few moments. The wee engine pulls its carriages through a rumpled patchwork of terrains – recently created in what used to be cattle pasture, much of it marshy. It whisks through willowy copses, winds along the lake shore with its diminutive castle, rushes through rushes, passes through newly planted woodland, coils around a magical spiral mound, chugs past a circle of Irish oaks and aspen, and – oh joy! – blasts its shrill whistle every couple of minutes.

For those who wish for a less boisterous experience, there are also plenty of walks in this less tame half of Oakfield Park. The diversity of habitats favours wildlife, and many creatures have come sneaking in to make their home here, among them otters, waterfowl and hares (whose ravages mean that all the young trees must have protection). And in the sky far above, buzzards hang, vast wings outspread, riding effortlessly on updrafts.

Back towards the Upper Gardens, the demesne retains its parkland character right up to the house. A path ambles through a bluebell-speckled beech wood with a rocky, watery cascade, and skirts around the small lake with the little Nymphaeum – which makes use of Donegal sandstone

ABOVE AND OPPOSITE
A stream meanders through the beech woodland, where in spring the floor is carpeted with bluebells.
RIGHT The lake is home to much wildlife; the castle is a recently built folly.

ABOVE LEFT The exquisitely maintained box parterre offers a moment of geometric formality next to the house.

ABOVE RIGHT The Robinsons have introduced – and carefully placed – several artworks, including Philip Jackson's *Reading Chaucer* and Carol Peace's bronze figure, both in the walled garden.

OPPOSITE A semicircular pergola in the walled garden supports hefty rambling roses and is bordered by sun-lovers such as sage, *Potentilla*, *Acanthus* and *Sedum*.

and granite in its construction. The elegant body of water here was once a silted up, boggy pond, fed by a flax-retting stream (the linen business was important in County Donegal in the eighteenth and nineteenth centuries). Part of the lakeside and a generous apron around the temple are heavily planted with royal fern and Portugal laurel, with smaller events of willow, strawberry tree, evergreen oak and English yew. All are species that would have been grown when the main house was built.

Nearby are two heritage trees, both listed by the Tree Council of Ireland: an ancient Spanish chestnut with a fantastically burred bole and spiraling trunk – reputed to be as old as the Battle of the Boyne (1690); and a fat horse chestnut whose dozen low-slung limbs give it the name of the 'Twelve Apostles'.

Up the hill – that beautifully striped hill – there is a single episode of formality next to the creamy, five-bay house – a geometric box parterre. Then, through an elaborate

wrought-iron gate set between a pair of red brick piers, is the intensively cultivated walled garden. When the Robinsons first came here there was little of interest besides a pear and a plum tree. But the architects were able to reinstate paths that they had identified from old Ordnance Survey maps. Now it is an area of perfection, charm and productivity, divided into many 'rooms'– each with its own particular character. A pair of velveteen lawns is divided by a tiny rill, flanked by a small guard of large yew topiary cones; a glasshouse is filled with tender plants (including agave, pelargonium, bougainvillea and *Tibouchinia*) expertly tended by head gardener Mark McConnellogue and his team; a tennis court, concealed behind a lime-trees-on-stilts hedge, has a dozens-strong and diverse audience of dwarf Japanese maples. And in an annex to the walled garden, a vegetable potager is filled with good things to eat.

Sir Gerry and Lady Robinson have carefully positioned sculptures about the place. (He was chairman of Arts Council England for six years – his knighthood was awarded for services to the arts and business.) Many visitors, especially smaller ones, love Philip Jackson's book-absorbed bronze lady with the teeteringly tall hat, *Reading Chaucer*. But my favourite is the vulnerable, yet serene, androgynous figure by Bristol artist Carol Peace, almost hidden away in a yew-hedged pond enclosure in the walled garden. The life-size bronze person rests head – ever so gently – on knees, with body folded over neatly like a human hairpin.

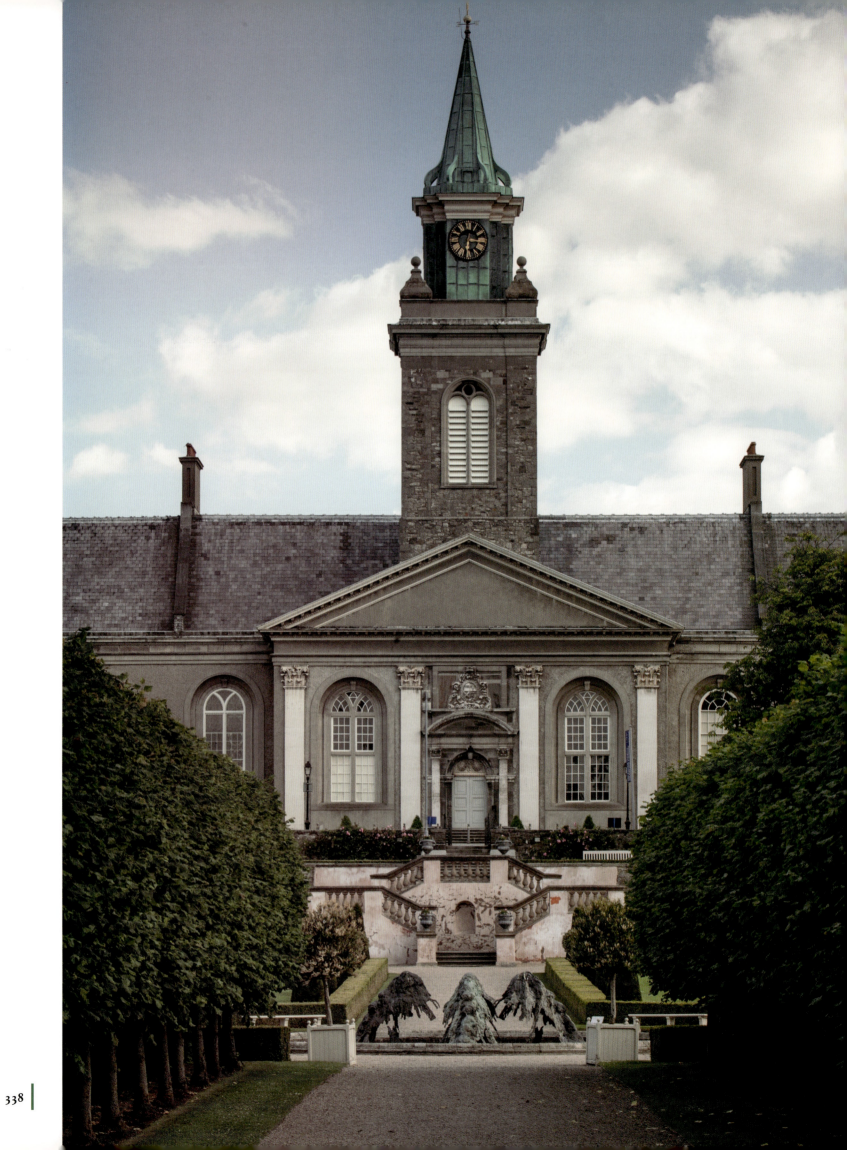

The Master's Garden, Royal Hospital

KILMAINHAM, DUBLIN

One of Ireland's more successful restorations is the Master's Garden at the Royal Hospital in Kilmainham, Dublin. The austere classical building was constructed between 1680 and 1684 upon the instigation of the viceroy to King Charles II, the first Duke of Ormonde. It was built as a home for retired soldiers of the British Army – a purpose that it served for over two centuries. In 1922 it was handed over to the Irish Free State Army. It subsequently acted as the headquarters for the Garda Síochána (the Irish police force) and as a national cultural centre. Finally, in 1991, it became the home of the newly founded Irish Museum of Modern Art.

There are records showing that the walled garden, on the north side of the building, was part of the original design. It went through a number of incarnations over the years, from the simple and geometric Anglo-French style of the seventeenth century to the over-elaborate fussiness of the nineteenth century. It remained productive until the 1960s (at which time it was operating as a market garden), before becoming derelict. Contemporary maps and drawings and the minute books of the Royal Hospital have been an aid in unravelling the garden's past. The documentation has helped the Office of Public Works' landscape conservation architects to construct a re-creation that is in keeping with the classical architecture of the building.

The design takes as its inspiration the garden's layout as seen on a 1773 map of Dublin by Bernard Scalé, and a plan from the fourth edition of *Sylva* (published in 1706), a treatise on trees by diarist John Evelyn. The resulting garden is divided by broad paths into four quarters, in turn divided again by smaller walkways. The two quadrants adjacent to the building take the form of minimal parterres

OPPOSITE The Royal Hospital was constructed in the 1680s. The sculpture in front is a water feature by the New York based artist Linda Benglis.

LEFT Topiarized yew shapes populate the gardens with green exclamation marks.

outlined in box hedging and populated with dark yew cones and variegated holly lollipops. The farther quadrants are bounded by pleached limes and contain 'wildernesses' of hornbeam hedging in the French *patte d'oie* (goose foot) pattern. The same arrangement can be seen at Killruddery, County Wicklow (see page 70), the home of the Earls of Meath. This is entirely appropriate, as the fourth Earl was the Master of the Hospital at the end of the seventeenth century, and he was known to be involved in the garden. A central fountain with a sculpture by contemporary American artist Linda Benglis and classical statuary complete the formal aspects. A tiny concession to modernity in the planting is made in the swathes of perennials that are confined within box-edged rectangles on two of the perimeters.

The garden is a delightful reiteration of the seventeenth- and eighteenth-century statement of man's mastery over nature through horticulture. All is resolutely organized and geometric, and clipped and snipped into orderliness. It is overlooked on one side by a sleek twenty-first-century cityscape of glass, steel and concrete, another symbol of man's supposed supremacy on this planet. The juxtaposition of the two scenes – which are both expressing the same idea, but through entirely different mediums – adds a deliciously ironic edge to the experience.

OPPOSITE Hornbeam hedging is arranged in the *patte d'oie* pattern; the classical figure represents *Painting*, and is a reproduction cast from the original statue at Stowe in Buckinghamshire.

ABOVE The cityscape of twenty-first-century Dublin makes a startling companion for the green formality of the Master's Garden.

LEFT Tulips, *Iris sibirica*, catmint and other herbaceous plants are barely confined by their box compartments. Wisteria, ivy and espaliered apples line the walls.

THE MASTER'S GARDEN, ROYAL HOSPITAL

Kells Bay Gardens

COUNTY KERRY

KERRY was one of the earliest parts of Ireland to attract tourists. Since the middle of the eighteenth century visitors came to marvel at the lakes and mountains around Killarney. Arthur Young in his *A Tour in Ireland, 1776–1779* goes into writerly ecstasies when describing the scenic approach to Muckross, just south of Killarney: '... the wildest and most romantic country I had anywhere seen; a region of steep rocks and mountains which continued for nine or ten miles, till I came in view of Mucruss. There is something magnificently wild in this stupendous scenery, formed to impress the mind with a certain species of terror.'

In 1853 the railway arrived into Killarney town, making mass tourism possible in the south-western county. Queen Victoria famously visited in 1861, travelling by train from Dublin, and spending three nights in the area. Her accommodation arrangements at Muckross House – where she slept two nights – reportedly sent her hosts tumbling into financial difficulties. Henry Arthur Herbert, local MP, spent a fortune extending and grandifying his house in preparation for the royal entourage.

While the Herbert family coffers may have been lightened by the Queen's stay, one of the world's first tourist trails, the 'Ring of Kerry', became more lucrative than ever for the hostelries and souvenir sellers along it. Visitors from all over came to travel the 179-kilometre (111-mile) circuit of the Iveragh peninsula, starting and finishing at Killarney. And they come even now. Its narrow and bouncing roads wind like rickrack braid through a grandeur that is still capable of filling our jaded twenty-first-century hearts with 'a certain species of terror'.

The Ring of Kerry is a place of wild excess and magical madness, with Ireland's tallest mountains, the Macgillycuddy Reeks, pushing intimidatingly through its centre. Their sandstone flanks, pleated and folded by glaciers during the last ice age, descend to moist valleys where the grass is preternaturally green, and where ferns and moss colonize every crevice. High above these mystical glens, dark tarns filled with bone-chillingly cold water feed the waterfalls that scurry and crash down over rough boulders.

The Reeks and the area around Killarney are home to the rare and secretive Kerry slug (*Geomalacus maculosus*), a species with two distinct forms. In woodland

The tallest palm tree in Ireland, *Jubaea chilensis*, towers over the surrounding garden at Kells Bay.

A forest of *Dicksonia antarctica* planted in the nineteenth century. The tree fern forest is 3 hectares/7½ acres in size and is suffused with eerie green light.

habitats it may be brown with yellow spots, whereas elsewhere it manifests a more jazzy livery – black with contrasting white dots. This benign creature lives only in particular kinds of wild areas: oak woodland, blanket bog, lake shores and open moorland. The species' other home outside Kerry and parts of west Cork and Galway is Spain and Portugal. Phenomenal, anomalous beast.

It was just off the northern loop of the Ring that Rowland Blennerhassett, from a successful merchant family in Tralee, bought land in 1837. There, 15 kilometres (9 miles) from Cahirciveen, he built himself a hunting lodge, Holly Mount, with views across the shimmering Dingle Bay to the distant peak of Mount Brandon and its rocky companions on the next peninsula. Two generations later, his grandson, Rowland Ponsonby Blennerhassett, extended and improved the house, renaming it Kells Lodge after the nearby town. Rowland was a magistrate and MP (for the campaigning Home Rule League) and – incidentally – second cousin of a much better-connected Sir Rowland Blennerhassett, who attended the banquet at Kenmare House to celebrate Queen Victoria's first night in Killarney.

Rowland – the Kells Rowland, that is – was keen on gardens, and began to impose order onto the rocky, peaty, dipping and diving lands of the estate. He put in a drive and paths, and a walled enclosure, the Ladies' Garden, where the womenfolk could stroll and take shelter in the summer house. The lumpy ground and the rocks crowding out of the soil everywhere made formality impossible. The Blennerhassett ladies and their friends had to content themselves with meandering along the many stony paths that tripped up and down between the sandstone walls.

Rowland's most dramatic addition to the demesne, however, was the planting of a huge forest of tree ferns. During the latter half of the nineteenth century *Dicksonia antarctica* was being imported in bulk from Tasmania and the south-eastern edges of Australia. Its massive green cartwheels became staples in conservatories throughout Britain and Ireland. Landowners in the more clement parts of the islands began to try the plant outside, and were mostly successful. And nowhere more so than in the south-

west of Ireland, where the high year-round rainfall and mild temperatures offered the ideal atmosphere for these fronded giants. At Kells Lodge, Rowland Blennerhassett's colony of tree ferns may well have been the most ambitious planting in the northern hemisphere.

Now, over a century after the brown, bristly rhizomes were first bedded into the spongy, acid soil, the ferns have increased spectacularly in size and numbers. Generations of *Dicksonia* cover 3 hectares (7½ acres) of the rising and falling ground.

The fern forest feels primeval, with its hundreds of dark and shaggy, moss-glazed columns topped with elaborate, antediluvian fronds. Decades of fallen tree-fern fibre have given the ground underfoot a shock-absorbent and dreamlike springiness. Shafts of watery light waver through the green murkiness. The air, uncannily still, is moved only by the wingbeats of birds flitting through the canopy. A family of long-tailed tits passes with flimsy, barely there movements, its members keeping solidarity with plaintive tsee-tsee-tsee calls. At dusk, it is the preserve of pipistrelle bats, who perform twisting aerobatics while hunting moths and midges.

Fern spores, given life by the damp air – 1,800 millimetres (71 inches) of rain falls per year – have produced plants all over the estate. Sheltered areas here act like propagation units so that ferns sprout out of walls and each other, and from between the rocks lining the small river that courses through the property.

When Billy Alexander, the present owner of Kells Bay House and Gardens (as it is now called), bought the 18-hectare (44-acre) property in 2006, it was near-wild and overgrown. The previous owners had been keen gardeners, but in this part of Ireland the volume and speed of growth is quick to overwhelm horticultural efforts. Turn your back for a season, and a green fur of seedlings and a veil of errant roots creeps across the soil. Yet, nature's urge to repossess the land can also be harnessed, if you know how. Scars heal quickly after excavations here. When Billy was using a digger to refashion parts of the garden, he let the rain do the work of smoothing away the rough gouges.

Kells Bay's owner is a fern man through and through. In 2000, he started a nursery, Dicksonia Direct, because he was finding it increasingly difficult to get the plants that he wanted for himself. Now he imports ferns, palms, restios, succulents and other exotics from Australia, New Zealand, South Africa, Brazil, Mexico, Chile and other far off places. In truth, he would not have been able to restore and develop the plantings at the one-time hunting lodge without such access to large numbers of specimens. Billy, in common with the previous owners, maintains the estate as a Robinsonian garden (after William Robinson, the Irish-born gardener and writer who preached 'wild gardening' in the nineteenth and twentieth centuries). Plants are arranged in naturalistic groupings: cascading down slopes, pooled into hollows and strung along paths and waterways. Such artlessness requires generous quantities of material. Billy's method, therefore, is to 'plant fifty ferns, or fifty restios, or fifty bamboos – and give them space to settle in'.

Silver tree ferns (*Cyathea dealbata*), for instance, which are usually displayed as proud singletons, are planted in a grove here. The 3-metre (10-foot) fronds of this New Zealand species are languidly luxuriant and backed with pale silver, giving them a ornate and filigreed look.

Dicksonia fibrosa, the golden tree fern, is also planted en masse: forty rust-coloured, hairy trunks topped with lime-green fronds make a bright splash in the landscape. Billy grows at least a hundred kinds of ferns at Kells Bay, including numerous *Cyathea*: 'nobody does cyatheas like we do them!' Members of this genus happily living in this Kerry outpost are the rough tree fern (*Cyathea australis*), Cooper's tree fern (*C. cooperi*), the slender tree fern (*C. cunninghamia*) and the soft tree fern (*C. smithii*) – all from the Antipodes. From southern Africa are the glossy-fronded and slender-trunked *C. capensis* and the yellow-stemmed *C. dregei* – 'a difficult plant'.

Billy has planted the more tender *Dicksonia squarrosa* in the shelter of a woodland (of holly, birch, sycamore, spruce, fir and lime), where he also anxiously minds his lone specimen of the rare *D. lanata*: 'Tuokara is the Maori name. The backs of the unfurling fronds are furry. It is very sensitive and precious.' Other pteridological rarities (of which there are many) include *Blechnum cycadifolium* and *Thyrsopteris elegans*, both from the Juan Fernandez Islands. The South Pacific archipelago is famous for having been the home of Alexander Selkirk, the marooned sailor on whom Daniel Defoe's *Robinson Crusoe* is based. Also from these islands is the world's rarest palm, *Juania australis*. It is hardy to -5°C (23°F) but doesn't like hot temperatures, says Billy. His Kerry garden, therefore, is perfect for it.

The most conspicuous plant at Kells Bay is a *Jubaea chilensis* 14 metres (46 feet) tall – Ireland's largest palm tree. The Chilean native arrived in 2007, having travelled from its home country in a refrigerated container which kept it in a chilled sleep as it passed across the torrid equator. It came down the Panama Canal, but the trickiest bit of its epic journey was squeezing along the narrow road outside the gates of Kells Bay Garden. Now, with two unseasonably harsh Irish winters under its considerable belt, it stands proud and tall, casting a lofty eye over the succulent garden outside the tearoom.

Southern hemisphere plants are abundant here. The Chilean evergreen fern, *Blechnum chilense*, is widely naturalized along a rocky stretch of the river. Billy has supplemented its numbers with *B. magellanicum*, which has red growth in spring, and with *Lophosoria quadripinnata*, another Chilean fern. The river has a changeable personality: most of the time it ambles cheerfully along, but after storms it turns into a raging torrent. Its level rises a metre or more,

OPPOSITE A *Dicksonia antarctica* crozier unfurling.
ABOVE *Blechnum tabulare*, a fern native to South Africa; one of the world's rarest ferns: *Thyrsopteris elegans* from the Juan Fernandez Islands.

ABOVE LEFT The oaks on the River Walk wear moss overcoats. *Polypodium* ferns and ivy sprout from the moist green folds.

ABOVE RIGHT Billy's waterfall provides the right conditions for filmy ferns, which are just one cell thick.

RIGHT Bright rhododendrons, their names unknown, survive on the old drive.

OPPOSITE Some of the demesne's abundant water is gathered into a gunnera-lined pond.

and its water is churned up into a white froth. At times the waterway disappears under a tunnel of vegetation, but its sound remains in the air. The River Walk was once the main drive of the house, and is lined with great oaks, their trunks covered in folds and wrinkles of moss, like the skin of a green Shar-Pei dog. *Polypodium* ferns run along the horizontal surfaces of the branches. There are tiny ecosystems all over this moist place.

Billy has channelled water from the river into a still pond margined with primulas and giant gunnera, and from there to a splattering, clattering waterfall. 'I had to go 350 metres up the river walk to get the levels, so it's gravity-fed, rather than with pumps – which is perfect, everything works off natural levels. We have sluices so that we can control the water, because water can be a dangerous thing.'

Dangerous it may be, but it is also fosters some of the most rarefied life in this garden. Living in the mist around the waterfall is a colony of tiny filmy ferns. Just one cell thick, they require near 100 per cent humidity to grow – and this is one of the few gardens in the world where they can get it.

Heywood

COUNTY LAOIS

Heywood, near Ballinakill in County Laois, is a garden that fills me with sadness. The house that presided over the historic and once-spectacular acreage was burned down in the 1950s, leaving the place with a forlorn and disorientated air. For half a century the garden was cared for – and kept from dereliction – by members of the Salesian Order, who bought the property in 1941.

Heywood is now managed by the state, which took ownership in the early 1990s. But, despite major restorations, this important garden – potentially one of the most beautiful in Ireland – seems to suffer from a persistent malaise (or so I have found on my many visits over the last two decades).

Nonetheless, if you are in the area, Heywood should not be missed, for it is full of unexpected gems. I have included it here because of that, and because I hope its beauties might have been revived in between the writing and the publishing of this book.

The 20-hectare (50-acre) demesne is set among Laois's gently swelling hills, and contains garden elements that were created during two distinct periods over two centuries apart. The earliest parts date from around 1780, and are the work of Frederick Trench. The barrister and amateur architect completed his house here in 1773 – possibly with the help of fellow architect James Gandon, who designed many of Ireland's notable buildings (including the Custom House and the Four Courts in Dublin).

Trench, the only son of a clergyman, was a man of great wealth, and was renowned for his interest in the arts. He was busily involved in the construction of Georgian Dublin, sitting on committees, submitting designs, and overseeing the expenditure for works.

After building his fine house in the country, he devoted many years to creating a poetic landscape of trees, lakes and hills and strategically placed follies that spread out from the house. His energy and enthusiasm were prodigious, and he carried out substantial land works, employing teams of men to move earth to create mounds and to cut through two existing hills to provide views of the water from the house. The lakes, lying at the bottom of the valley that rolled down from the house, were made by building a series of dams.

The garden at Heywood culminates in Lutyens's famous tiered oval enclosure.

The grand plan of his romantic landscape remains – although rather frayed around the edges – and almost all his follies are extant (to some degree), as is his castellated gate lodge at the entrance to the estate. The most finely wrought of his garden buildings is an orangery or summer house: a red and yellow brick building with elegant gothic arches that sprouts determinedly out of the scrub and weeds on a lane off the main drive. A little further down is Trench's sham ruin, with magnificent mediaeval windows, which were said to have been taken from the nearby priory, Aghaboe Abbey. The intended view through the delicate stone tracery is a commanding vista of the lakes but, alas, it is obscured by a tangle of unmanaged rowan, hazel, sycamore and pheasant berry. Across the lane, a tiny ivy-clad castle boasts four circular towers, one at each corner. Trench, his family and his numerous friends must have enjoyed many strolls and entertainments among these and the several other follies across the demesne.

At the beginning of the twentieth century more major garden developments took place, at the instigation of Lieutenant-Colonel William Hutcheson Poë (he was awarded a baronetcy in 1912, becoming Sir Hutcheson Poë). His wife was Mary Adelaide Domvile, the great-granddaughter of Frederick Trench. The colonel, although he lost his right leg after fighting in the Sudan, was an avid huntin'-shootin'-fishin' man, and he hosted many sporting gatherings at his estate in Queen's County (as Laois was then known). The first shooting party of 1907, according to the *Irish Times*, welcomed thirteen guests, including Sir Neville Chamberlain (not the man who later became prime minister of Britain, but the Inspector General of the Royal Irish Constabulary – who was credited with inventing snooker while serving in India). Over a period of three days the party bagged a multitude of animals: '1,102 pheasants, 223 rabbits, 70 woodcock, and 9 various'.

Hutcheson Poë was often in the newspapers, and not just in the social pages, for he was active in Irish politics. He was a prominent member of the short-lived Irish Reform Association and was deeply involved in the birth of the independent Irish nation. He was a member of the first Seanad Éireann (Irish Senate) when the Irish Free State was formed in 1922.

While he was at Heywood, he spent £250,000 in renovations and improvements to the estate. In 1906, he

ABOVE Frederick Trench's eighteenth-century follies include a miniature castle, an orangery and a sham ruin built around windows which may have been taken from a nearby mediaeval priory.
RIGHT A corridor of pleached limes sits on Lutyens's terrace.
OPPOSITE Almost hidden from view at the back of the loggia are four Ionic capitals, which may have been salvaged from Dublin's Houses of Parliament.

commissioned Edwin Lutyens to design a garden that wrapped around three sides of the now enlarged Georgian house. It is one of four gardens that the great architect made in Ireland. As well as designing the National War Memorial Gardens in Dublin city, he carried out architectural works that included gardens at Howth Castle in County Dublin and at Lambay Island, off the coast of north County Dublin.

The garden at Heywood was completed in 1912, but the association between the two men was not an entirely happy one. Lutyens found his client to be bad-tempered and with questionable taste (they argued over a fountain and other things), while Hutcheson Poë was unhappy about the cost of the project.

Still, aside from the brutish fountain (the designer was right), Lutyens's garden at Heywood is quite beautiful – an Italianate creation with Art Nouveau embellishments. Although it now lacks its mansion, its presence is monumental, and its situation – with a miles-long view over the rolling fields of Laois – is stately. Because the land fell steeply from the house, Lutyens built the compartmentalized garden on several levels. The massive retaining walls and buttresses that keep the terraces from tumbling down into the surrounding landscape are solidly and expertly built – and were tremendously expensive.

To the south of the house, the garden steps downwards in grassy slopes and long terraces. It culminates in an expansive rectangular lawn that floats – thanks to those buttresses and the wall they support – above the green patchwork of Laois fields. Along one side, and at a lower level, a pergola with powerful oak crossbeams resting on Ionic columns overlooks the lakes and woodland. The main terrace above the lawn leads into a shady corridor of pleached limes. Behind its high stone wall is a garden of yew compartments.

Lutyens's showpiece is at the end of the lime *allée*: a sunken, tiered oval garden built on three levels. The vast stone enclosure has a tremendous sense of occasion, like a horticultural amphitheatre. Its tall walls are pierced by oval eyelets that gaze on to the fields outside. At the centre is a pond where eight bronze turtles spit contemptuous parabolas of water towards the ungainly fountain in the middle. A tile-roofed Tuscan loggia, with its lintels sheltering four fat Coade stone putti, overlooks the scene, and offers a place of shelter.

Round the back of this summer house – and unseen by most visitors – four Portland stone Ionic capitals are

incongruously embedded into the rough stonework. Historian Jane Meredith, in the *Irish Arts Review* yearbook (2001), makes a good case that these were originally part of Dublin's Houses of Parliament, designed by Edward Lovett Pearce, and partially destroyed by fire in 1792. An exchange of letters from 1804, between Frederick Trench, Heywood's first garden-maker, and Thomas Williams, secretary of the Bank of Ireland (which had acquired the old parliament building), has Trench asking to purchase (and receiving) 'Ten Capitals which were attached to the Columns of the late Parliament House'. It is unknown to what use he put them – although it is thought that he included them in his now destroyed Temple of the Winds folly. Meredith measured the capitals in Lutyens's loggia, compared them with those in Francis Wheatley's 1780 painting *The Irish House of Commons*, and found them to be a perfect match. One of Meredith's theories is that Lutyens may have been pressurized by Hutcheson Poë to include them in the summer house, and that he popped them around the back where they would not interfere with his design.

It is believed that Gertrude Jekyll, who often worked with Lutyens, prepared a planting plan for his garden at Heywood, but no such plan can be found. The current planting – albeit dreadfully gappy – is reminiscent of her style, and includes some of her specials, such as grey-leaved herbaceous perennials, the scented pink floribunda rose 'Nathalie Nypels' and her signature anchor plant, bergenia.

Glenarm Castle Walled Garden

COUNTY ANTRIM

The road from Larne to Glenarm in County Antrim is famous. Narrow, winding and rocky, it skirts along the coast with the sea splashing and spuming on one side, while chalk and basalt cliffs rise on the other, with tufts of grass and harebells clinging to their dappled flanks. It is a road for bowling along in an open-topped car, with Cary Grant or Grace Kelly at your side. Certain stretches along here date from 1970, but the original route was a renowned piece of civil engineering, designed by the Scottish-born William Bald. It was constructed between 1832 and 1842 – using liberal amounts of dynamite to blast away the layers of the cliff face (an ecological crime that would be forbidden today).

Before the road, the Glens of Antrim were almost inaccessible to the rest of the island. At the beginning of the nineteenth century, the Commissioners of Public Works in Ireland described the Glens as 'cut off from any reasonable communication by the badness of roads over mountains and slopes varying from 1 in 6 to 1 in 12'. It was 'a barren waste, asylum of a miserable and lawless peasantry'. In those days, it was less hazardous to sail across the North Channel to Scotland for trade, rather than attempting to travel to elsewhere in Ireland. Perhaps because of this long association with the other island, this section of Antrim is more like a little piece of Britain than many other parts of Ulster.

In the days when the 'lawless peasantry' roamed the mountains, Glenarm Castle, the seat of the Earls of Antrim, was a world apart, with a fine house and deer park, and a newly built walled garden and adjoining frame-yard. The estate, which flows down to the sea in the first of Antrim's nine glens, had been home to the MacDonnell clan (now McDonnell) since the beginning of the sixteenth century, and had been much improved over the ages. Rebuilt in the middle of the eighteenth century, the house was a grand and elegant Palladian pile. Less than a hundred years later it was heavily Gothicked, with the addition of mullioned windows, stepped gables, lofty chimneys, an extravagant porch and a quartet of towers – each garnished with a weather vane. Ornate finials sprouted from every possible apex and soared skywards.

It is this self-important, overwrought building that peers out from behind a shield of oak and lime trees at the garden at Glenarm today. It is both a watchful and somewhat forbidding presence, so that the visitor is alternately entranced and cowed by its fairytale appearance and seigneurial air. It's not hard to believe that the ground underfoot has been owned by a single family for over half a millennium.

The 600-hectare (1,500-acre) estate is now in the guardianship of Randal and Aurora McDonnell, Viscount and Viscountess Dunluce – he took over the property in 1992.

OPPOSITE A section of the Upper Garden at Glenarm Castle in springtime.
LEFT The castle keeps an eye on the walled garden through the trees.

ABOVE The Victorian glasshouse is frilled with catmint, while the hot border glows with dahlias, lilies, *Potentilla*, *Crocosmia*, *Helenium* and other fiery characters.

OPPOSITE In the kitchen garden, sensible artichokes, brassicas and broad beans are mingled with sweet peas and marigolds.

The 1.6-hectare (4-acre) walled garden, which dates from around 1820, has been open to the public since 2005, and is nearing the end of an extensive and thoughtful refurbishment, which started in the mid-1990s.

Prior to its restoration, the limestone-walled enclosure at Glenarm was blessed with a number of existing plants and structures – and these have been carefully conserved. An immensely long (perhaps 100 metres) lean-to Victorian glasshouse clothes the middle third of the south-facing wall. At its back, in the attached frame-yard, a lengthy row of sheds originally comprised the boiler room for the hothouse, potting sheds, tool houses and fruit stores, as well as bothies for garden staff (in its heyday, fifteen or twenty men would have worked here). The sheds are unusual in that the doors and windows follow the line of the garden's slope, so that they are slanted at top and bottom. These skewed parallelograms would have served as a novel demonstration of the skill of the Victorian joiners and masons.

At present this smaller enclosure is run as a highly ornamental kitchen garden. Sensible cabbages and carrots are interspersed between towering wigwams of sweet peas, including the historic and fragrant 'Matucana'. A gathering of cartoonishly bright dahlias pays homage at the foot of a huge and thriving fig on the south-facing wall. Planted in the late nineteenth century, it once had its own hothouse, but now, protected only by a narrow awning of glass, it is proof of how mild this sheltered corner of County Antrim is.

In the main walled garden, a sombre and imposing yew circle in the Lower Garden – the more easterly half – dates from the 1850s. It was around this time that the new railways and roads in Ireland made transporting of produce easier, so big houses did not have to be as self-sufficient as previously. Parts of walled gardens, therefore, were given over increasingly to the cultivation of ornamental plants. At Glenarm, by the end of the nineteenth century, the walled garden was well furnished with substantial and elaborate herbaceous borders – as can be seen in contemporary paintings by Louisa, wife of the 11th Earl. The countess took her gardening seriously, and around this time invited Ellen Willmott, the great English gardener, to Glenarm to advise on the roses.

By the 1990s, however, when the present Lord Dunluce took over, the gardens had mainly been grassed over for easy maintenance, and presented a near blank canvas, ready for restoration. Besides the dark yew circle, there was a matching beech circle – which forms the centre of the more westerly Upper Garden. It was planted in the 1950s, and has a delightful crinkle-crankle hedge peeling off from it. Surviving trees included good specimens of Yulan magnolia (*M. nudata*), myrtle (*Luma apiculata*), *Sorbus* 'Mitchellii' and eucryphia.

Lord Dunluce set about recreating structure in the gardens, first restoring the long glasshouse, and then planting hedges of pleached limes, which enfold the Lower Garden in a stern and manly embrace. Their muscularity

RIGHT A limestone madonna and child, sculpted by Angela Sykes.
BELOW The west-facing border is a mixture of robust perennials and flowering shrubs.
OPPOSITE The planting inside the stern yew circle is unexpectedly light-hearted and cottagey.
OVERLEAF The double herbaceous border is a confection of *Lysimachia*, *Penstemon*, *Phlox*, *Salvia*, *Dierama* and other white, pink, mauve and purple perennials.

is nicely balanced by the flamboyant planting in this area: much of it is the work of Nigel Marshall, the former head gardener at Mount Stewart, who worked closely with the family for several years. On the south-facing wall a herbaceous border is filled with hot-coloured flowers that really start exploding in late summer: *Lobelia cardinalis* 'Queen Victoria', *Potentilla nepalensis* 'Roxana', *Helenium* 'Moerheim Beauty', *Crocosmia* 'Citronella' and 'Lucifer' and a gaudy display of fiery dahlias. Earlier in the year this space is gloriously fussy with the plump dowager flowers of the lactiflora peonies, including 'Bunker Hill', 'Arabian Prince' 'Félix Crousse', 'Buckeye Belle' and 'Kelway's Majestic'. And before that, this bed, and almost all the other beds in both halves of the garden, start the year with a trumpet blast of tulips: over eight thousand of them. Their blocks of crazy colour add episodes of pointillistic radiance to the spare bones of the springtime garden.

The west-facing wall is fronted by a mixed border where robust herbaceous plants, such as eupatorium, *Anemone* x *hybrida* 'September Charm' and *Geranium* 'Patricia' mingle with hydrangea, fuchsia, tree peony and other flowering shrubs. Nestled in the middle, and backed by a fountain of *Miscanthus* x *giganteus*, is a limestone sculpture of a madonna and child carved by Angela Sykes when she was a teenager. She later became the wife of the 13th Earl of Antrim.

The main event in this half of the garden is a double herbaceous border, directly opposite the entrance gate. It is a deliciously sugary confection: a floral dessert of pink, mauve and blue phlox, hardy geranium, polemonium, salvia, penstemon, campanula, stachys and other pretties. The border's pale luminescence is set off by dark yew hedges on either side and by the fortress-like yew circle at its end with formidably high, curved walls. Enter the opening in its dusky foliage ramparts, and you find an unexpectedly

BELOW The Upper Garden, designed by Catherine FitzGerald, contains a spiral mound, which is neatly coiffed and shaggy by turns. In a section devoted to medlars the awns of *Stipa gigantea* catch the evening light, while an oak obelisk rises proudly in the newly planted orchard.

exuberant herb garden – a cottagey throng of orange marigolds, purple agastache, wild strawberries, sunflowers, bay, rosemary and santolina.

Lord and Lady Dunluce have worked with many experts to bring the walled garden back to life: Reg Maxwell, former curator of the Belfast Botanic Gardens, is an advisor, while brothers James and Bill Wharry are the gardeners who look after the space. Most recently, designer Catherine FitzGerald has worked on the more westerly part – the Upper Garden – to create a contemporary garden of rooms. There are six beech-delineated divisions: three on either side of the central beech circle and its crinkle-crankle corridor. Five of the spaces pay homage to the garden's previous use as a place to grow food, and are planted with apples, quince, medlar and pears, all in formal arrangements. The sixth

'room' has a spiral turf mount like a vast grassy blancmange. Its peak commands a view across the adjacent deer park.

Hidden away in a beech passageway, a double rill trickles down a gentle slope. It was designed by architect Jill Lambert. The water hops musically over a mosaic of black and white pebbles brought from the Glenarm coast. The collecting of the beach stones (which are also laid on the ground in the frame-yard) is an ancient right of the Earls of Antrim. This walled garden is but a beach-stone's throw from the ragged Irish coast, yet there is little, besides those very stones and the wafts of sea mist, to connect it with the world outside. Its highly organized space is a triumph of man's ability to impose order on a wild landscape.

ABOVE The fountain and rill were designed by local architect Jill Lambert.
RIGHT The Glenarm estate retains an ancient right to collect the black and white pebbles from the nearby beach.

GOOD ENOUGH TO EAT

Productive Patches

There have been productive gardens in Ireland since at least the early Christian period. Monastic settlements and well-off farmers had enclosures in which they grew brassicas, beans, peas, leeks, onions and grains such as wheat, oats and barley. There were also herbs (including chives, coriander and dill), apple and plum trees, grape vines and beehives. In the centuries following the Norman invasions (their main incursions were between 1169 and 1171), food growing became more sophisticated, with a greater range of crops, among them cardoons, garlic, carrots, parsnips, radishes, pumpkins, cherries and pears.

Yet, in the sixteenth century, Irish gardens were still mostly relatively simple affairs, even in the 'stately castles of the chieftains', according to the eighteenth-century historian Joseph C. Walker. In his *Essay on the Rise and Progress of Gardening in Ireland* published by the Royal Irish Academy in 1792, he noted that 'the perturbed state of the kingdom' had made it impossible for gardening to prosper. He quotes Fynes Moryson, secretary to Lord Mountjoy (commander of the English army in Ireland), who notes that rebels – 'not only idle themselves, but in natural malice destroying the labours of other men' – were wont to cut up or burn fruit trees. 'Under such circumstances,' laments Walker, 'it was impossible that the art of gardening would make any considerable advances in Ireland. The hand of rapine restrained it.'

J.C. Loudon, in *An Encyclopaedia of Gardening* (published in 1824), observed that Irish gardens were still not as developed as those of their British neighbours: 'As far as respects hardy fruits and culinary vegetables, the gardens of the principal proprietors in Ireland may be considered as approaching those of Scotland or England, as they are generally managed by gardeners of those countries; but in respect to exotic productions, Irish gardens are far behind those of the sister kingdoms.' Moreover, he remarked, 'The gardens of the minor nobility and gentry of Ireland are poor in horticultural productions; many content themselves with cabbages and potatoes, and perhaps a few pears, onions and apples.'

Ireland's history is inextricably linked with the potato. It has been said that Sir Walter Raleigh, who lived for a while in Youghal, County Cork, first brought *Solanum tuberosum* to Ireland, but Sir Francis Drake and John Hawkins have likewise been credited with this. It has also been suggested that it came to these shores through trade with Spain. In any case, the historic tuber entered Irish diets sometime around 1600, and by the middle of the nineteenth century it, along with milk – which in combination made a near perfect food – was the main sustenance of the greater part of the population. A farm labourer would consume up to fourteen pounds of potatoes a day. The potatoes, along with a few cabbages, were grown in half-acre or acre holdings by their cottages.

By the middle of the nineteenth century, kitchen gardens in large Irish country houses were extensive and intensive, measuring anything from 0.8–2 hectares (2–5 acres). But seventy years later almost all had become derelict or put to pasture. The First World War, the ensuing collapse of the economy, soaring death duties and income tax, and Ireland's own troubled birth as a nation, all combined to put an end to – or at least seriously curtail – the privileges of the Big House.

One of the country's most famous Big Houses is Lissadell, erstwhile home to the Gore-Booth family, including Eva Gore-Booth and her sister Constance, Countess Markievicz – both political activists and friends of W.B. Yeats. After the house was bought in 2003 by Edward Walsh and Constance Cassidy, and massively refurbished, the 0.9-hectare (2.2-acre) kitchen garden was restored and managed by Klaus Laitenberger, and then by Dermot Carey. The garden opened in 2006, but less than five years later both house and garden closed again because of a right-of-way dispute. The walled kitchen garden was sown over with a grass-and-clover mix. Lissadell has recently reopened, but at the time of writing the kitchen garden remains grassed over, except for the planting of the Lissadell-Langford Collection of Heritage Potatoes, curated by Dermot Carey: an important genetic resource of two hundred heirloom and landrace varieties.

A happier restoration is that of the Victorian walled garden in Dublin's Phoenix Park. The 1-hectare (2.5-acre) enclosure provided fruit, vegetables and cut flowers for the since-demolished Ashtown Lodge, the residence of the Under-Secretary for Ireland. The Office of Public Works began renovating the structure in 2003, and planting commenced in 2008. Now, with its strict Victorian layout re-established, it is a model of productivity, with neat beds of vegetables, herbs and soft fruit, espaliered fruit trees and a double herbaceous border.

As the Big House in Ireland declined, the allotment movement grew. In the first years of the new century, the St Vincent de Paul Society established 'Workingmen's

Gardens' in Navan, Cork and Killarney. And in 1913 the Vacant Land Cultivation Society obtained land throughout Dublin city. The charitable organization was chaired by the Jesuit Reverend Joseph McDonnell and had a Miss S.C. Harrison as its honorary secretary. In 1917, the society had 487 plots in thirteen locations. Dublin Corporation also made allotments available: in 1925, there were 334. During the 'Emergency' – as the Second World War was known in Ireland – the Corporation managed a veritable, if fragmented, urban farm of 7,413 plots. Some were set up on the city's own stock of land, while two thousand were acquired over forty-eight hours in 1941 by Emergency Powers order.

Unemployed men were offered concessionary rents of one shilling (instead of one pound), and were given seeds and manure, and loaned implements. According to a report presented to the Dublin City Council in 1946, the main reason for these concessions was not to relieve hardship: 'It is well to make clear that the Government's declared intention in starting the scheme was to enable idle men to remain physically fit and so be enabled to undertake manual work when offered.' Accordingly, the scheme did not provide for 'old age pensioners, delicate people or persons with scanty means'.

The numbers of allotments steadily dwindled from the 1950s onwards, as land was handed back for development and, later, as food became cheaper and Irish people became more prosperous. By the 1970s and 1980s there were few allotments; homegrowing of food was likewise diminishing.

PREVIOUS PAGES The ornamental potager at Ballymaloe Cookery School.
BELOW Orderly ranks of herbs in the Victorian walled garden in Dublin's Phoenix Park.

In a land where a large portion of the population had been raised on farms, or was one generation removed, the *not* growing of one's own food was often seen as a sign of success. Fruit and vegetables were now conveniently and cheaply available, and the family cabbage-onion-and-spud plot became a rarity. In many cases it was grassed over, or planted with heathers and dwarf conifers. There were exceptions, of course, especially in the minority Protestant section of the community. The ethic of efficiency, sufficiency and thrift – as well as an abiding connection to life lived outdoors – meant that vegetables, soft fruit bushes and fruit trees persisted in the gardens of the Anglo-Irish.

A slow resurgence of food growing began in the 1990s, a decade that saw the founding of the Irish Seed Savers Association by the American Anita Hayes in 1991 (initially in County Carlow, and then in County Clare); and Leitrim's Organic Centre by English harpsichordist Rod Alston in 1995. These initiatives were driven by commitment to future food security and sustainability, as well as by the conviction that produce grown organically is more wholesome for both man and planet.

In the first decade of the new millennium demand for allotments grew again, and city councils gradually made hundreds of new plots available (although still not nearly enough), while entrepreneurs started up private allotment schemes. Some of these latter are well managed and vibrant places; others could be described as cynical attempts to cash in on people's desire to get back to the land – even unsuitable land at inflated rents.

The same decade also saw the arrival in Ireland (in 2002) of Joy Larkcom, the undisputed queen of organic vegetable growing. With her husband, Don Pollard, she moved to west Cork to 'retire' – which she didn't. Instead, her presence added an injection of energy and expertise into the Irish home-growing movement.

Not far away, near Skibbereen, in west Cork, Madeline McKeever started her organic seed production business in 2004, Brown Envelope Seeds. And in 2009, a year after Ireland's property bubble burst, and as the country hit a grim recession, journalist Michael Kelly founded GIY (Grow It Yourself) Ireland, a thousands-strong network of growers. Members are connected through their local GIY groups, and through an online community and a many-layered website.

Irish people are once again returning to the land.

OPPOSITE Purple-podded bean in the Cork garden of Joy Larkcom; and traditional Donegal ridges at Salthill House in Mountcharles.
LEFT AND BELOW Lissadell Kitchen Garden: pollinators' patch; old apple trees and rugosa roses line the rows of saladings.

Ballymaloe Cookery School

COUNTY CORK

On a summer morning in the glasshouses at Ballymaloe Cookery School, in Shanagarry, the air is perfumed with warm basil, tomatoes and compost. A few bumblebees have found their way in through the open doors and are hard at work nuzzling the blossoms of the dozens of squash plants that clamber towards the sky. Farm manager Haulie Walsh is writing carefully on white adhesive labels and sticking them on a series of curious-looking tomatoes. 'White Beauty' is lemon-coloured and broadly rumpled, 'Purple Calabash' is richly toned, ribbed and flattened, while 'San Marzano', a historic Italian paste kind, is an elongated plum shape. The tomatoes – there are thirteen heritage varieties being fitted with name tags – are on their way to Darina Allen's classroom at the far end of the gardens, where they will be examined and sampled by the students. Education is as much a function of this east Cork plot of land as is the growing of food.

The bulk of the tomato crop, though, is made up of commercial Dutch varieties, bred for vigour and for resistance to tomato mosaic virus. That other disease-prone crop, cucumber, is also a modern Dutch kind. The area under glass is 0.4 hectare (1 acre), an immense space that has most visitors green with envy. The soil has been bulked up with home-made compost (made in a huge seven-bay operation), and is both fertile and moisture-retentive: 'We don't have to water half as much since we've been adding our own compost,' says head gardener Eileen O'Donovan. Compost is the fuel that runs this place, and its importance is broadcast proudly and urgently: the first recipe that the cookery students are given is the one for compost.

The cropping is mighty in the organic glasshouse, with areas the size of an ordinary back garden devoted to a single fruit or vegetable: besides those already mentioned there are courgettes, peppers, aubergines, sweetcorn, beetroot (three kinds), beans and peas (grown indoors to thwart the pigeons), leeks, spinach and chard. Scores of sweet peas have just finished, and their place on the network of cords has been taken by pumpkins and squashes, including the near-crimson 'Potimarron' and 'Ushiki Kuri'. Overhead, the struts of the greenhouse are garlanded with bunches of onions, shallots and garlic, their dried leaves hanging down in buff-coloured tresses. Peaches, nectarines, cherries, apricots, oranges and lemons have been planted as an experiment, explains Eileen.

The herb garden is enclosed in deep and tall beech hedges planted around 1870. The box compartments hold a mixture of culinary herbs and floriferous annuals and perennials.

A Place to Grow

Ballymaloe Cookery School, which was started in 1983, is on Tim and Darina Allen's 40-hectare (100-acre) farm at Kinoith. The tiny townland of Shanagarry takes up a small parcel, the equivalent of just a few fields, at the heart of the property. The name Ballymaloe means 'old garden' in Irish (*sean garraí*), so it seems that plants were cultivated here in distant times. In the seventeenth century the lands were confiscated from Irish Catholics by Oliver Cromwell and given to the English admiral Sir William Penn. His famous son, also William Penn – the founder of Pennsylvania – lived here for a time, attending Quaker meetings not far away, and espousing Quakerism.

Since then, it is said that the lands have always passed from Quaker to Quaker. Before the Allens owned it, the farm belonged to Wilson Strangman, who in 1932 hired the seventeen-year-old Ivan Allen (Tim's late father), then fresh out of the Quaker school Newtown, in Waterford. Within six years, the two had set up a limited company, Imokilly Orchards (named after the barony) to 'acquire the business of farmers, fruit and vegetable growers and dealers, market gardeners, florists, etc.', according to a notice in the *Irish Times* on 11 May 1938.

Prior to that the farm had been a mixed operation, with everything from livestock to violets, but 'the only thing making money was the apple orchard, so, sometime in the 1930s and 40s, my father planted the whole farm down to apples,' according to Tim. Ivan also built the extensive glasshouses – for tomatoes, cucumbers and cut flowers – at around the same time. Mushrooms were also grown here and exported to England and Wales.

Ivan and his wife, Myrtle, bought the much larger farm at nearby Ballymaloe House in 1947, and in the 1960s they started a country house restaurant and hotel there. When his friend Strangman died in 1966, Ivan inherited the farm and house at Kinoith. It is now the home of Tim and Darina, who have been developing the gardens here since the 1980s.

Experimentation (as well as education) is continual here. One of Tim Allen's projects, 'my legacy to my grandchildren', is a vegetable field next to the glasshouse range which is being compartmentalized using long north–south lines of alder. The ensuing corridor-like divisions will provide the optimum amount of shelter and sunlight for food growing. Already there are plots of leeks, turnips, kohl rabi, romanesco and cauliflower which – along with the greenhouse crops – supply produce for the cookery school, the restaurant at Ballymaloe House and the market in Midleton. Darina is at the forefront of the local and slow food movements, and has done much to raise awareness in these areas.

The veg field is one of many fresh endeavours on the Allens' estate: a new fruit field with numerous kinds of soft fruit was planted in early 2009, and a new orchard is being planned at the time of writing. Expansion is continual, keeping pace with the increase in family members. The ever-extending Allen clan, through its industriousness and public-relations acumen, enjoys a position akin to that of Cork royalty. The Ballymaloe model is dynastic and demanding of loyalty. Hard work and long hours are the norm for all.

Most of the recent horticultural projects have been to do with food, as Tim admits: 'I'm fed up with flower gardens, I'm only interested in vegetable or fruit gardens.' He is unmoved by the lavish double herbaceous border which does an impressive 91-metre (300-foot) song-and-dance along the centre of the garden: 'I think of all that bloody hard work, and then you can't eat the damn thing!' You can't eat the Celtic maze next to it either, which Eileen replanted the previous winter with a thousand beech and hornbeam, after the original yew failed.

There are around 3 hectares (7½ acres) of gardens at Kinoith, as well as a species-rich wildlife meadow and farm walk. The soil is a slightly heavy, free-draining loam, being progressively lightened with compost and seaweed from the nearby seashore. The oldest part – known as Lydia's Garden, after previous owner Lydia Strangman – is an enclosure with lawns and mixed borders. A pretty little summer house has a mosaic floor dating from 1912, with shards of china depicting a shamrock, a rose and a thistle, the symbols of Ireland, England and Scotland. A viewing platform looks into a herb garden encompassed within voluminous nineteenth-century beech hedges. At one time Tim's father, Ivan Allen, used to propagate

tomato plants within this sheltered microclimate. The herb beds are laced around with box hedging, a tribute to the gardens at Château de Villandry in the Loire. 'We designed it ourselves,' says Tim. 'It started out as a series of rectangular beds, but they looked so boring on paper. So I went around cutting all the corners off.' The result, although only a couple of decades old, looks baroque and consequential. Dozens of culinary herbs are neatly buttoned up in their *Buxus* overcoats while the occasional froth of echinacea and Russian sage (*Perovskia*) erupts from the strict framework. In the central roundel, a formidable *Ugni molinae* with an impressive embonpoint watches over the humble herbs. Previously known as *Myrtus ugni*, it was planted in honour of Myrtle Allen, Tim's mother.

Soon after completing the herb garden, the Allens started on a decorative potager, a thoroughly pretty creation whose herringbone red brick paving and tumbling nasturtiums regularly appear in gardening publications. Triangular and

ABOVE, CLOCKWISE FROM TOP LEFT A herbaceous border picks up the last rays of the late-summer evening; Cape gooseberry, peppers, basil, tomatoes and cucurbits in one of the glasshouses; the water garden offers a quiet place to sit, while pondering the monstrous size of the gunnera leaves; the box-edged divisions in the herb garden were conceived after the Allens visited Château de Villandry.

OPPOSITE The ornamental potager is productive as well as pretty. Its yield includes red cabbages, artichokes and nattily striped marrows.
FAR LEFT Old apples grow in the tiny fruit garden outside the dining room.
LEFT Shallots drying in the warmth of the glasshouse.

diamond-shaped beds edged with edible flowers hold cos lettuce, leeks, chard, beet, cabbage and other handsome crops. Standard bay trees, sunflowers and wigwams of purple-podded climbing French beans, pink-splashed Barlotti beans and sweet peas add height. The garden is almost private and is ringed with tall sycamore, beech and pine. Wood pigeons, cooing antiphonally, perch in the trees like vultures and look longingly at the netted brassicas.

In 1990, the Allens employed Jim Reynolds, then gardening correspondent of the *Irish Times*, to design an ornamental fruit garden outside the cookery school dining room. In contrast to the sensibly ordered parade lines of fruit bushes in Tim's big new field, this tiny square is a pomicultural jewel box. Old apples – including 'Beauty of Bath', 'Winston', 'McIntosh Red' and 'Pitmaston Pineapple' – are trained over four arches, while a black mulberry spreads its branches in the centre. Strawberries, hardy geraniums, *Rudbeckia* 'Goldsturm' and other herbaceous fancies edge the beds. Worcesterberry, jostaberry, gooseberry and cobnut bushes fill the outer margins. A circular gravel path bids you to walk contemplatively through this diminutive patch of plenty. Peace is short-lived, however, as several roosters billeted nearby are usually engaged in a crowing competition.

The noisy cockerels and their more demure wives are all old breeds. They are mainly for show, rather than for eggs or eating. But there are working hens elsewhere on the farm, who process waste from the cookery school and lay copious amounts of eggs. Much of the estate is managed in this way, with an ornamental veneer – which dispenses an appealing dollop of education – layered on top of a serious food-raising enterprise. With enticing features such as fancy fowl and pretty potagers, visitors can pass through the twin gateposts of sustainability and future resilience while hardly noticing.

Glebe Gardens

COUNTY CORK

THE FISHING VILLAGE of Baltimore sits on the upper side of Ireland's most southerly peninsula. During winter its population numbers barely three hundred, but in summertime it is thronged with visitors who arrive for the sea angling, diving and sailing.

Four centuries ago it was visitors of a different stripe who came one summer, and with disastrous consequences. In June 1631, pirates from the Barbary Coast in North Africa attacked the sleeping west Cork village just before dawn, breaking down cottage doors and carrying off at least a hundred of the inhabitants. Their victims were transported to Algiers to be sold into slavery. The Sack of Baltimore was the only known instance of a slaving raid in Ireland, and the event took a grim toll on the village.

Nowadays, it is a considerably more jolly place, with an approach road lined with hot pink fuchsia and blazing orange montbretia. These unlikely but cheerfully

BELOW The nineteenth-century Glebe is a solid presence among the trees, just a beach pebble's throw from the sea.
RIGHT A glimpse of Church Strand Bay is visible above the griselinia hedge.

THE IRISH GARDEN

noisy bedfellows are characteristic of the south-west of Ireland, and are the delight of tourists who marvel at these 'Irish' plants. In fact, *Fuchsia magellanica* is a native of South America, while *Crocosmia* x *crocosmiiflora* is a nineteenth-century hybrid of two South African species (*C. pottsii* and *C. aurea*) bred by Victor Lemoine in France.

Yet these naturalized foreigners symbolize perfectly the cultural diversity of this part of Ireland. West Cork has been colonized by people from all over the globe, drawn by its almost frost-free climate and by the historic and handsome scenery along a rugged coastline pinched in and thrust out by frequent bays and peninsulas.

In 1989, Jean and Peter Perry and their four young daughters arrived from Gloucester, and moved into the pleasingly square former rectory on the edge of the village. The 1820 house came with a 2.5-hectare (6-acre) wedge of pasture, sloping gently down to the rocky seashore at the north-east end of the property.

In England, the couple had been pioneering members of the Organic Growers' Association, an organization that was later absorbed into the Soil Association. They left behind a successful organic market garden and farm shop. But the business had been so all-consuming that they were on call all the time, and never had a holiday. In Ireland, they would do things differently. Peter would fulfil his ambition to paint, and Jean 'wasn't going to do any gardening, ever again!'

But gardeners don't stop gardening, and before too many seasons had elapsed, Jean again had her hands in the soil ('light, acid and rocky, with no humus'). Within a decade of buying the Glebe, the couple had transformed the cattle-grazed fields into an organic garden of extraordinary productiveness and prettiness. Now, there is also an award-winning café that opens during the tourist season, run by three of the Perry daughters, Tessa, Keziah and JoJo. Jean gardens full time (after getting up at dawn to bake bread for the café) and Peter, between the garden and the café, has

little time to paint. Thaddeus O'Regan, who lives nearby, helps in the garden and with winter projects. Hard work is abundantly in evidence about the place, which feels wholesome and holistic and utterly worthwhile. With different parts of the operation feeding into each other, nothing is wasted, and common sense and forethought are joint rulers.

The Glebe, being next to the sea, is constantly challenged by salt-laden winds. When the Perrys arrived there was already a first line of defence of sycamore and hawthorn. They added a cordon of alder and willow, and then – to protect the most intensive growing area – hedges of pea-green, waxy-leaved *Griselinia littoralis*, the New Zealand plant that thrives so well in coastal Ireland. At the heart of the garden is the potager: two dozen beautifully organized raised beds filled with crops – carefully planted, precisely spaced and watchfully tended. It is a small world of handsomeness and industry: a poem to vegetables in twenty-four stanzas.

OPPOSITE AND ABOVE Twenty-four raised beds are kept in constant service during the growing season, supplying fresh vegetables and salads for the restaurant. In autumn the soil in the empty beds is protected with a duvet of mulch.

TOP Rainbow chard; the flower of the old French mangetout pea 'Carouby de Maussane'; 'Striped Roman' tomato (for sauce). ABOVE The Glebe's own strain of *Papaver somniferum*, known as 'Plums and Custard'.

The soil in the long rectangles is minded with exquisite concern. Each bed bears at least three crops during the year – which Jeans charts in advance on a large plan. She doesn't follow a traditional rotation, but makes sure to move things around, paying special attention to disease-prone groups. Potatoes and brassicas, for example, don't land in the same bed again for at least four years. At the end of the growing season, where there are no overwintering plants, the beds are snuggled up for winter under a layer of mulch. This can be all or any of the following: seaweed, compost, lawn mowings mixed with fallen leaves, and well-rotted goat manure. The 'duvet' insulates the soil, shielding it from pounding winter rain. In time, the worms incorporate the material into the soil, so that the beds never need to be dug.

This no-dig method of cultivation saves time, but it also preserves the soil structure, which has been built up by the gazillions of mini-creatures and micro-organisms living in it. In springtime, 'we pull aside the mulch, and plant through it,' says Jean. Later, when the worms have done their work and the soil surface is bare, the crops are mulched again, with grass clippings, to keep the weeds down and to prevent moisture loss. Rainfall in this part of west Cork averages around 1,200 millimetres (47 inches) per annum, but Baltimore is considerably drier, as showers often bypass it and dump on Skibbereen, 13 kilometres (8 miles) away.

The thoughtful regime at the Glebe keeps the beds super-fertile and early producing: one year there were ripe courgettes at the end of May – the earliest I've ever seen them outdoors. I've learned more about growing food and managing the soil from this garden than anywhere else.

The potager supplies the bulk of the produce for the café, so Jean chooses some of her cultivars for prolificness, as well as disease-resistance and flavour. Courgettes are the yellow-fruited 'Atena' and the old commercial hybrid 'Ambassador', while spinach is another fast-maturing F1 hybrid, 'Emelia'. Yet, old open-pollinated varieties are still on the list. Jean has grown the purple-podded French mangetout 'Carouby de Maussane' for years, and she also favours the venerable pea 'Hurst Greenshaft', with its 'good long pods, each with about ten peas: really good peas'.

Old-fashioned sweet peas scramble happily up the wigwams that sprout among the vegetables. Every summer without fail, the air is sweetened by the sugary scent of the purple 'Matucana', the white 'Dorothy Eckford', and the claret-coloured 'Black Knight', as well as other complementary varieties. Jean picks bunches of their daintily chintzy blooms for the café tables, and to sell at Skibbereen market.

There are beans in plenty here, growing up rows of V-shaped supports. It is a sensible configuration for picking, as the beans hang out freely from the foliage. And, there

TOP In one of the polytunnels: onions drying; the Italian heirloom tomato 'Costoluto Fiorentino'; Black Hamburgh grapes.
ABOVE One of the Glebe's goats, supplier of milk for a good tangy cheese, and of manure for the soil.

is lots of room in the soil below for crops such as rainbow chard, beetroot, oriental leaves, rocket, lettuce and other saladings, and for leeks and shallots.

'Enorma' runner beans are 'foolproof', as are the poignantly named pole beans 'Cherokee Trail of Tears'. This heirloom pulse was supposed to have accompanied the Cherokee people when they were forcibly relocated to Oklahoma by the US government in the 1830s. The climbing bean 'Blauhilde' is an old German variety with long purple pods.

Jean grows the crimson-flowered broad bean, an eighteenth-century variety saved from extinction by the Henry Doubleday Research Association in the UK. It has small pods, and is not as productive as the white-flowered 'Express' (also here), but the blossoms sit preciously among the foliage, like floral rubies. The broad beans are secured in cages made from blue baling twine wrapped around stout poles. The poles are goat willow thinnings, cut from the shelter belt by Peter and Thaddeus. They are processed – appropriately enough – by the Perrys' twin nanny goats, who strip the bark, leaving pale and smooth stakes, ready for use. The goats' manure is an important part of the gardening operation, while their milk makes a tangy cheese. A large enclosure full of busybody hens, meanwhile, sees choice bits of garden waste going in, and eggs and manure coming out. The 'engine room of the garden', as Jean calls it, is an enviable five-bay compost depot. 'We use about three bins a year. All the beds get some of our compost every year. Even an inch makes a difference.'

The potager is bounded on one side by cordons of spur-fruiting apples, including 'Winston' and 'Lord Lambourne', while plantings of cottage flowers crowd in from all sides. Their blooms attract pollinators, and help to maintain a healthy balance of wildlife.

There is more food in two polytunnels on the far side of the chicken run. It is tomato heaven: Jean grows at least thirty varieties each year. She is never without the old hybrids 'Shirley' and 'Harbinger' for the café's lively breakfast trade, while 'San Marzano', 'Principe Borghese' and 'Striped Roman' all go into the sauce pot. Small and sweet kinds include 'Black Cherry', 'Brown Berry', 'Sungold' and the Polish 'Malinowy Ozarowski'. The old Italian 'Costoluto Fiorentino' is pompously puffed and corrugated (and has a good, deep flavour), while 'Paul Robeson' has dark skin and a distinctive smoky taste. (Surprisingly, the last is a Russian heirloom, named after the famous singer for his tireless human rights advocacy.)

Also in the tunnels are Black Hamburgh grapes, as well as tender peppers, cucumbers, gourds and basil. Early beans, courgettes, lettuces and strawberries are cosseted here, while carrots hide out from their nasty little nemesis, carrot fly. Many other crops are started off here before going outdoors. Self-seeded flowering tobacco (*Nicotiana sylvestris*) and the Glebe's own strain of opium poppy, the well-named 'Plums and Custard', add impudent floral notes among the useful crops.

The garden at the Glebe is always changing. A few years ago the Perrys carved a turf amphitheatre out of a slope at the seaward end of the property. In order to reach it, you amble across a wooden bridge, built by Peter over a now-defunct railway cutting. The train, which stopped running in the 1960s, used to take fish (mainly pilchards) from Baltimore and thence – via Cork and Rosslare – to Billingsgate in London. Now, the cutting is filled with water and verged by the big wheels of the tree fern, *Dicksonia antarctica*. On the far side of the bridge mown paths loop through a long scented meadow which catches the sea mist in the morning and the last golden syrup rays of the sun in the evening.

At the time of writing, Jean is eyeing up the cut flower garden next to the potager and is planning to transform it into a Mediterranean herb garden and a physic garden. This from the woman who was never going to garden again. I know that I am just one of thousands who are delighted she didn't keep her word.

ABOVE The meadow is full of wildflowers, including orchids. When the grass needs 'mowing', Peter and Jean bring the goats down in the evening.
LEFT Peter's wooden bridge over the cutting where the 'Baltimore to Billingsgate' train used to run.

Dunmore Country School

COUNTY LAOIS

THE IRISH SAINT FIACHRA, patron of gardeners (and cab-drivers), upped stakes and moved to the Brie area of France, to lead a life of solitude tending his plants in a clearing in the forest. There is a pleasing symmetry (although it took over thirteen centuries to be realized), in that the same part of France sent a rather good gardener to Ireland, to live not far from where Saint Fiachra himself once resided.

Tanguy de Toulgoët came to County Laois in 1995 with his wife, Isabelle, not to garden, but to fly-fish in the 'Three Sisters': the Suir, Nore and Barrow rivers. He worked as a guide for visiting fishermen, but the foot-and-mouth disease outbreak of 2001, and its resulting restrictions on movement in the countryside, had a catastrophic effect on his business. Before leaving France, however, Tanguy had managed his family's 325-hectare (800-acre) tillage farm (including a walled garden where he grew vegetables for a restaurant on the estate), so it was natural for him to move back to the soil. He became head gardener at the upmarket hotel, Castle Durrow. Several later years he left, after having set up his own smallholding down a quiet road, a mile north of Durrow.

Here, on a 0.5-hectare (1¼-acre) site, in a field leased from the neighbouring farmer, he grows food and flowers, keeps bees, raises hens and other poultry, and stables a pair of ponies for his and Isabelle's two young daughters. The family is almost self-sufficient, and the operation has an appealing Gallic blend of practicality and elegance. A few years ago the couple set up their Dunmore Country School to impart their expertise (his in the garden, and hers in the kitchen), in both English and French, to small groups of people.

Most of Tanguy's growing takes place in a 400-square-metre (4,300-square-foot) plot, just above the newly built, many-gabled house, which itself stands where there was once an inn. The soil in this intensively gardened rectangle was already good and fertile: Tanguy surmises that in times past it had served as a billet for cattle, horses and other animals, and that their manure had enriched the ground. It is massively productive, in the prettiest way: the rows of workaday cabbage and carrots are interspersed with cottage garden annuals and biennials. The gleaming flowers of calendula, mallow, cornflower, cosmos and hollyhock spangle the plot, while the bronze and yellow discs of sunflowers float above the

LEFT AND OVERLEAF Edible and ornamental plants, mingled together, flourish in the rich soil of Tanguy de Toulgoët's garden.

RIGHT Cornflowers attract pollinators and are 'good to give to your wife', says Tanguy; crimson clover provides nectar, and is also used as a cover crop to protect the soil.
OPPOSITE ABOVE Roses lean over walls, while waves of catmint wash across the ground.
OPPOSITE BELOW Phacelia acts both as a cover crop and as a nectar plant for Tanguy's bees.

drills of crops. Young cordons of apple trees loop through the space, beaded with the impossibly red and polished 'Katy' and the rosy, mottled 'Beauty of Bath'.

It all looks carefree and ingenuous, but its charm hides a system that is complicated and thoughtful. Tanguy gardens organically, using some biodynamic practices (such as rotating according to roots, leaves, fruits and flowers), and some traditional French techniques, taught to him when he was young by his grandparents' gamekeeper and gardener.

He is constantly vigilant, refining and adapting his strategies as he goes along. He pays minute attention to the rhythms and energies of nature: the movements of the sun and moon, the power of plants to heal or harm, the throb of the earth's life force. Although this may sound somewhat airy-fairy, his methodology is, in fact, intensely grounded in good sense and observation. The garden, for example, faces south-east – 'in the morning there is always some blue sky, so you get some heat that you wouldn't get otherwise' – and the crop rows run north–south so that they receive the most even light all day ('otherwise the plants at one end will be larger than those at the other'). The earth, he also explains, 'breathes in during the evening, and out during the morning'. This is a vivid description of the minuscule changes in pressure at either end of the day – it is lower in the evening and higher in the morning. Tanguy uses these fractions of millibars to the garden's advantage. In dry weather he hoes as night approaches, so that the exposed soil can draw in moisture from the cool air.

He is particular about his water use in the garden, and completely eschews tap water: it 'smells like a swimming pool' and is harmful to beneficial micro-organisms. Instead, a rainwater harvest system collects the run-off from the house and outbuilding roofs into a 8,000-litre (1,760-gallon) storage tank. Even with his own reserve, he waters rarely. His soil, carefully minded and fed with meticulously made, well-aged compost (cured in heaps 2 metres long and 1 metre wide – 6½ x 3¼ feet), is nutritious and water-retentive. 'You don't grow plants,' he says. 'You grow soil.' All the same, Tanguy is not averse to treating his crops with a range of home-made sprays and potions. In hot summers, he uses a concoction made from burdock, which helps the cells retain moisture. His knowledge of the properties of individual weeds is impressive. Those with strong root systems, such as dandelion, dock and thistle, are able to extract and store soil minerals that less brawny plants cannot access. Other commonly misunderstood and undervalued plants that offer up their hidden goodness in home-made sprays and feeds are comfrey, nettles, horsetail and yarrow. Garlic and lavender, meanwhile, may both be used to repel unwanted pests.

390 | THE IRISH GARDEN

Tanguy never puts manure, even well-rotted stuff, directly on to the soil, as he believes that it promotes too much growth too quickly. Instead, manure, and sometimes seaweed, are sent through the compost heap, so that they are melded into more complex and balanced provender for the soil. Time, he advises, is one of the most important ingredients in compost.

This County Laois French garden (well stocked with roses and herbs, of course) thrives on its diet of vintage compost and choice potions. The diversity of produce is wide, with many of the varieties being old cultivars from Tanguy's native land. They do well in this inland spot, where the climate is more continental than Irish, with hotter summers and colder winters than is the norm in most other parts of the island. The tiny, winey blackcurrant 'Noir de Bourgogne', which Tanguy uses to make his own *crème de cassis*, flourishes here, as do other French currants, including the translucent pink 'Gloire de Sablon'. Among his French apples are the centuries-old 'Patte de Loup', which has a a matt buckskin surface, curiously scarred – it used to be said – by the claws of wolves. Some of the apples grow in the main garden, while others are trained against the house and barn.

The site is also punctuated with fig, medlar, quince, plum and pear trees. On these last, fruits are trapped in bottles tied onto the branches. Introduced as fertilized flowers, they have magically swelled in their glass prisons, and are destined to flavour the pear liqueur, Poire William. In a polytunnel tucked into a sheltered corner, grape, kiwi and peach bear fruit, while melon vines climb upwards, heavy with the green-striated sandy orbs of the variety 'Cyrano'. This domed plastic enclosure is not just home to tender food crops such as aubergine, tomato, pepper, cucumber, squash and basil, it also acts as a place to dry and process seeds. Sheaves of brown and buff stalks, laden with pods and capsules, rustle gently in the breeze drifting through the polythene cocoon. On a shelf are jars and glasses of interesting yellow and pinkish gelatinous gloop – the innards of the tomatoes that Tanguy is fermenting in order to save their seed.

He likes heirloom tomatoes, for their old-fashioned flavour and eccentric looks. 'Voyage' is many-lobed and grotesque, not unlike a shiny red brain; the yellow and red 'Pineapple' is streaked and ruched; and 'Brown Berry', 'Yellow Pear', 'Red Pear' and 'Red Zebra' are all well named. 'Bloody Butcher' is one of the earliest tomatoes to ripen, and, because it is a potato-leaved variety, it is more resistant to blight, says Tanguy. Among the many others filling the tunnel with their sharp resinous scent are two from the Irish Seed Savers Association: 'Yellow Scotland' and the Russian 'Silver Fir Tree' – the latter so named because of its finely cut greyish foliage.

Back in the main garden, there are more tomatoes, each backed by a right-angled, terracotta roofing tile standing on its end. The warm clay reflects the heat back on to the plant, while also giving it shelter. Leafy vegetables do well here, the good soil and the 850 millimetres (33.5 inches) of rain per year – not especially high for Ireland – suit them. Besides cabbages and Brussels sprouts (both green and red) and kale ('Maribor', a highly ornamental pink-centred one), Tanguy grows several varieties of spinach (mostly old French kinds). There are plenty of saladings: rocket (both wild and cultivated), New Zealand spinach (*Tetragonia*), oriental leaves, and winter and summer purslane. He grows many lettuces, with the old French (despite its name) 'Frisée d'Amérique' being a favourite.

In fact, there isn't much that he doesn't grow. Think of any vegetable – turnip, kohl rabi, parsnip, leek, onion, sweetcorn, beans, beetroot, scorzonera perhaps? – and you are bound to find at least half a row (and usually more) of it here. Tanguy doesn't like to see unproductive ground: 'I don't leave empty spaces, so I don't get weeds.' Green manures, such as the highly structured, heraldic-looking, blue-tipped phacelia and the pink-tailed crimson clover, are planted as cover crops when the ground is not producing food. Preoccupied bees move between their nectar-rich flowers, creating a many-layered, thrumming accompaniment that is just right for this busy and beautiful garden.

OPPOSITE, CLOCKWISE FROM TOP LEFT A pear captured in a bottle – the resulting potion will be the liqueur Poire William; tomato seeds and pulp macerating in water, as part of the seed-saving process; a harvest basket including 'Potimarron' and 'Gemini' squash, 'Voyage' tomatoes, and 'Chinese Five Color' chilli peppers.

The Gardens: Contact Information

Some gardens are open by appointment only, so please check the website or contact the owner before planning a visit. Note: GPS coordinates are given in decimal degrees, not in minutes or seconds.

Airfield, Overend Way, Dundrum, Dublin 14; airfield.ie (53.288205, -6.237082)

Altamont, Bunclody Road, Tullow, Co Carlow; altamontgarden.com (52.734018, -6.723421)

Annes Grove, Castletownroche, Co Cork; annesgrovegardens.com (52.189641, -8.467762)

Antrim Castle, Randalstown Road, Antrim, Co Antrim, BT41 4LH; antrim.gov.uk/antrimcastlegardens (54.720605, -6.225006)

Ardcarraig, Oranswell, Bushypark, Co Galway; oranswell@eircom.net (53.303416, -9.120694)

Ballymaloe Cookery School, Shanagarry, Co Cork; cookingisfun.ie (51.860406, -8.033541)

Bantry House, Bantry, Co Cork; bantryhouse.com (51.678503, -9.463802)

The Bay Garden, Camolin, Co Wexford; thebaygarden.com (52.608664, -6.443644)

Belvedere House, Mullingar, Co Westmeath; belvedere-house.ie (53.477064, -7.353851)

Birr Castle, Birr, Co Offaly; birrcastle.com (53.096202, -7.91416)

June Blake's Garden, Tinode, Blessington, Co Wicklow; juneblake.ie (53.21179, -6.484576)

Blarney Castle, Blarney, Co Cork; blarneycastle.ie (51.931459, -8.568803)

Botanic Gardens (Tropical Ravine and Palm House) Belfast, College Park, Botanic Avenue, Belfast, BT7 1LP; belfastcity.gov.uk (54.581116, -5.928436)

Caher Bridge Garden, Fermoyle West, Fanore, Co Clare; caherbridgegarden@gmail.com; tel: + 353 (0)65 707 6225 (53.118651, -9.25109)

Corke Lodge, Woodbrook, Bray, Co Wicklow; corkelodge.com (53.2163, -6.119537)

Derreen, Lauragh, Kenmare, Co Kerry; tel: + 353 (0)64 6683588; (51.765582, -9.77492)

The Dillon Garden, 45 Sandford Road, Ranelagh, Dublin 6; dillongarden.com (53.321486, -6.24694)

Drishane House, Castletownshend, Co Cork; drishane.com (51.527576, -9.180516)

Dunmore Country School, Swan Road, Durrow, Co Laois; dunmorecountryschool.ie (52.857944, -7.401193)

Carmel Duignan, 21 Library Road, Shankill, Co Dublin; dublingardens.com (53.234132, -6.127158)

Emo Court, Emo, Co Laois; heritageireland.ie (53.10616, -7.201413)

Farmleigh, Castleknock, Dublin 15; farmleigh.ie (53.366661, -6.36231)

Florence Court, Enniskillen, Co Fermanagh, BT92 1FN; nationaltrust.org.uk/florence-court (54.262605, -7.717532)

Fota House, Arboretum and Gardens, Fota Island, Carrigtwohill, Co Cork; fotahouse.com (51.889818, -8.303651)

Glebe Gardens, Baltimore, Co Cork; glebegardens.com (51.48439, -9.360913)

Glenarm Castle, Glenarm, Ballymena, Co Antrim, BT44 0BQ; glenarmcastle.com (54.968672, -5.95633)

Glenveagh Castle Gardens, Glenveagh National Park, Churchill, Letterkenny, Co Donegal; glenveaghnationalpark.ie (55.053049, -7.93448)

Glin Castle, Glin, Co Limerick; olda.fitzgerald@icloud.com; tel + 353 (0)87 2383883 (52.568904, -9.287141)

Heywood Gardens, Ballinakill, Co Laois; heritageireland.ie (52.889098, -7.308722)

Hunting Brook Gardens, Lamb Hill, Blessington, Co Wicklow; huntingbrook.com (53.220259, -6.486993)

Ilnacullin (Garinish Island), Glengariff, Bantry, Co Cork; heritageireland.ie (ferry: 51.74967, -9.542748)

The Japanese Gardens, Tully, Co Kildare; irishnationalstud.ie (53.144118,-6.900648)

Kells Bay Gardens, Kells, Co Kerry; kellsgardens.ie (52.022105, -10.102274)

Kilfane Glen and Waterfall, Stoneen, Thomastown, Co Kilkenny; kilfane.com (52.553081, -7.088096)

Killruddery, Southern Cross Road, Bray, Co Wicklow; killruddery.com (53.185773, -6.1023)

Kylemore Abbey, Kylemore, Connemara, Co Galway; kylemoreabbeytourism.ie (53.558309, -9.890486)

Lakemount, Barnavara Hill, Glanmire, Co Cork; lakemountgarden.com (51.92484, -8.406001)

Lakeview, Mullagh, Co Cavan; daphnelevingeshackleton.com (53.814424, -6.978702)

Larchill Arcadian Garden, Kilcock, Co Kildare; larchill.ie (53.441334, -6.655597)

Lismore Castle, Lismore, Co Waterford; lismorecastlegardens.com (52.138203, -7.932736)

Lissadell, Ballinfull, Co Sligo; lissadellhouse.com (54.344063, -8.577772)

National Botanic Gardens, Glasnevin, Dublin 9; botanicgardens.ie; (53.371722, -6.269396)

National Botanic Gardens, Kilmacurragh, Kilbride, Co Wicklow; botanicgardens.ie (52.934168,-6.152476)

Mount Congreve, Kilmeaden, Co Waterford; mountcongreve.com (52.237605, -7.212444)

Mount Stewart, Portaferry Road, Newtownards, Co Down, BT22 2AD; nationaltrust.org.uk/mount-stewart (54.549106, -5.596259)

Mount Usher Gardens, Ashford, Co Wicklow; mountushergardens.ie (53.008638, -6.108101)

Oakfield Park, Raphoe, Co Donegal; oakfieldpark.com (54.877483, -7.574905)

Phoenix Park (Victorian Walled Kitchen Garden), Dublin 8; phoenixpark.ie (53.364664, -6.331453)

Powerscourt Gardens, Enniskerry, Co Wicklow; powerscourt.com (53.185514,-6.186714)

Rathmichael Lodge, Ballybride Road, Shankill, Co Dublin; dublingardens.com (53.232104, -6.135468)

Rowallane Garden, Saintfield, Co Down, BT24 7LH; nationaltrust.org.uk/rowallane-garden (54.452252, -5.823315)

Royal Hospital (The Master's Garden), Military Road, Kilmainham, Dublin 8; heritageireland.ie (53.342622, -6.301456)

Salthill Gardens, Mountcharles, Co Donegal; donegalgardens.com (54.631518, -8.210898)

Talbot Botanic Gardens, Malahide Castle, Malahide, Co Dublin; malahidecastleandgardens.ie (53.443427, -6.163503)

Tullynally Castle, Castlepollard, Co Westmeath; tullynallycastle.ie (53.68461, -7.315957)

Warble Bank, Newtownmountkennedy, Co Wicklow; warblebank@yahoo.ie; tel: + 353 (0)1 2819298 (53.086157, -6.105771)

Woodstock Gardens and Arboretum, Inistioge, Co Kilkenny; woodstock.ie (52.484766, -7.068761)

Selected Bibliography and Sources

Jonathan Bell & Mervyn Watson, *Rooted in the Soil: A history of cottage gardens and allotments in Ireland since 1750*, Four Courts Press, 2012

Patricia Butler and Mary Davies, *Wicklow through the Artist's Eye: An Exploration of County Wicklow's Historic Gardens c. 1660 – c. 1960*, Wordwell, 2014

Sybil Connolly and Helen Dillon (eds), *In an Irish Garden*, Weidenfeld & Nicolson, 1986

Vandra Costello, *Irish Demesne Landscapes: 1660–1740*, Four Courts Press, 2015

Nigel Everett, *Wild Gardens: The Lost Demesnes of Bantry Bay*, Hafod Press, 2000

Aubrey Fennell, *Heritage Trees of Ireland*, The Collins Press, 2013

Olda Fitzgerald, *Irish Gardens*, Conran Octopus, 1999

James Howley, *The Follies and Garden Buildings of Ireland*, Yale University Press, 1993

Keith Lamb and Patrick Bowe, *A History of Gardening in Ireland*, The Stationery Office for the National Botanic Gardens, Glasnevin, 1995

Shirley Lanigan, *The 100 Best Gardens in Ireland*, Liberties Press, 2011

Samuel Lewis, *A Topgraphical Dictionary of Ireland*, S. Lewis & Co., 1837

Edward Malins and Patrick Bowe, *Irish Gardens and Demesnes from 1830*, Barrie & Jenkins, 1980

Edward Malins and The Knight of Glin, *Lost Demesnes*, Barrie & Jenkins, 1976

E. Charles Nelson, *A Heritage of Beauty: The Garden Plants of Ireland, An Illustrated Encyclopaedia*, Irish Garden Plant Society, 2000

Viscount Powerscourt, *A Description and History of Powerscourt*, Mitchell and Hughes, 1903

Terence Reeves-Smyth, *Irish Gardens and Gardening Before Cromwell*, The Barryscourt Trust, in association with Cork County Council and Gandon Editions, 1999

E.H. Walpole (compiler), *Mount Usher: 1868–1952: a short history of the origin and development of the gardens*, privately published by E.H. Walpole, 1952

Arthur Young, *A Tour in Ireland, 1776–1779*, Cassell & Company, 1887

Periodicals and Newspapers

The Belfast Telegraph; *Curtis's Botanical Magazine*; *The Gardeners' Chronicle*; *History Ireland*; *International Dendrology Society Yearbook*; *The Irish Arts Review*; *The Irish Garden*; *Irish Gardening*; *Irish Historical Studies*; *The Irish Times*; *Journal of Enniskerry and Powerscourt Local History*; *The Journal of Horticulture and Cottage Gardener*; *Moorea: The Journal of the Irish Garden Plant Society*; *The Spectator*; *The Transactions of the Royal Irish Academy*

Websites

archiseek.com: online magazine of Irish architecture
buildingsofireland.ie: National Inventory of Architectural Heritage
dia.ie: Irish Architectural Archive, Dictionary of Irish Architects, 1720–1940
dib.cambridge.org: Dictionary of Irish Biography (Royal Irish Academy)
downsurvey.tcd.ie: The Down Survey of Ireland
landedestates.nuigalway.ie: Landed Estates Database, Moore Institute, National University of Ireland, Galway.
lordbelmontinnorthernireland.blogspot.ie: Lord Belmont in Northern Ireland
treeregister.org: The Tree Register

A more complete list of sources can be found at onebeanrow.com

Index

Page numbers in **bold** refer to captions of illustrations.

Acton family *see* National Botanic Gardens (Kilmacurragh)
Acton, Janet **215**, 220, 222, 224
Acton, Lieut-Col. William 217, 220
Acton, Thomas 220, 224, **224**
Acton, Thomas II 217
Adair, Cornelia (*née* Ritchie) 142–4, 146, **146**, 149, 153
Adair, John George 112, 144
Addison, Joseph 263
Airfield, Dundrum, Co Dublin 11, **11**
Alexander, Billy *see* Kells Bay House and Garden; *see also* 329
Allen, Darina 371–3, 375
Allen, Ivan 372
Allen, Myrtle 372, 373
Allen, Tim 372–3, 375
allotments 366–8
alpine plants 101, 139, 169, **169**, 258, 271
Alston, Rod 368
Altamont, Co Carlow 10, 85, 90–5, **90**, **93**, **94**
Anglo-Dutch influence 18, 217, 220
Annes Grove, Co Cork 85–6, **85**
Annesley, Hugh, 5th Earl 86, 135
Annesley, Patrick and Jane 85
Annesley, Priscilla Cecilia, Countess (*née* Moore) 135–6
Annesley, Richard Grove 85–6
Annesley, William Richard, 4th Earl 135
Antrim Castle, Co Antrim 18, **19**
Antrim, Earls of 355
Antrim, Louisa, Countess of 357
arboreta, significant *see* Altamont, Birr Castle, Fota, Killruddery, Mount Congreve, Mount Stewart, Mount Usher, National Botanic Gardens (Glasnevin), National Botanic Gardens (Kilmacurragh), Powerscourt, Rowallane, Talbot Botanic Gardens, Tullynally Castle, Woodstock
Ardcarraig, Co Galway 280, 320–5, **320**, **322**, **325**
Ashdown Lodge, Dublin 366
Ashlin, George Coppinger 287
avenues, beech 62, 92, **93**, 288; lime 18, **19**, 62, 72, 73; monkey puzzle (*Araucaria*) **69**, **203**, 206, 224; noble fir (*Abies procera*) 206, **206**; oak 209, **209**, 217–20, **220**, **348**, 349; rhododendron **215**, 222 ; Wellingtonia (*Sequoiadendron*) 200–1, **201**; yew 53, **81**, 90, 211, 217, 231, 263, **263**

Avoca company 101
Awbeg, River 85–6, **85**
azalea, significant collections 42, **102**, 103, 139, 153, 162, 325

Bald, William 355
Ballawley nursery, Dundrum, Co Dublin 95
Ballymaloe Cookery School, Co Cork **367**, 371–5, **371**, **373**, **375**
Baltimore, Co Cork: sack of (1631) 376
bamboo 85, **85**, 143, 185, 232, 254, 275, 346
Bann, River 309
Bantry Bay, Co Cork 26, **27**
Bantry House, Co Cork 10, 14, **14**, 24–32, **24**, **27**, **30**, **33**
Bantry, Earls of 24, 26
Bantry, Mary, Countess of (*née* O'Brien) 26
Bantry, Richard White, 2nd Earl of (*earlier* Viscount Berehaven) 24, 26, 32
Barbezat & Cie (foundry) 73, **76**, 78
Barry, Arthur Hugh 198
Barry, James Hugh 198
Barry, John Smith 198
Bay Garden, the, Co Wexford 280, 308–14, **309**, **310**, **315**
Beattie, Thomas 39
Beaumont, Rex 242
bedding-out 40, **65**, **124**, 126, **131**, 133
Bede, Venerable 8
Beech Park, Co Dublin 281
Belfast Botanic and Horticultural Company (Limited) 276
Bell, Dorothy 198
Beloeil, Château de, Belgium 48
Belvedere House, Co Westmeath 59, 228, **228**, 238–42, **238**, **240**, **243**
Belvidere, George Augustus Rochfort, 2nd Earl of 242
Belvidere, Mary, Countess of (*née* Molesworth) 240, 242
Belvidere, Robert Rochfort, 1st Earl of (*earlier* 1st Baron and Viscount Belfield) 228, 238, 240, 242, **243**
Benedict, Sister 125
Benglis, Linda **339**, 340
biodynamic gardening 388
Birr Castle, Co Offaly 14, **16**, 47–57, **47**, **49**, **53**, **54**, **55**, **57**, 139, 329; telescope ('Leviathan') 48, **49**
Blackmore and Langdon (of Bristol) 181
Blackwater, River 228
Blake, Jimi *see* Hunting Brook; *see also* 157

Blake, June *see* June Blake's Garden; *see also* 184;
Blake, Kathleen 297
Blarney Castle, Co Cork 232, **232**, 234
Blennerhassett, Rowland 345–6
Blennerhassett, Rowland Ponsonby 345
Blennerhassett, Sir Rowland 345
Bolas, Thomas 44
Bonnet (Bonet or Bonel; Huguenot) 71
Borror, Dawson 90, 95
Botanic Gardens, Belfast 228, 275–6, **275**, **276**
Bowe, Paddy 236
Boyle, Robert 228
Brabazon family 71, 81
Broomfield, Assumpta 95
Brown Envelope Seeds 368
Bruce, Maye E. 44
Bruger, Walter 144, 153
Bryce, John Annan 113, 129–31, 133
Bryce, Roland L'Estrange 133
Bryce, Violet (*née* L'Estrange) 113, 129–31, 133
Budina, Charles (or Karl) 216–17
Burbidge, Frederick William 221, 224, 275
Burn, William 80
Burren, the, Co Clare 112, **113**, 115, **115**, **116**, 120
Burscough, William, Bishop of Limerick 332
Bushe, Henry Amias 246

Caha Mountains, Co Cork 26, **129**, 130, **132**, 133
Caher Bridge Garden, Co Clare **113**, 115–20, **115**, **121**
Caher River 120, **121**
canals *see* water
Carey, Dermot 366
Carteret, John, 2nd Baron (*later* Earl Granville) 332
cascades *see* water
Cassidy, Constance 366
Castle, Richard 59, 238, 242
Castlereagh, Robert Stewart, Viscount *see* Londonderry, 2nd Marquess of
Castlewellan, Co Down 86, 135, 136
Chamberlain, Sir Neville 351
Chaplin, Sir Henry 39
Cholmeley-Harrison, Major Cholmeley Dering 200
Church Strand Bay, Co Cork **376**
Churchill, Sir Winston 36, 39
Clark, Eithne **118**
Clifden, Co Galway 125
Clive, Robert, 1st Baron 246

Cochrane, Alfred, *see* Corke Lodge; *see also* 228
Cochrane, Sir Stanley 251
Cogan, William Henry Ford 287
Colthurst, Sir Charles 232
Condell, Anne *see* Warble Bank
Congreve, Ambrose *see* Mount Congreve, *see also* 157
conifers, significant collections *see* Mount Usher, National Botanic Gardens (Kilmacurragh), Powerscourt, Woodstock; *see also* **199**, 234, 264
Connolly, Sybil 246
Conolly's Folly, Castletown, Co Kildare 10
cordyline, in Irish gardens 8, **9**, 98, **113**, **251**, 254
Cork, Richard Boyle, 1st Earl of 228
Corke Lodge, Co Wicklow 250–4, **251**, **252**
Corrib, Lough 322
Costello, Vandra: *Irish Demesne Landscapes, 1660–1740* 72
Costin, John Joe 296
cottages ornés 228, 245, **245**
Cotterell, Revd William (*later* Bishop of Ferns and Leighlin) 332
Cowan, John 125
Croaghan Hill, Co Donegal 330
Cross, Brian and Rose *see* Lakemount; *see also* 280
Cross, H.G. 172
Cross, Peggy 317
Crowther, William 221
cultivars, Irish: bulbs 172, **217**; herbaceous 95, 137, **149**, 159, 185, **188**, 283, **294**, 296, **296**, 297; woody **9**, **53**, 105, 137, **149**, 175, 222, **222**; *see also* yew, Irish
Cunningham, Barbara 167
Curtis, Winifred: *Endemic Flora of Tasmania* (illus. Margaret Stones) 167
Cutler, Paul 95

Daisy Hill Nursery, Newry 136
Dangan Castle, Co Kildare 236
de Valera, Éamon 217
Defoe, Daniel: *Robinson Crusoe* 347
Delaney, John 205
de Las Casas, Micheal and Louisa 234, 236
de Toulgoët, Isabelle 385
de Toulgoët, Tanguy *see* Dunmore Country School
Derreen, Co Kerry 10, 87–8, **88**
Devonshire, Charlotte, Duchess of (*née* Boyle) 228
Devonshire, Dukes of 228, 332
Devonshire, William Cavendish, 4th Duke of 228–31
Devonshire, William George Spencer Cavendish, 6th Duke of 231
Diamond Hill, Co Galway 125

Dicksonia Direct nursery 346
Dillon Garden, Dublin **156**, 175–82, **175**, **176**, **180**, **182**
Dillon, Helen *see* Dillon Garden; *see also* 95, 157
Dillon, Julie 175
Dillon, Val 175
Donegal Bay 280, 301, **301**, **307**
Dool, Herman 165
Dorrien Smith, Commander Tom 168
Doughruagh Mountain, Galway 125
Douglas, David 203
Down Survey (Ireland) 72, 87
Drake, Sir Francis 366
Drishane House, Co Cork **85**, 86–7, **87**
Druery, Charles T. 275–6
Duignan, Carmel **9**, **156**, 158–9
Duncan, Brian 172
Dunluce, Aurora, Viscountess 355, 362
Dunluce, Randal McDonnell, Viscount 355, 357, 362
Dunmore Country School, Co Laois 385–91, **385**, **388**, **391**
Dunn, Malcolm 65
Dunrobin Castle, Scotland 38

Edgeworth, Maria 213
Eida, Saburo 257, **258**, 261
Emo Court, Co Laois 199–201, **201**
Ennell, Lough, Co Westmeath 238, 242
Enniskillen, William Willoughby Cole, 1st Earl of 231
eucalyptus, significant 37, **102**, 103, 172
European Union Cultural Commission 248
Evelyn, John 211; *Sylva* 339
Exbury, Hampshire 161

famine *see* Great Famine
Fanore, Co Clare 115
Farmleigh, Phoenix Park, Dublin 18, 20, **20**, 22, **23**
Farren, Daragh 73
Farrer, Reginald **9**
Fawkes, Ernest 125
ferme ornée 234, 236, **236**
ferneries *see* Botanic Gardens, Belfast; *see also* 53, 54, 199, **199**, 232, **232**
Fernhill, Co Dublin 11
Fiachra, Saint *see* Saint Fiachra'a Garden; *see also* 385
Finnegan, Lorna 26
Fish, Margery 120
Fish, R. 8–9
FitzGerald, Catherine 197, 362, **362**
FitzGerald, Desmond, 29th Knight of Glin 197
FitzGerald, John Frauncels, 25th Knight of Glin 195, **195**, 197
FitzGerald, Olda (*née* Willes) 197

Florence Court, Co Fermanagh 231, **231**
Foerster, Karl 181
follies *see* Belvedere, Larchill Arcadian Garden; *see also* 10, **10**, **96**, 197, 228, **228**, 232, **232**, 331, 351, 352, **353**
Forde, Noel 20
Forrest, George 136
Fota House, Fota Island, Co Cork 197–9, **199**, 264
fountains *see* water
Fownes, Sir William 203
French influence *see* Antrim Castle, Dunmore Country School, Killruddery, Master's Garden (Royal Hospital)
French, Percy 332
Fuller, James Franklin 123

Gandon, James 199, **201**, 351
Gardeners' Chronicle 8, 88, 201, 206, 221, 224, 242, 258, 264, 275
Garinish Island *see* Ilnacullin
Garnier, James 125
Gathorne-Hardy, Captain Geoffrey 143
Gayer, Dr Arthur E. 264
Geiss of Berne (company) **76**
Giambologna (born Jean Boulogne) 131
Gillespie, Sean 305
GIY (Grow It Yourself) Ireland 368
Glasnevin, Dublin *see* National Botanic Gardens, Glasnevin
glasshouses *see* Botanic Gardens, Belfast, National Botanic Gardens (Glasnevin), Talbot Botanic Gardens; *see also* 22, 53, 113, **124**, 125, 126, **180**, 182, 204–5, **205**, 211, 228, 337, 356, **356**, 371, 372, **373**
Glebe Gardens, Co Cork 376–82, **376**, **379**, **380**, **381**, **383**
Glenarm Castle, Co Antrim **328**, 329, 354–63, **355**, **356**, **358**, **362**, **363**
Glendalough House, Co Wicklow **251**, 254
Glenveagh Castle, Co Donegal 112, **113**, 142–53, **143**, **145**, **146**, **148**, **151**, **152**
Glin Castle, Co Limerick 195, **195**, **196**, 197
Glin, Knights of *see* FitzGerald
Gohlke, Anja 126
Gore-Booth family 366
Gormley, Antony: *Learning to Be I* (sculpture) **228**, 231
grasses 4, **158**, 159, 187, **188**, 270, 289, 310, 311, 314, 317, **317**
Great Gardens of Ireland Restoration Scheme 126, 236, 329
Great Famine (1845–50) 264; famine relief projects 10
Great Sugar Loaf mountain, Co Wicklow **11**, 59, **59**, 63

grottoes (and hermitages) 62, 67, 248, 275, 195, **196**, 197
Guinness, Mariga (*née* Princess Marie Gabrielle of Urach) 53

ha-has 73
Hagen, Hugo **64**
Hall-Walker, Colonel William 257–8, **257**, 261
Hall, Mr & Mrs S.C.: *Handbooks for Ireland* 69
Hallinan, Martin 261, **261**
Harrison, Miss S.C. 367
Hawkins, Sir John 366
Hayes, Anita 368
Headford, Co Meath 264
hedges, architectural 41, **41**, 45, 48, **53**, 78, **79**, 80, 81, 211, 288, **296**, 298, 357, **358**, 359, 362
Heffernan, Sean 101
Henry Doubleday Research Association 382
Henry, Augustine 48, 288
Henry, Margaret 123, 125
Henry, Mitchell 112, **113**, 123, 125–6
herbaceous borders, notable 67–9, **69**, 94, 95, **124**, 125, 126, 205, **205**, **356**, 357, **358**, 359, 366, 372, **373**
Herbert, Henry Arthur 343
hermitages *see* grottoes
Hewat, Corinne and Richard *see* Rathmichael Lodge
Heywood, Co Laois **328**, 329, 351–3, **351**, **352**
Hoche, General Lazare 26
Hodson, Sir George 80, **81**
Hooker, Sir Joseph **220**, 221
hosta, collections **118**, 309, 314, 325
Howard-Bury, Lieut-Col. Charles Kenneth 242
Howe, James 62
Howley, James: *The Follies and Garden Buildings of Ireland* 236
Hunting Brook, near Blessington, Co Wicklow **156**, 157, 184–90, **185**, **187**, **188**, **191**
Hurricane Charley (1986) 245, 248

Iford Manor, Wiltshire 129
Ilnacullin (or Garinish Island), Co Cork 113, **113**, 129–33, **129**, **131**, **132**
Imokilly Orchards (company) 372
International Conifer Conservation Programme 217
invasive species 146; *Rhododendron ponticum* 142, 146, 245
Ireland: British influence in 10; climate 8–11, 48; economic/political conditions 11
Irish Arts Review yearbook (2001) 353
Irish Gardening 98, 261
Irish Museum of Modern Art, Dublin *see* Royal Hospital, Kilmainham, Dublin 339
Irish Reform Association 351

Irish Seed Savers Association 368, 391
Irish Times 217, 257, 261, 351, 372
Italian influence *see* Bantry House, Ilnacullin, Mount Stewart, Powerscourt
Iveagh, Edward Cecil Guinness, 1st Earl of 18
Iveagh, Gwendolen, Countess of (*née* Onslow) 22
Iveagh, Miranda, Countess of (*née* Smiley) 20

Jackson, Philip: *Reading Chaucer* (sculpture) **336**, 337
Japanese Gardens, the, Co Kildare 228, 257–61, **257**, **261**
Jay, Madelaine 98, 101, 105
Jebb, Dr Matthew 263
Jeffereyes, James St John 232
Jekyll, Gertrude 44, 353
Journal of Horticulture and Cottage Gardener 8, 205–6
Jullian, Philippe 149
June Blake's Garden 280, 286–98, **287**, **289**, **292**, **294**, **296**, **298**

Kahl of Potsdam (company) **77**
Kells Bay House and Garden, Co Kerry **328**, 329, 343–9, **343**, **345**, **347**, **348**
Kelly, Michael 368
Kenmare River 87
Kerry, Ring of 329, 343–5
Kilbride, Co Wicklow *see* National Botanic Gardens, Kilmacurragh
Kilfane Glen and Waterfall, Co Kilkenny 228, 245–8, **245**, **247**, **249**
Killarney 343
Killiney Hill, Co Dublin 10, **11**
Killiskey River 108
Killruddery House, Co Wicklow **14**, 16, 18, 71–81, **71**, **73**, **74**, **76**, **79**, **80**, **81**, 329, 340
Kilmacurragh, Co Wicklow *see* National Botanic Gardens, Kilmacurragh
Kilmakilloge Harbour, Co Kerry 87
King, Brian 22, **23**
King, James, Dean of Raphoe 332
Kingdon-Ward, Frank 48, 86, 136
Kirk, John 272
kitchen gardens *see* Ballymaloe Cookery School, Dunmore Country School, Glebe Gardens; *see also* **113**, 127, **127**, 146–9, 284, **284**, 357, **357**, 366–9
Kylemore Abbey, Co Galway 112, **113**, 123–6, **123**, **124**, **127**

Laitenberger, Klaus 366
Lakemount, Co Cork 280, 316–18, **316**, **319**
lakes, ornamental *see* water
Lakeview, Co Cavan 280–1, **281**, 283
Lambert, Jill 363, **363**

landforms 18, **19**, 22, **23**, 292, **328**, 334, **362**, 363
Lanne, William 221
Lansdowne, Henry Petty-Fitzmaurice, 5th Marquess of 87–8
Lanyon, Charles 276
Larchill Arcadian Garden, Co Kildare 234, **235**, 236, **236**
Larkcom, Joy 368, **369**
le Nôtre, André 71
le Poer family 59
Lecky Watson family 90, 92
Leigh-White, Edward 32
Leitrim, Charles Clements, 5th Earl and Anne Mary, Countess of (*née* Vanneck) 144
Lemoine, Victor 378
Lennox-Boyd, Arabella 11
Lindley, John 201
Lismore Castle, Co. Waterford 10, 228, **228**, 231, **231**
Lissadell-Langford Collection of Heritage Potatoes 366
Lissadell, Co Sligo 11, 328–9, 366, **369**
Little Sugar Loaf mountain, Co Wicklow 73, 74
Lobb, William 200, **203**, 206, 220–1, **220**, 224
Londonderry, Charles Stewart, 3rd Marquess of 36
Londonderry, Charles Vane-Tempest-Stewart, 7th Marquess of 34, 36–7, 39
Londonderry, Edith, Marchioness of (*née* Chaplin) *see* Mount Stewart; *see also* 14
Londonderry, Frances Anne, Marchioness of (*née* Vane-Tempest) 36
Londonderry, Robert Stewart, 1st Marquess of 36, **44**
Londonderry, Robert Stewart, 2nd Marquess of (Viscount Castlereagh) 36
Londonderry, Theresa, Marchioness of (*née* Chetwynd-Talbot) 37–8
Longford, Earls of (Pakenham family) **209**
Loudon, John Claudius 211; *An Encyclopaedia of Gardening* 10, 366
Ludlow, Edmund 115
Lutyens, Sir Edwin **328**, **351**, **352**, 353

MacDonald, Frances and Iain *see* Bay Garden; *see also* 280
MacDonnell (McDonnell) clan 355
Macgillicuddy Reeks (mountains), Co Kerry 343
Mackenzie, Murdo 133
MacMahon, Lorna *see* Ardcarraig; *see also* 280
Magan family 253
magnolia, significant collections *see* Birr Castle, Glenveagh, Mount Congreve, Mount Usher, National Botanic Gardens (Kilmacurragh), Rowallane
Maguire, Ned 292

Malahide Castle, Co Dublin 157, 167–72, **167, 169, 171, 172**
Malahide, Milo Talbot, 7th Baron 157, 167–70, 172
Manchester, William Angus Drogo Montagu, 9th Duke of 125
Mapas, John **11**
maples (*Acer*), significant collections 93, 97, 101, 105, 139, 163, 164, 211, **213**, 323, **325**, 337
Markievicz, Constance, Countess (*née* Gore-Booth) 366
Marlay, Charles Brinsley 242
Marlfield Nurseries, Co Dublin 323
Marshall, Nigel 359
Martin, Violet ('Martin Ross') 87
Massereene, Clotworthy Skeffington, 3rd Viscount 18
Massereene, John Skeffington, 2nd Viscount 18
Maxwell, Reg 362
Maxwell, Sir Herbert 34
maze 372
McConnellogue, Mark 337
McCrum, Bridget: *Poised bird* (sculpture) 231; *Hunting* (sculpture) 231, **231**
McDonald, Charles (head gardener, Woodstock) 8, 205–6
McDonnell, Revd Joseph, SJ 367
McIlhenny, Henry **113**, 143–6, **145**, 153
McKeever, Madeline 368
McKimm, Charles 275
meadows, pictorial **11**
meadows, wildflower 4, 48, 73, 120, 137, 190, **195**, 213, 216, **217**, 280–1, **281**, 301, **301**, 331, 372, 382, **383**
Meath, Captain Edward Brabazon, 4th Earl of 72, 340
Meath, Earls of 340
Meath, Harriot, Countess of (*née* Brooke) 80
Meath, John Anthony, 15th Earl of ('Jack') 71, 74, 81
Meath, John Chambré Brabazon, 10th Earl of 79
Meath, William Brabazon, 11th Earl of 80
Meath, William Brabazon, 1st Earl of 71
Menzies, Archibald 206
Meredith, Jane 353
Messel, Lieut-Col. Leonard 48
Millard, F.W. 101, 103
Miller, Robert 95
Milligan, Averil 139
Molesworth, Richard, 3rd Viscount 240
Moore family, of Glasnevin 86
Moore, Dr David 220–1, 263–4, 269
Moore, Hugh Armytage 112, 136–7, 139
Moore, Phylis, Lady 136

Moore, Revd John Robert 112, 135, **135**, 136, 139
Moore, Sir Frederick 92, 98, 136, 220, **223**, 264–5
Morrison, Richard 79
Morrison, William Vitruvius 79
Moryson, Fynes 366
Mosse, Nicholas and Susan 245–8
Mount Congreve, Co Waterford **156**, 157, 161–5, **161, 163**, 325
Mount Stewart, Co Down 14, **16**, 34–45, **34, 36, 39, 40, 42, 44**, 359
Mount Usher, Co Wicklow 85, 97–108, **97, 98, 100, 102, 104, 105**, 264
Muckross House, Co Kerry 343
Mulcahy, Sean 247
Mullagh Lake, Co Cavan 280
Murphy, Michael 165

Nash, David: *Three Lismore Columns* (sculpture) 231, **231**
National Botanic Gardens, Glasnevin, Dublin 8, 98, 133, 136, 220, **223**, 228, 263–73, **263, 265, 269, 270, 272**; Central China Expedition (2004) 224
National Botanic Gardens, Kilmacurragh, Co Wicklow 9, **195**, 195, 215–25, **215, 217**, 220, **223**, 264
National Trust 34, 36, 48, 53, 112, 137, 231
native plants *see* Caher Bridge Garden; *see also* 54
Nevill, Jacob 286
New Naturalism *see* Hunting Brook, June Blake's Garden; *see also* 4, **310**, 311–4
Nore, River 203
North, Corona (*née* Lecky Watson) 92–3, **93, 94**, 95
North, Garry 95
Nymans, West Sussex 48, 53

Ó Gaoithín, Seán 142, 146, **152**, 153
O'Brien, Seamus 159, 217, 221–2
O'Connell, Eilis: *Over and Under* (sculpture) 231, **231**; *Wrapt* (sculpture) 231
O'Donohue, John 297, **298**
O'Donovan, Eileen 371
O'Regan, David 198
O'Regan, Thaddeus 378, 382
Oakfield Park, Co Donegal 328–9, **328**, 330–7, **331, 333, 334**
Office of Public Works 18, 95, 145, 198, 216, 339, 366
orangeries 80, **81**, 149, 198, **199**, 351, **352**
orchards 22, 81, **85**, 247, **249**, 283, **362**, 369, 372, 391
orchids, tropical, breeding 264
Organic Centre, Leitrim 368
Organic Growers' Association 378

Ormonde, James Butler, 1st Duke of 339
Oxmantown, Anna Lin, Lady (*née* Xiaojing) 57
Oxmantown, Patrick Parsons, Lord 57

Paine, W.H. 259
Pakenham, Henry 211
Pakenham, Thomas *see* Tullynally Castle; *see also* 195
Pakenham, Valerie 209
Parsons family *see* Rosse, Earls of 465
Parsons, Sir Laurence 47
parterres 24, **24**, 38, 48, **79**, 80, 172, 251, 336, **336**, 339
Peace, Carol **336**, 337
Pearce, Edward Lovett 353
Penn, Sir William 372
Penn, William 372
Penrose, Francis Cranmer 64, **65**
perennial planting style *see* New Naturalism
Perry, Jean and Peter *see* Glebe Gardens
pet cemetery 67
Peto, Harold 113, 129–31, 133
Petty, Sir William 72, 87
Phepotstown, Co Kildare 234
Phoenix Park, Dublin 366, **367**
Plant Heritage 54
Poë, Colonel Sir (William) Hutcheson 351, 353
Poë, Mary Adelaide, Lady (*née* Domvile) 351
Pollard, Don 368
polytunnels 297, **381**, 382, 391
pools, formal *see* water
Portarlington, John Dawson, 1st Earl of 200
Porteous, Neil 42
Porter, Arthur Kingsley 143
Porter, Lucy 143
potato: blight 264; introduced to Ireland 366
potatoes, collection 366
Power family (of Kilfane) 246
Power, Captain Sir John 246, 248
Power, Harriet, Lady (*née* Bushe) 246, 248
Power, Richard 246
Power, Seamus and David 204
Powerscourt, Co Wicklow 10, **11**, 16, **16**, 59–69, **59, 63, 65, 66, 69**
Powerscourt, Mervyn Patrick Wingfield, 9th Viscount 59
Powerscourt, Mervyn Richard Wingfield, 8th Viscount 67
Powerscourt, Mervyn Wingfield, 7th Viscount 59, 62–5, **64**, 67, 69; *A Description and History of Powerscourt* 62
Powerscourt, Richard Wingfield, 1st Viscount 59, 62, 67
Powerscourt, Richard Wingfield, 6th Viscount 59, 62, 64, **64**, 79

Pratt family 101
Prentice family 234, 236
Pye, William: *Vessel* (sculpture) 247

Raleigh, Sir Walter 366
Raphoe, Co Donegal: deanery 332
Rathmichael Lodge, Co Dublin 283–4, **284**
Rauch, Christian Daniel **64**
Reynolds, Jim 245, 375
Reynolds, Mary 22, **23**
Reynolds, Sir Joshua 332
rhododendrons, Himalayan *see* Annes Grove, Glenveagh, Mount Congreve Mount Stewart, Mount Usher, National Botanic Gardens (Kilmacurragh), Powerscourt, Rowallane
Richmond, Charles Lennox, 4th Duke of 204
Ritchie, Montgomery Wadsworth 143
river gardens *see* water
Roberts, Samuel Ussher 123, 125
Robertson, Alexander 62, 65
Robertson, Daniel 16, 62, 79, **81**
Robertson, William 246
Robinson, Sir Gerry and Heather, Lady *see* Oakfield Park
Robinson, Sir William (architect) 215
Robinson, Sir William (gardener) 98, 105, 264–5, 271, 346; *The English Flower Garden* 98
Rochfort House *see* Tudenham Park
Rochfort, Arthur 240, 242
Rochfort, George 242
Rochfort, Mary *see* Belvidere, Mary, Countess of
Rocque, John 62
Rollisson, Messrs (nursery, Tooting) 221
Roper, Lanning 20, 22, 144, 146, **146**, 149, **151**
rose gardens 22, 32, 80, 95, **152**, 153, 283, 301–2, 391
Ross (of Bladensburg), Sir John 34
Rosse, Alison, Countess of (*née* Cooke-Hurle) 53, **54**
Rosse, Anne, Countess of (*née* Messel) 48, 54
Rosse, Earls of (Parsons family) 16, 47
Rosse, Lawrence Parsons, 2nd Earl of 47, 54
Rosse, Mary, Countess of (*née* Field) 53
Rosse, Michael Parsons, 6th Earl of 48, 54
Rosse, William Brendan Parsons, 7th Earl of 16, 47–8, 53–5, **54**, 211
Rosse, William Edward Parsons, 5th Earl of ('Ocky') 48, 54
Rosse, William Parsons, 3rd Earl of 48, **49**
Rothschild, Lionel de 161–2, 164
Rowallane, Co Down 54, 112, **113**, 135–9, **135**, **136**, **137**, **138**, **141**
Royal Dublin Society 263, 264
Royal Hospital, Kilmainham, Dublin **328**, 329; The Master's Garden 339–43, **339**, **341**
Russborough House, Co Wicklow 11, 59, 238

Russell, James 144, 149
Ruxton, Sophy 213

Saint Fiachra's Garden, Tully, Co Kildare 261, **261**
Salthill House, Co Donegal 280, **281**, 301–7, **301**, **302**, **305**, **369**
Sayers, Brendan 273
Scalé, Bernard 339
Scott, Sir Walter: *St Ronan's Well* 78–9
Selkirk, Alexander 347
Shackleton, Daphne and Jonathan *see* Lakeview
Shackleton, David 281
Shankill, Co Dublin 158–9, 251, 283
Shannon Heritage 167
Sheehan, David 246
Shelswell-White family 26
Slaney, River 90
Slazenger family 59
Slieve Donard Nursery, Newcastle 136, 137, 139
Slinger, Leslie 137
Smyth, Dr Noeleen 268
Smyth, Revd Arthur (*later* Archbishop of Dublin) 332
snowdrops, significant collections 95, 120
Soil Association 378
Somerville, Edith 87
Somerville, Tom and Jane *see* Drishane House
southern beech (*Nothofagus*), significant collections 93, 97, 105, 170
southern hemisphere plants, significant collections *see* Glenveagh, Ilnacullin, Kells Bay, Mount Stewart, Mount Usher, National Botanic Gardens (Glasnevin), National Botanic Gardens (Kilmacurragh), Talbot Botanic Gardens; *see also* 157
Spectator, the (magazine) 263, 264
St Vincent de Paul Society 366
statues and sculpture 39, 59, **59**, 64–5, **64**, 73, **76**, 78, **152**, 153, **180**, **228**, 231, **231**, 246–7, **247**, **336**, 337, **339**, 340, **341**, **358**, 359
Stewart, Alexander 36
Stewart, Samuel Alexander: *A Flora of the North-East of Ireland* 275
Strangman, Lydia 372
Strangman, Wilson 372
Stratheden House, Knightsbridge, London 123, 125
stream and bog gardens *see* water
Stuart, James ('Athenian') **44**
Sugar Loaf Mountains, Co Wicklow *see* Great Sugar Loaf Mountain; Little Sugar Loaf Mountain
Sugarloaf Mountain, Co Cork 130
Suir, River 161
Sunningdale Nursery, Surrey 144

Sutton, Sam 97
Swift, Jonathan 332
Sykes, Angela **358**, 359

Talbot Botanic Gardens, Malahide, Co Dublin **156**, 157, 166–74, **167**
Talbot, Milo, Lord *see* Malahide, 7th Baron
Talbot, Richard 167
Talbot, Rose 167
Temple family **281**, 301
Temple, Elizabeth *see* Salthill House; *see also* 280
Temple, Lynn 304
temples **44**, **93**, 95, **132**, 133, 165, **235**, 236, 330, 336, 353
theatres, outdoor 78–79, **80**, 382
Thomas, William Brodrick (or Broderick) 62
Thomson, David: *Woodbrook* 10
Thomson, Thomas 221
Tickell, Thomas 263
Tighe, Lady Louisa (*née* Lennox) 204–5, **205**, 246
Tighe, William Frederick Fownes 204–6, **206**, 246
Tinode House, Co Wicklow 185, 287, 289, 292, 297
Tone, Theobald Wolfe 26
Tonygarra, Glencree 64
topiary 20, **23**, 40, **41**, 337, **339**
Trankner, P. 217
Tree Council of Ireland 336
tree ferns *see* Derreen, Kells Bay; *see also* 88, **88**, 133, **151**, 172, **172**, 199, **199**, 232, 234, 271, **275**
Tree Register of Great Britain and Ireland 48
trees, champions: significant collections *see* Birr, Mount Usher, National Botanic Gardens (Glasnevin), National Botanic Gardens (Kilmacurragh), Powerscourt, Tullynally, Woodstock; tallest in Ireland 66
Trench, Frederick 351, **352**, 353
Trench, John Townsend 144
Tresco Abbey Gardens, Scilly Isles 168
Trinity College Botanic Garden 221, 264, 275,
Tropical Ravine and Palm House, Belfast *see* Botanic Gardens, Belfast
Tudenham Park (*earlier* Rochfort House), Co Westmeath 242
Tully, Co Kildare *see* Japanese Gardens, The
Tullynally Castle, Co Longford 195, 208–13, **209**, **210**, **213**, 224
Turner, Richard 204, 265, **265**, 268, 276
Turrell, James: *Air Mass* (sculpture) 247
Tweedie, John 264

Vacant Land Cultivation Society 367
Vartry, River 97, 101, 103, **104**, 105, 108
Veagh, Lough 143, **143**, 144, 149, **151**
Veitch nursery 139, 200, 221, **265**
Victoria, Queen: in Ireland, 343, 345

Victorian Walled Garden, Phoenix Park, Dublin 366–7, **367**
Villa Farnese, near Rome 38
Villa Gamberaia, near Florence 38
Villa Trabia, Sicily (*formerly* Villa Butera) 62
Villandry, Château de (France) 373, **373**

Walker, Joseph C.: *Essay on the Rise and Progress of Gardening in Ireland* 366
walled gardens, significant *see* Altamont, Glenarm Castle, Glenveagh, Kylemore, Powerscourt, Rowallane, Talbot Botanic Gardens
Walpole, (Edward) Horace 98, 101, 103; (ed.) *Mount Usher 1868–1928: a short history* 98, 101
Walpole, Edward 97
Walpole, Edward, Jr 97–8
Walpole, George 97–8
Walpole, Robert Basil 98
Walpole, Thomas 97–8, **98**
Walsh, Edward 366
Walsh, Haulie 371
Warble Bank, Co Wicklow 283, **283**
water
　canals, ornamental *see* Antrim Castle, Dillon Garden, Killruddery; 217
　cascades *see* Kilfane Glen and Waterfall; *see also* 54, 69, **69**, **164**, 165, 332, 275, 334, **348**, 349
　fountains 20, 24, **24**, 59, 65, **65**, 67, 73, **79**, 210, 211, **338**, 340, 353, **363**
　lakes, ornamental *see* Altamont, Larchill, Oakfield Park, Powerscourt; *see also* **36**, 42, 45, 47, 54, **57**, **135**, 198, **199**, 258, 351
　pools, formal **16**, **19**, 24, 38, 67, 78, **79**, 95, 131, **131**, 265, 188, 211, 217, **223**, **289**, 247, 311, **317**, **328**, **337**, 353, **373**
　river gardens *see* Annes Grove, Birr Castle, Kells Bay, Mount Usher
　stream and bog gardens *see* Ardcarraig, Caher Bridge Garden; *see also* **105**, 108, 213, **213**, 232, **261**, 314, **315**
　water gardens, oriental *see* Japanese Gardens; *see also* 32, **33**, **66**, 67
Watson family 236
Watson, Robert **236**
Watson, William 8
Watson's nursery, Killiney, Co Dublin 92
Webb, Captain 269
Wellesley family 236
Wellington, Arthur Wellesley, 1st Duke of 201, 203
Wells, H.G.: *Food of the Gods* 276
West Dean House, West Sussex 129
Wharry, James and Bill 362

Wheatley, Francis: *The Irish House of Commons* (painting) 353
Whitbourn, Adam 234
White, Michael 165
White, Richard 24
Wicklow Mountains 74, 184, **185**, 190,
wildernesses, artificial **76**, 78, 125, **127**, 340
wildlife 101, **108**, 115, 118, 120, 198, **199**, 322, 334, **334**, 382
Williams, Jeremy 245
Williams, Thomas 353
Willis, George 231
Willmott, Ellen 357
Wilson, Ernest Henry 136, 139
Wilson, Guy 172
Wingfield family *see* Powerscourt, Viscounts
Woodbrook, Co Wicklow 251
woodland gardens, significant *see* Ardcarraig, Birr Castle, Corke Lodge, Glenveagh, Kells Bay, Kilfane Glen and Waterfall, Mount Congreve, Tullynally Castle; *see also* 74, **76**, 78, 85–6, 87, **87**, 88, **88**, 98, 101, **104**, 105, 120, 133, 172, **172**, 184, 190, **191**, 197, 334, **334**
woodland, native 54, 120, **120**, 144, 146
Woodrow, Bill: *Rut* (sculpture) 246, **247**
Woodstock, Co Kilkenny 8, 195, 203–6, **203**, **205**, **206**, 246
Woodtown Park, Rathfarnham, Dublin **118**
Wright, A & E. (Belfast architects and garden designers) 332
Wright, Carl *see* Caher Bridge Garden; *see also* 112
Wright, G.N.: *A Guide to the County of Wicklow* 74
Wright, Thomas **238**, 242

Yeats, William Butler 366
yew, Irish (*Taxus baccata* 'Fastigiata'), original **231**, 231
Young, Arthur, *A Tour in Ireland* 10, 85, 86, 238, 343
Young, Charles D. & Co, of Edinburgh 276

Zimmerman, Eugene 125

Acknowledgments

Both Jonathan and I are grateful to the many people who helped us with this book. Our joint thanks go first to the owners and guardians of the gardens in its pages. We have tramped through their plots at dusk and dawn, dined at their tables and slept in their houses. We are especially obliged to Billy Alexander, Olda FitzGerald, Seán Ó Gaoithín, Lynn and Elizabeth Temple and Ballymaloe Cookery School.

Jo Christian, who commissioned this book, showed heroic levels of good humour and tact. Anne Wilson, who designed it, has been meticulous and stupendously patient. We are profoundly grateful to both of them.

Mary Davies read every word before publication, and has been a constant and wise presence. I am forever in her debt. I also owe thanks to the following people who provided precious nuggets of information: Vandra Costello, Brian Eida, Jill Raggett, Simon Suter and Tony Wright.

I am grateful to Catriona Brennan, Cathy Burke, Rebekah Burke, Grainne Devaney, Helen and Val Dillon, Fidelma Farley, Pam Joyce, Frances MacDonald, Sara Macken, Koraley Northen, Judith Spring, Jonny Taylor, Milo de Paor and Lily Hession – all of whom helped in many ways. And, a big thanks to the members of my book club, who give me advice, entertainment and non-garden-related reading.

Jane Powers